Mini Treats
& Hand-Held
Sweets

Mini Treats & Hand-Held Sweets

100 Delicious Desserts to Pick Up and Eat

Abigail Johnson Dodge

The Taunton Press

Text © 2012 by Abigail Johnson Dodge
Photographs © 2012 by Miki Duisterhof except for the following:
pp. ii, 11, 18, 56, 63, 78, 79, 97, 123, 144, 148, 149, 176, 189, 194, 195, 200, 209 by
Scott Phillips © The Taunton Press, Inc.

The Taunton Press
Inspiration for hands-on living®

The Taunton Press, Inc., 63 South Main Street, PO Box 5506,
Newtown, CT 06470-5506

email: tp@taunton.com

Editor: Carolyn Mandarano
Copy Editor: Li Agen
Indexer: Heidi Blough
Cover design: Alison Wilkes
Front cover photographers: Miki Duisterhof (top row, second from left and second
from right; center) and Scott Phillips (top row, left , center, and right; bottom)
Back cover photographer: Miki Duisterhof
Cover photo of author: Winne Abramson
Interior design & layout: Laura Palese
Interior photographers: Miki Duisterhof, Scott Phillips
Food stylists: Mariana Velasquez, Adrienne Anderson
Prop stylists: Nan Whitney, Paige Hicks

The following names/manufacturers appearing in *Mini Treats & Hand-Held
Sweets* are trademarks: Absolut®, After Eight®, Applejack®, Bigelow®, Cointreau®,
Cuisinart®, Dufour®, Dunkin' Donuts®, Fluff®, Ghirardelli®, Gold Medal®, Grand
Marnier®, Guittard®, Hershey's®, Ho Ho®, Kahlua®, Kencraft®, King Arthur®,
KitchenAid®, Kraft®, La Salamandra®, M&M's®, McCormick Gourmet®,
Microplane®, Nabisco® Famous® Chocolate Wafers, Nutella®, Pyrex®, Quaker®,
Reese's® Peanut Butter Cups®, Rubbermaid®, Salter®, Scharffen Berger®, Spice
Islands®, Sugar in the Raw®, Sunbeam®, Swans Down®, Wonder®, Ziploc®

Library of Congress Cataloging-in-Publication Data in Progress
ISBN 978-1-60085-467-5

Printed in the United States of America
10 9 8 7 6 5 4 3 2 1

For Chris,

Love and laughter, family and friendship have been the hallmark of our first 25 years together. Cheers to our next quarter century and beyond. ~ Dude

Acknowledgments

I'm honored and proud to be a small part of the food world that has shaped my life and influenced my work. I have learned from every situation, every chef, every teacher, every editor, every success, and every failure. I am forever grateful for the privilege of working in a field that inspires, invigorates, humbles, and, at times, intimidates me. My mom always said that when it came to choosing a career, I should follow my passion and love what I do. Thanks, Mom.

Sending my warmest thanks to my friends in the international food blogging community. You inspire me daily with your endless energy and love. I stand in awe of your talents, and I'm grateful for your friendship, guidance, and support as I meander down my blogging road.

My wonderful friend Claire Van de Berghe tested and retested many of the recipes in this book. Thank you, Claire, for your patience, taste buds, attention to detail, as well as your hard work. I can't imagine doing a project without you, and I hope I never do.

I'd be lost without my wonderful agent, Stacey Glick. Thanks, Stacey, for never mincing words, for always pushing me to do better, and protecting me along the way.

Once again, it was an honor and a pleasure to work side by side with my wonderful editor, Carolyn Mandarano. Thank you, Carolyn, for being such a wonderful person as well as a gifted and creative editor. Your suggestions and guidance are always spot-on and always delivered in a caring, creative way.

Few cookbook authors are fortunate to have a true home with their publisher, and I am one of them. This is my second book with The Taunton Press, but I began working for *Fine Cooking* magazine (published by Taunton) with their first issue, published in 1994, and I have loved and learned from every issue and every person that has graced their staff. With heartfelt thanks to the entire Taunton family, your work is an inspiration, and I'm grateful for your continued support and belief in me.

Thanks to the all-star design and production team for working your magic on this book. Laura Palese and Alison Wilkes created the beautiful look and layout of this book—gorgeous! Thanks to photographers Miki Duisterhof and Scott Phillips, food stylists Mariana Velasquez and Adrienne Anderson, and prop stylists Nan Whitney and Paige Hicks for their hard work to create the photos that bring these recipes to life. And, last but never least, Li Agen is a friend, a trusted colleague, and a true goddess of a copy editor. We've been working together for so long that I think Li can finish my sentences in her sleep.

I am fortunate to count Barbara Kiebel from Kineticwebs.com and Creative-Culinary.com as a friend and colleague. Barb designed my beautiful website and I am so lucky that she's always willing to swoop in to fix what I have broken. TY B!

Through the course of developing, testing, and retesting these recipes, my kitchen and counters have been flooded with all things sweet. Thankfully, my brother, Tim Johnson, swooped in on many occasions and collected the goods to share with his colleagues at LabCore in Shelton, Connecticut. Thanks to the team for all your wonderful feedback!

Thanks to the cast and crew of "cabana one" for tasting and critiquing these desserts. We are all a bit heavier for it, and I appreciate your sacrifice for the greater good.

And lastly and lovingly, to my two beautiful babies, Alex and Tierney. You have grown up in a home filled with more desserts than most kids taste in a lifetime. I hope you've enjoyed this sweet ride as much as I have loved sharing it with you.

Introduction

Serving up a dessert from this book means no plates, no forks, no spoons—no kidding. I designed these easy-to-make and even-easier-to-serve desserts that will dazzle guests, spark every palate, and, as an added benefit, leave you with less cleanup. Plus, they're fun and flavorful in a small package, making them perfect for an after-dinner sweet, desserts-only party, or on-the-go treat.

The recipes range from last-minute wonders and make-ahead marvels to show-stopping projects. You'll find classic, homespun treats as well as innovative, playful sweets; many have intriguing, contemporary flavor combinations with unique variations. Within this broad range of recipes, you'll find gluten-free, non-dairy, vegan, egg-less, and low-fat desserts. They speak to home bakers of all experience levels who are seeking sweets that offer flavor, variety, and depth, and, most important, that are finger-licking good.

Like all of my books, each recipe includes simply worded, easy-to-follow directions that are conversational in tone and include many sensory clues for doneness, along with tips and shortcuts, when appropriate. Step-by-step directions are numbered to keep things crystal clear and bakers on track.

For bakers who like to plan ahead, recipes will include, when appropriate, Do Ahead suggestions for when and how recipes can be broken down into manageable steps, along with storage information to help keep the desserts at their best.

While many of these recipes are stand-alone stylish, Finishing Touches options are perfect for those times when you want to dress up a dessert with a sauce, a drizzle, or a dollop.

In all of my recipes, inspiration and experimentation are encouraged! I want home bakers of all skill levels to think beyond the flavors I have given in the recipe and try something new. In the Twists sections, you'll find flavor variations (including seasonal fruit swap-outs) for key ingredients as well as baking variations, allowing you some flexibility to experiment and make the recipes your own. It's part of what makes baking fun.

I've also included some of my personal Kitchen Wisdom throughout the book. Here, I'll lend a hand with a technique or offer an explanation of an ingredient. A little insider knowledge makes everyone a better, more successful baker.

And, remember, if you have questions or need some recipe advice, please visit me at www.abbydodge.com and "Ask Abby."

—Abby

Baking Wisdom

Over the years, I've accumulated a lot of intel about what works and what doesn't in baking, and it's this insider knowledge that I pass on to you to help you become a better baker. Throughout the book, I've called these little nuggets Kitchen Wisdom, but in this Baking Wisdom section, you'll find information that's particularly appropriate to baking. While much of what you read here can apply to all types of cooking, these things are especially important in baking, so you can achieve the same sweet success that I have when I'm baking in my own kitchen.

General Information

Read the recipe before you start baking. You should always make sure you have all the ingredients and equipment you need before diving in. For newer bakers, I suggest you read the recipe through a second time so that you're more familiar with it.

Get to know your oven. It's important to know how your oven heats. Oven temperatures can vary widely, so put a mercury-filled oven thermometer (the most accurate, in my opinion) in your oven. Check the temp occasionally to be sure it's in sync with the temperature controls. If

not, adjust up or down accordingly. Also, keep an eye out for "hot spots" in your oven—these pockets are hotter than other areas of your oven and can cause overbrowning and overcooking. If you have them, simply rotate your pans about halfway through the suggested baking time.

Get to know your refrigerator and freezer. Your fridge and freezer temperatures are just as important as your oven temp. Set the controls to 38°F for the fridge and 0°F for the freezer. Place a thermometer in the center of both compartments (not on or near the door, as the temperature in those areas will fluctuate as the compartments are opened) and check the reading after about 24 hours. If the reading isn't in sync with the controls, adjust up or down accordingly.

Get to know your candy thermometer and instant-read thermometer. Before you use either of these tools in a recipe, check that their readings are accurate. For the candy thermometer, clip onto the side of a pan and adjust the probe so that it isn't touching the bottom. Fill the pan with 2 to 3 inches of water and bring to a boil. Once boiling, the reading should be 212°F (for sea level). In the same pan of boiling water, dip the probe end of the instant-read thermometer into the water. Again, it should read 212°F (for sea level). Make note of any inaccuracies and adjust your recipe accordingly.

Measure carefully and follow the directions. If you aren't using a scale to weigh your ingredients (it's the most accurate), using the appropriate measuring cups—metal for dry ingredients and glass for liquid—and following the directions will ensure consistent and delicious results.

Pay attention to the doneness test and use the timing as a guide. Recipe instructions offer sensory clues to help you know when to move onto the next step or when you are finished. The timing is a suggested window but, depending on your equipment, kitchen and oven temp, and ingredients, your dish might take a bit longer or a bit less. Make sure to mark down any changes in the margins so you will remember the next time.

Roll like a pro. Even experienced bakers struggle with sticky doughs, so I recommend rolling doughs with the help of parchment. Using two pieces of parchment (top and bottom with the dough sandwiched in between) avoids the need for adding extra flour to the dough and allows you to easily turn and flip the dough so it rolls easily to an even thickness.

Here's how to do it: Put a large piece of parchment on the counter. Put your dough onto the center of the paper and top with another piece of parchment. Roll as directed on top of the paper and rotate the dough a quarter-turn after a few passes and flip the dough over. When the paper begins to crinkle up, carefully peel it away, dust lightly with flour, and reposition the paper. Using the paper, flip the dough and repeat on the other side. Continue rolling, turning, flipping, and repositioning the paper as needed.

Line a pan with foil. For easy removal of baked goods as well as easy cleanup, line the baking pans with foil. Tear off a long sheet of foil, making sure you'll have enough for a 1-inch overhang on the two shorter sides, and lay it flat on the counter. Center the baking pan on top of the foil. Press the foil up against the sides of the pan and fold the corners neatly. Lift the pan from the foil and set it on the counter. Carefully press the prefab foil liner into the baking pan.

Measure sticky ingredients. For easy, clean removal, lightly spray the inside of a measuring cup with baking spray before adding sticky ingredients like peanut butter, molasses, honey, and cane syrup.

Ingredients
FLOUR
There are many different varieties and brands of flour on the market, but for these recipes you need only white unbleached all-purpose flour and cake flour. For all-purpose, I like King Arthur® and Gold Medal® brands, and Swans Down® for cake flour. Store flour in an airtight container at room temperature to keep it fresh and bug-free.

Measuring flour Proper measuring of all types of flour is of the utmost importance to ensure accurate baked results. For the most consistent results, I urge you to buy a digital kitchen scale. They are inexpensive and easy to use (see Essential Equipment on p. 211). I've given weight measurements for the flour as well as all dry ingredients. If you don't use a scale, use the spoon-and-sweep method: Stir the flour in the container, lightly spoon into the appropriate metal measuring cup—no scooping, packing, or tapping—and sweep off the excess with a flat edge (a ruler, knife, or spatula handle).

SALT
I use table salt in all of my recipes. Because the granules are small and relatively uniform, I get a consistently accurate measurement every time. On occasion, I call for a sprinkle of fleur de sel as a finishing touch.

FLEUR DE SEL

Traditional French sea salt is very coarse in texture and, because of the sand collected with salt, it can often have a slight gray tinge. Its intriguing flavor comes from the minerals. It's available in a number of forms and flavors, and you can find it in specialty stores and online. Buy a small quantity of a few varieties so you can sample and choose one or two to always have on hand.

BROWN SUGAR

Light and dark brown sugar vary only in the slightly higher molasses added to the darker variety, which makes the flavor slightly more pronounced and the color, well, darker. In these recipes, I specify light or dark but, in a pinch you can substitute one for the other; just keep in mind the color and flavor differences. Left at room temperature, brown sugar will turn dry and hard, so it's important to keep it in an airtight container (I use a Rubbermaid® container and store it in my pantry).

UNSALTED BUTTER

I use only unsalted butter in my recipes. Without the salt, the butter lacks the longer shelf life so it tends to be fresher. Using unsalted also means I can accurately control the salt level in the recipes. Don't be tempted to leave out or reduce the salt—it's imperative to the dessert's flavor and will taste flat without it. When I'm developing and testing recipes, I use the store brand butter for consistency but, much like chocolate, there are many types available, so feel free to experiment.

Softening butter Many recipes call for the butter to be softened in order for the batter to mix up thoroughly and properly. This means that the butter shouldn't be too hard or too soft, or worse, melted. If you haven't been able to plan ahead and your butter is still cold from the fridge, use the microwave, but use it judiciously. Put the wrapped butter stick in the microwave, and cook in short 5-second blasts, turning and rotating, until the butter is soft enough to give slightly when pressed with a finger. If you've gone too far, pop the stick back into the fridge and start again with a fresh one.

EGGS

Size matters. I use large eggs for all of my recipes and, unless otherwise directed, they should be used at room temperature. Don't be tempted to use a different-size egg, as it will affect the baked results. If you are in a rush and your eggs are cold, take a few minutes to warm the eggs in a bowl of warm water.

Separating eggs While it's easiest to separate the egg whites when the eggs are cold, they get the most volume when at room temperature. So, separate first and then warm to room temp before beating. Tap the eggshell against the rim of a small bowl or ramekin. Working over the bowl, separate the shell into two halves, being careful to keep the yolk in one half. Pass the yolk from shell to shell, allowing the white to drop into the bowl. Put the yolk and white in separate mixing bowls. Using the same method, separate any remaining eggs over an empty bowl or ramekin before adding to the mixing bowl to avoid any yolk contamination.

Beating egg whites Impeccably clean beaters and a stainless-steel or glass bowl are a must for beating whites—even a touch of grease makes for flat, unbeatable whites. Beat slowly at first, until the whites are foamy, then gradually increase the speed and proceed as directed in the recipe. Be careful not to overbeat or they will be dry and possibly deflate.

MILK

I used whole milk when developing and testing the recipes for this book, and I urge you to follow my lead at home. That said, 2% milk will yield similar results, but I wouldn't go any lower than that, as anything else might adversely affect the texture and depth of the dessert.

HALF-AND-HALF

Half-and-half is made with half milk and half heavy cream. If you have both heavy cream and milk in the fridge, feel free to use equal parts of each for the amount of half-and-half called for in a recipe. Do not, however, substitute half-and-half for heavy cream—it can't be whipped.

CHOCOLATE

I test and develop my chocolate recipes using Ghirardelli® chocolate that is 60% cacao Most brands, but not all, call this "bittersweet," so double-check the label. For example, Scharffen Berger®'s (one of my favorites) "semisweet" is 62% cacao, which is very close to Ghirardelli's bittersweet, which is 60%. The higher-percentage chocolate will give a stronger, more bitter flavor. For chips, I like Guittard® and Ghirardelli brands. Bittersweet chips can be substituted for bar chocolate. There are many bittersweet and semi-sweet chocolate varieties out there, so I encourage you to sample and experiment. I prefer not to substitute chips for chopped chocolate (the chips have added ingredients to stabilize them) but, in most cases, it can be done successfully. My rule of thumb is 6 ounces equals 1 cup of chips.

Melting chocolate Chopped chocolate can be melted in the microwave or on the stovetop. To melt in the microwave, put the chopped chocolate in a heatproof or microwave-safe bowl. Microwave on full power in short, 30-second bursts (to avoid scorching) until the chocolate is soft and shiny but not completely melted. Stir until smooth. For stovetop melting, use a traditional double boiler (two nesting saucepans) or a saucepan or skillet and a heatproof bowl. Fill the bottom saucepan with water and bring to a simmer. Put the chopped chocolate in a heatproof bowl and set it over the simmering water, stirring occasionally, until the chocolate is almost completely melted. Remove from the heat and stir until smooth.

COCOA POWDER

Made from roasted cocoa beans pulverized into a paste and then dried and ground, this fine powder is unsweetened. Not to be confused with sweetened cocoa mix, it is available in natural or Dutch-processed forms. Dutch-processed cocoa is treated with an alkaline to neutralize the acid, giving it a smoother taste. The varieties aren't always interchangeable, so it's best to use what's called for in the recipe. I have tested the recipes here using natural, Hershey's® brand as it's the most commonly available, but feel free to experiment with other brands. If your cocoa is lumpy, sift before measuring.

LIGHTLY SALTED NUTS

I like using these types of nuts in all my baking because the nut flavors are bolder than the dry-roasted and unsalted types, and the added salt kicks up the sweet flavors in the dessert to push the sweet-savory line.

Toasting nuts and shredded coconut Toasting heightens the flavor of nuts and shredded coconut. Heat the oven to 350°F. Spread the nuts or coconut on a baking pan in an even layer. Bake, stirring once or twice, until golden brown and fragrant, 7 to 12 minutes (depending on size and variety). Let cool completely before using. Stow in heavy-duty zip-top bags in the freezer.

FLAVORINGS

Use only pure extracts and pass over the subpar imitation varieties. Vanilla and almond are two that I always have on hand. Small jars of ground spices like cinnamon, ginger, and nutmeg will taste vibrant for up to 6 months. After that, I'd urge you to crack open a new container or your dessert's flavor may be limp and weak.

PHYLLO (OR FILO)

This flour-based, commercially made dough is carefully stretched and pulled until it's so thin that it's practically transparent. Cut into rectangles, the layers or sheets are stacked and rolled together and frozen. Recipes typically use many sheets layered with butter (or other fat) and sometimes sugar, which bake up into crisp, flaky pastries, shells, or toppings. A cautionary word: When working with phyllo, cover any dough sheets not in use with plastic wrap to keep them from drying out and becoming brittle.

GELATIN

Unflavored powdered gelatin is used to thicken and set many chilled desserts. Soften the granules in liquid, as directed, until plump and moist. Unless otherwise directed in a recipe, heat gently in a microwave or over simmering water until the liquid is clear and no granules remain. Avoid boiling, as that can affect its thickening power.

·1·
Cookies

SENSATIONAL SQUARES, CUTOUTS,
SANDWICHES & MORE

- 1¼ cups (11¼ ounces) smooth peanut butter, at room temperature
- ¾ cup (5¼ ounces) firmly packed light brown sugar
- ½ teaspoon baking soda
- 1 large egg, at room temperature
- 1 teaspoon pure vanilla extract

FOR THE PEANUT BUTTER FILLING

- ½ cup (2 ounces) confectioners' sugar
- ⅓ cup (3 ounces) peanut butter, smooth or chunky
- 4 tablespoons (2 ounces) unsalted butter, at room temperature

Makes 14 sandwich cookies or 28 individual cookies

twists

- **MAKE THE FILLING CHOCOLATE:** Melt 5 ounces chopped bittersweet chocolate and 4 tablespoons (2 ounces) unsalted butter in the microwave or in a medium metal bowl set over a pot of simmering water, stirring with a rubber spatula until smooth. Remove from the heat and set aside until cool and thickened.
- **MAKE THE FILLING JAM OR PRESERVES:** Instead of the peanut butter filling, use ⅔ cup jam or preserves—any flavor!

do ahead

- The cookies can be prepared through Step 3 in Make the Cookies. Layer the baked and cooled cookies between sheets of parchment or waxed paper in an airtight container. They can be stowed for up to 5 days at room temperature or for up to 6 weeks in the freezer.
- The filled sandwich cookies can be stowed between sheets of parchment or waxed paper in an airtight container for up to 5 days.

Gluten Free

Double Peanut Butter Sandwiches

I have never liked peanut butter sandwiches. Of course, when growing up, most of my friends—and especially my oldest brother, Darv—inhaled peanut butter at any given chance. It wasn't until I was older and began baking with peanut butter that I embraced this rich, buttery spread as an excellent flavoring that adds depth, texture, and—when used appropriately—sophistication to my desserts.

These flourless cookies are perfect unadorned, but when sandwiched with a creamy, sweet peanut butter filling or a rich chocolate ganache, they really shine. And if you happen to be a PB&J lover, you can opt to sandwich these cookies with a dab of your favorite jam.

make the cookies

1 Position an oven rack in the center of the oven and heat the oven to 350°F. Line two cookie sheets with parchment or nonstick liners.

2 Put the peanut butter, brown sugar, and baking soda in a large bowl. Beat with an electric mixer fitted with the paddle attachment on medium speed until well blended and smooth, about 2 minutes. Add the egg and vanilla and mix on low speed until just blended. Don't overmix.

3 Using a 1-tablespoon mini scoop, shape into balls and arrange about 1½ inches apart on the prepared cookie sheets. *Do not* press down. Bake, one sheet at a time, until the cookies are puffed and crackled but still moist looking, about 11 minutes. Transfer the cookie sheet to a rack to cool for about 5 minutes. Using a spatula, lift the cookies from the sheet and onto a rack until completely cooled.

make the filling and assemble the sandwiches

1 Put the confectioners' sugar, peanut butter, and butter in a small bowl. Mix with an electric mixer (hand-held is fine) until well blended and fluffy, about 2 minutes.

2 Turn half of the cooled cookies over so they are flat side up. Spoon 1 tablespoon of the filling onto the center of each cookie. Top with the remaining cookies, flat side down. Press gently on each cookie to spread the filling almost to the edge.

Toasted Pistachio–Cherry Biscotti Straws

I've always loved the crisp texture and bold flavor of biscotti, but as a tea drinker, I always felt left out of the whole "dunking" experience. While dipping a biscotti in tea made the cookie easier to bite into, it seemed to dilute the flavor. The compromise lies in these slender biscotti straws. They have the same great texture of the traditional version but are thin enough that you can bite right into one without breaking a tooth. Dunking is optional.

1   Position an oven rack in the center of the oven and heat the oven to 325°F. Line one large cookie sheet with parchment or a nonstick liner.

2   Put the flour, brown sugar, baking powder, and salt in a large bowl and beat with an electric mixer fitted with the paddle attachment on medium-low speed until well blended. Add the nuts and cherries and mix briefly to combine.

3   In a 1-cup glass measure (the spout makes it easy to pour), whisk the egg, egg white, brandy or water, and vanilla extract. With the mixer on low speed, slowly pour in the egg mixture. Continue mixing until a sticky, moist dough forms, about 1 minute. Dump the dough onto the center of the lined cookie sheet. Using slightly wet hands, press the dough roughly into a rectangle. Cover with a large piece of plastic and, using your hands and a rolling pin, press and roll into a 7x11-inch rectangle. Lift the plastic wrap occasionally and reposition it on the dough until you have an even layer.

4   Bake until the rectangle is golden brown on top and slightly darker brown on the edges, about 25 minutes. Transfer the cookie sheet to a rack and set aside until the rectangle is just cool enough to handle, about 10 minutes. Keep the oven set at 325°F. Using a metal spatula, loosen the rectangle from the liner and set it on a cutting board. Using a serrated knife, cut crosswise into thin slices about 1/3 to 1/2 inch thick. I use a gentle sawing motion to break through the crust and then push down firmly on the knife. Return the biscotti to the baking sheet and arrange them cut side down—it's fine if they're touching. Bake until the biscotti are light golden brown and dried to your taste, 10 to 14 minutes. Let cool completely before adding the Orange-White Chocolate Drizzle, if using.

recipe continues

1¼ cups (5½ ounces) unbleached all-purpose flour

½ cup (3½ ounces) firmly packed light brown sugar

1   teaspoon baking powder

¼ teaspoon table salt

¾ cup (3 ounces) pistachios, toasted

½ cup (3 ounces) dried cherries

1   large egg, at room temperature

1   white from a large egg, at room temperature

1   tablespoon brandy or water

¾ teaspoon pure vanilla extract

Orange-White Chocolate Drizzle (recipe on p. 12; optional)

Makes 22 cookies

Press and roll the dough into a rectangle.

twists

Instead of the pistachio, cherries, and brandy, use one of the following combinations: 3/4 cup (3 ounces) slivered almonds, toasted, 1/2 cup (2 1/2 ounces) dried apricots, chopped, and 1 tablespoon Grand Marnier®, brandy, or water; or 3/4 cup (3 1/2 ounces) toasted, chopped macadamias, 3 ounces chopped semisweet or white chocolate, and 1 tablespoon Grand Marnier, brandy, or water.

do ahead

Layer the baked and cooled straws between sheets of parchment or waxed paper in an airtight container. They can be stowed for up to 3 weeks at room temperature or for up to 6 weeks in the freezer (without the drizzle).

finishing touches

ORANGE-WHITE CHOCOLATE DRIZZLE Combine 3 ounces chopped white chocolate and 1 teaspoon canola or vegetable oil in a small heatproof bowl. Melt over simmering water or in a microwave. Add 1 teaspoon finely grated orange zest and stir until well blended.

Scrape the melted chocolate into one corner of a heavy-duty zip-top bag, press out the air, and seal. Arrange the cooled biscotti straws on their sides—they should be touching—on a wire rack or lined cookie sheet. Snip off a small piece of the corner of the bag and drizzle the chocolate casually over the straws. Set aside until the chocolate firms up, about 30 minutes.

FOR THE BISCOTTI

1 cup (4½ ounces) unbleached all-purpose flour

1 teaspoon baking powder

¼ teaspoon table salt

4 tablespoons (2 ounces) unsalted butter, softened

½ cup (3½ ounces) granulated sugar

1 large egg, at room temperature

1 teaspoon pure vanilla extract

¼ teaspoon pure almond extract

⅔ cup (2⅝ ounces) slivered almonds, toasted

3 ounces milk chocolate, chopped

FOR THE MILK CHOCOLATE DRIZZLE

3 ounces milk chocolate, chopped

1 teaspoon canola or vegetable oil

Makes 24 biscotti

twists

- Instead of the almond extract, almonds, and a milk chocolate drizzle, use 3 ounces bittersweet chocolate, chopped, ⅔ cup (3⅜ ounces) toasted and chopped macadamia nuts, and 2 teaspoons finely grated lemon zest.

- **MAKE 'EM STRAWS:** For more slender biscotti, prepare the dough as directed and then follow the directions for shaping into straws on p. 11.

do ahead

Layer the baked and cooled biscotti between sheets of parchment or waxed paper in an airtight container. They can be stowed for up to 3 weeks at room temperature or for up to 6 weeks in the freezer (without the drizzle).

Milk Chocolate–Almond Biscotti

Unlike traditional biscotti, which have a crisp—even hard—texture that's perfect for dunking into hot chocolate or a latte, these are made with butter. The added fat makes for a more tender, crumbly cookie that doesn't need dunking and is much easier on your teeth. I've used the classic biscotti technique of shaping into logs and cutting on a sharp angle, but feel free to shape this into "straws" (see p. 11).

make the biscotti

1 Position an oven rack in the center of the oven and heat the oven to 325°F. Line one large cookie sheet with a nonstick liner. (You can use parchment, but it makes shaping the dough more challenging.)

2 In a medium bowl, whisk the flour, baking powder, and salt until well blended. Put the butter and sugar in a large bowl and beat with an electric mixer fitted with the paddle attachment until smooth and creamy, about 3 minutes. Add the egg, vanilla, and almond extract to the sugar mixture and beat on medium until blended, about 1 minute. Add the flour mixture, almonds, and chocolate and beat on low speed until the dough forms moist clumps.

3 Dump the dough onto the center of the prepared cookie sheet. Using slightly wet hands, press and shape the dough into an even 10x2½-inch log. Bake until the log is golden brown around the edges and pale brown on top, 30 to 32 minutes. Transfer the cookie sheet to a rack and set aside until the log is just cool enough to handle, about 10 minutes. Keep the oven set at 325°F.

4 Using a metal spatula, loosen the log from the liner and set on a cutting board. With a serrated knife, cut crosswise and on the diagonal into ½-inch-thick slices. Use a gentle sawing motion to break through the crust and then a firm push down on the knife. Return the biscotti to the baking sheet and arrange cut side down—it's fine if they're touching. Bake until the biscotti are light golden brown and dried to your taste, 10 to 15 minutes. Let cool completely before adding the milk chocolate drizzle, if desired.

make the drizzle

1 Put the chopped chocolate and oil in a small heatproof bowl. Melt over simmering water or in a microwave and stir until well blended.

2 Scrape the melted chocolate into one corner of a heavy-duty zip-top bag, press out the air, and seal. Arrange the cooled biscotti on their sides—they should be touching—on a wire rack or lined cookie sheet. Snip off a small piece of the corner and drizzle the chocolate casually over the biscotti. Set aside until the chocolate firms up.

Gingerbread Biscotti

One of the fringe benefits of writing a cookbook is the chance to travel and meet with readers. Even with email and all the social media to connect us, I love the chance to connect to home bakers IRL (in real life).

Another benefit of my business travel is sampling the best foods from the local restaurants. A few years back, I was in Chicago to promote *The Weekend Baker,* and I had a little time to kill. Knowing that a proper meal wasn't in my future that night, I tucked myself into Blackbird for a snack. I sampled a few incredible appetizers, but the most spectacular was the seared foie gras served with gingerbread toast and cranberry compote. It was phenomenal and all at once sweet yet savory.

Like its inspiration, this biscotti is slightly sweet, filled with mellow spices, nuts, and dried fruit. It's a perfect accompaniment to a cup of tea or coffee or served alongside a warm fruit compote.

1 Position an oven rack in the center of the oven and heat the oven to 350°F. Line one large cookie sheet with a nonstick liner or parchment. Measure the molasses in a 1-cup measure and add the eggs and zest. Using a table fork, mix until blended.

2 Put the flour, brown sugar, ground ginger, baking powder, cinnamon, salt, nutmeg, and baking soda in a large bowl and beat with an electric mixer fitted with the paddle attachment on medium-low speed until well blended. Add the pecans, apricots, and crystallized ginger and mix briefly. With the mixer on low speed, slowly pour in the egg mixture. Continue mixing until the dough is well blended and comes together in large, moist clumps, 1 to 2 minutes.

3 Dump the dough onto the counter or work surface. Divide into two equal piles (about 1 pound each). Shape each pile into an even 10x1½-inch log, lightly flouring your hands as needed (the dough is a bit sticky). Repeat with the other pile of dough.

4 Arrange the logs on the lined cookie sheet about 4 inches apart. Bake until the tops are cracked and spring back slightly when gently pressed, 30 to 35 minutes. Transfer the sheet to a rack and let cool until the logs are cool enough to handle, about 10 minutes. Keep the oven set at 350°F.

5 Carefully peel the biscotti logs from the liner and set on a cutting board. With a serrated knife, cut crosswise and on the diagonal into ¼-inch-thick slices. Gently saw through the crust and then firmly push down on the knife. Return the biscotti to the cookie sheet and arrange them cut side down (it's fine if they are touching).

6 Bake until the biscotti are dried to your taste, about 10 minutes (for slightly moist and chewy) to 20 minutes (for super-dry and crunchy). Move the cookie sheet to a wire rack and let the biscotti cool completely. The biscotti will still give slightly when pressed but will harden as they cool. When cool, store in an airtight container.

- ¼ cup molasses
- 2 large eggs, at room temperature
- 2 teaspoons finely grated orange zest
- 2¼ cups (10⅛ ounces) unbleached all-purpose flour
- 1¼ cups (8¾ ounces) firmly packed dark brown sugar
- 2 teaspoons ground ginger
- 1¼ teaspoons baking powder
- 1 teaspoon ground cinnamon
- ½ teaspoon table salt
- ¼ teaspoon ground nutmeg
- ¼ teaspoon baking soda
- 1 cup (4 ounces) pecans, coarsely chopped
- ⅓ cup (3 ounces) lightly packed dried apricots, coarsely chopped
- 3 tablespoons finely chopped crystallized ginger

Makes about 24 biscotti

finishing touches
Garnish the cooled biscotti with Milk Chocolate Drizzle (see the recipe on the facing page).

twists
Instead of the pecans, apricots, and crystallized ginger, use 3 ounces white chocolate, chopped, ⅔ cup (2⅝ ounces) toasted and chopped walnuts, and ⅓ cup (2 ounces) dried cherries.

do ahead
Layer the baked and cooled biscotti between sheets of parchment or waxed paper in an airtight container. They can be stowed for up to 3 weeks at room temperature or for up to 6 weeks in the freezer (without the drizzle).

1½ cups (6¾ ounces) unbleached all-purpose flour

¼ cup unsweetened, flaked coconut, toasted (see Kitchen Wisdom below)

½ teaspoon table salt

¼ teaspoon baking powder

12 tablespoons (6 ounces) unsalted butter, softened

1¼ cups (8¾ ounces) granulated sugar

1 vanilla bean, split and scraped

2 large eggs, at room temperature

FOR THE ORANGE CREAM

2 ounces cream cheese, softened

¾ cup (3 ounces) confectioners' sugar

2 teaspoons finely grated orange zest

Makes about 3 dozen individual cookies or 18 sandwiches

twists

- Substitute 1½ teaspoons pure vanilla extract or pure vanilla bean paste for the vanilla bean seeds.

- Substitute ⅔ cup raspberry preserves or dulce de leche (see p. 65) for the orange cream.

do ahead

Store the cookies at room temperature for up to 2 days before filling.

Toasted Coconut– Vanilla Cookies

These soft, delicate cookies have a heady vanilla perfume and a soft, delicate texture. The cookies can be eaten plain (my preference), or you can sandwich them with a bit of orange cream, raspberry preserves, or dulce de leche.

make the cookies

1 Position oven racks in the top and bottom thirds of the oven and heat the oven to 375°F. Line two to four large cookie sheets with parchment or nonstick liners.

2 Whisk the flour, coconut, salt, and baking powder in a medium bowl until blended.

3 Put the butter in a large bowl. Beat with an electric mixer fitted with the paddle attachment on medium speed until well blended and smooth, about 3 minutes. Add the sugar and vanilla bean seeds and continue beating until well combined, about 2 minutes. Add the eggs, one at a time, beating until just blended between additions. Add the flour mixture and mix on low speed until a soft dough forms, about 1 minute.

4 Using a 1-tablespoon mini scoop, shape the dough into balls and arrange about 2½ inches apart on the prepared cookie sheets. Bake two sheets at a time, swapping the sheets' positions halfway through baking, until the edges are golden brown, about 12 minutes. Move the sheets to wire racks and let the cookies sit for 5 minutes, then transfer the cookies to a wire rack and let cool completely. Repeat with the remaining cookie dough using cooled cookie sheets and liners.

make the orange cream and assemble the cookies

1 Put the cream cheese, confectioners' sugar, and orange zest in a small bowl. Using a hand-held mixer or a spoon, beat until well blended and smooth.

2 Spread about 1 teaspoon of the orange cream on the flat side of one cookie, then gently press another cookie, flat side down, on top of the filling. The filled cookies can be prepared and kept at room temperature for up to 2 hours before serving.

KITCHEN WISDOM ◎◎ **more about coconut**

This recipe calls for unsweetened, flaked coconut, *not* the sweetened, shredded kind you usually find in the grocery store. This coconut, sometimes called "desiccated," can be found in health- or specialty-food stores.

To toast coconut, spread it on a small cookie sheet and bake in a 350°F oven until golden brown, about 8 minutes. Let cool completely before using.

White Chocolate Filled Orange–Pistachio Macarons

If you ever have the opportunity to visit Paris, you must visit two of the city's most famous pâtisseries: Ladurée and Pierre Hermé (right after you visit the Jeu de Paume and the Musée d'Orsay, of course). Both pâtisseries are filled with a stunning array of macarons in a bouquet of colors and flavors. It's impossible to taste them all, so I suggest selecting a few classic flavors (chocolate, coffee-vanilla, chocolate-chocolate ganache, and caramel are my favorites) and then choose a few that are more color- and flavor-forward (rose, hibiscus, green tea, or port wine). This way you get a broad taste of what Parisians can indulge in daily. Fortunately for those of us in the metro New York area, Ladurée has opened a shop on Madison Avenue.

Pistachio flour can be ordered from a number of Internet sources.

make the shells

1 Line three large heavy baking sheets with nonstick liners. Set aside.

2 Put the confectioners' sugar and pistachio flour in a food processor. Process until the pistachio flour is very fine, 45 to 60 seconds. Set a fine-mesh sieve over a medium bowl and add the confectioners' sugar mixture. Sift and discard any remaining pistachio bits.

3 Put the egg whites and salt in a large bowl (be sure the bowl and beater are nice and clean; see p. 41). Beat with an electric mixer fitted with the whisk attachment on medium speed until the whites are frothy and opaque, about 1 minute. Increase the speed to medium high and beat until the whites form medium-soft peaks, about 2 minutes. Continue beating while gradually sprinkling in the sugar, 1 tablespoon at a time. When all the sugar is added, increase the speed to high and whip until firm, glossy peaks form. Using a spatula, scrape down the sides of the bowl and add the orange zest, orange extract, and food coloring and beat until just barely blended (it will mix more when you are folding), about 10 seconds.

4 Add half of the confectioners' sugar-pistachio mixture to the meringue and, using a large rubber spatula, fold until most of the mixture is combined. Add the remaining sugar-flour mixture and continue folding until completely combined and the meringue is no longer stiff. It should be glossy and slowly flow off the spatula when lifted.

recipe continues

FOR THE ORANGE PISTACHIO SHELLS

- 1½ cups (6 ounces) confectioners' sugar
- ¾ cup (2½ ounces) pistachio flour
- 3 whites from large eggs, at room temperature
- Pinch of table salt
- 5 tablespoons (2⅛ ounces) granulated sugar
- 1 teaspoon finely grated orange zest
- ¾ teaspoon pure orange extract
- ⅛ to ¼ teaspoon orange food coloring or gel (see Kitchen Wisdom on p. 18)

FOR THE WHITE CHOCOLATE FILLING

- 12 ounces white chocolate, chopped
- ½ cup heavy cream
- Pinch of table salt

Makes 38 sandwich cookies (76 shells)

finishing touches
Just before baking, sprinkle the tops of half of the shells with a little finely crushed fleur de sel and use these for the tops of the macaron sandwiches.

twists
Substitute the same amount of almond flour for the pistachio flour.

do ahead
Store the shells, unfilled, in an airtight container for up to 1 month.

Pour the meringue into the pastry bag.

Hold the bag perpendicular to the sheet when piping. Squeeze from the top and use the opposite hand to guide the bag.

5 Using a wide plastic scraper or spatula, scoop or pour the meringue into a large pastry bag fitted with a ½-inch-wide plain tip (Ateco #806). Holding the pastry bag perpendicular to the lined baking sheet, pipe small flat mounds about 1¼ inches in diameter and no higher than ⅓ inch onto the sheet, about 1½ inches apart. Release the pressure on the bag and flick the tip away from the batter. Once the baking sheet is filled (I get 30 mounds on my sheet), firmly rap it on the counter several times to release any air bubbles and to flatten the mounds slightly. Repeat with remaining meringue and baking sheets.

6 Set the baking sheets aside until the meringue is no longer sticky when lightly pressed with a finger, 1 to 3 hours (depending on the humidity). If some meringue still sticks to your finger, continue to let them dry out before baking.

7 Position oven racks in the top and bottom thirds of the oven and heat the oven to 300°F. Slide two sheets of the meringues into the oven. Bake for 9 minutes, then rotate the sheets in the oven. Continue to bake until the shells are very pale golden, another 5 to 6 minutes. Move the sheets to wire racks and set aside until completely cool. Repeat with the remaining sheet of meringues.

make the filling

Melt the white chocolate, heavy cream, and salt in the microwave or in a small bowl set over a pot of simmering water, stirring with a rubber spatula until smooth. Remove from the heat and set aside until cool and thick enough to spread or pipe, 1 to 2 hours.

assemble the macarons

1 Spoon or pipe about 1½ teaspoons of the chilled filling onto the center of the flat side of one shell, then gently press the flat side of another shell onto the filling until it is just at the edge of the shells. Repeat with remaining shells.

2 The filled macarons can be prepared and kept at room temperature for up to 1 day before serving. The longer they sit, the softer the macaron shells will be.

KITCHEN WISDOM ⚙ **coloring macarons**

I like my flavored macarons to have a matching bold color, so I don't shy away from using the larger amount of food coloring listed on p. 17; if you prefer a more subtle color, use the lower amount. Also, I think the best colors come from gels or pastes. You can find these types of food colorings at your local baking shop or online.

1½ cups (6 ounces) confectioners' sugar

¾ cup (2½ ounces) almond flour

3 whites from large eggs, at room temperature

Pinch of table salt

5 tablespoons (2⅛ ounces) granulated sugar

1½ vanilla beans (see Kitchen Wisdom on the facing page), split and scraped

FOR THE FILLING

⅔ cup raspberry preserves

Makes 38 sandwich cookies (76 shells)

finishing touches

Just before baking, sprinkle the tops of half of the shells with a little finely crushed fleur de sel and use these for the tops of the macarons.

twists

• Substitute 1½ teaspoons pure vanilla extract or pure vanilla bean paste for the vanilla bean seeds.

• Substitute White Chocolate Filling (see p. 17) for the raspberry preserves.

do ahead

Store the shells, unfilled, in an airtight container for up to 1 month.

Gluten Free

Vanilla Bean Macarons with Raspberry Filling

I have always been fascinated with vanilla. As a kid, I could never understand how something that smelled as delicious as vanilla extract could taste so terrible straight from the bottle (I tasted it many times just to be sure and, indeed, it does taste terrible). Yet when baked into a cookie or cake or stirred into ice cream custard or pudding, the aroma and flavor are unmistakable and heavenly.

For the biggest flavor and prettiest appearance, these macarons use the seeds scraped from the pods (see the facing page). Though you can substitute pure vanilla extract for the seeds, the flavor won't be as deep and the macarons won't have the visual beauty of the tiny seeds. If you've never used real vanilla beans before, this is a great recipe to start with.

make the shells

1 Line three large heavy baking sheets with nonstick liners.

2 Put the confectioners' sugar and almond flour in a food processor. Process until the almond flour is very fine, about 45 to 60 seconds. Set a fine-mesh sieve over a medium bowl and add the confectioners' sugar mixture. Sift and discard any remaining almond bits.

3 Put the egg whites and salt in a large bowl (make sure the bowl and beaters are nice and clean, see p. 41). Beat with an electric mixer fitted with the whisk attachment on medium speed until frothy and opaque, about 1 minute. Increase the speed to medium high and beat until the whites form medium-soft peaks, about 2 minutes. Continue beating while gradually sprinkling in the sugar, 1 tablespoon at a time. When all the sugar is added, add the vanilla bean seeds, increase the speed to high, and whip until firm, glossy peaks form. Using a spatula, scrape down the sides of the bowl and beat until just barely blended (it will mix more when you are folding), about 10 seconds.

4 Add half of the confectioners' sugar-almond flour mixture to the meringue and, using a large rubber spatula, fold until most of the mixture is combined. Add the remaining sugar-flour mixture and continue folding until completely combined and the meringue is no longer stiff. It should be glossy and slowly flow off the spatula when lifted.

5 Using a wide plastic scraper or spatula, scoop the meringue into a large pastry bag fitted with a ½-inch-wide plain tip (Ateco #806). Holding the pastry bag perpendicular to a lined baking sheet, pipe small flat mounds about 1¼ inches in diameter and no higher than ⅓ inch onto the prepared sheet, about 1½ inches apart (see the photos on p. 18). Release the pressure on the bag and flick the tip away from the batter. When the baking sheet is filled (I get 30 mounds on my sheet), firmly rap it on the counter several times to release any air bubbles and to flatten the mounds slightly. Repeat with remaining meringue and baking sheets.

6 Set the baking sheets aside until the meringue is no longer sticky when lightly pressed with a finger, 1 to 3 hours (depending on the humidity). If some meringue still sticks to your finger, continue to let the mounds dry out before baking.

7 Position oven racks in the top and bottom thirds of the oven and heat the oven to 300°F. Slide two sheets of the meringues into the oven. Bake for 9 minutes, rotate the sheets in the oven, and then continue to bake until the meringues are very pale golden brown, another 5 to 6 minutes. Move the sheets to wire racks and set aside until completely cool. Repeat with the remaining sheet of meringues.

assemble the macarons

1 Spoon about 1½ teaspoons of the preserves onto the center of the flat side of one shell, then gently press another meringue, flat side down, onto the filling until it spreads just to the edge of the shells. Repeat with remaining shells.

2 Serve immediately or keep at room temperature for up to 1 day before serving. The longer macarons sit, the softer the shells will be.

KITCHEN WISDOM ☺☺
more about vanilla beans

You can find vanilla bean pods in the grocery store alongside the other spices, but you'll get better pricing by buying them online and in larger quantities. Penzeys.com is a reliable source, but shop around to get the best pricing for the smallest amount.

The perfect vanilla bean is about 5 to 7 inches long, plump, and supple and has a very dark brown appearance. To get the seeds out of the bean, hold the bean at one end and, using the tip of a small knife, cut the bean in half lengthwise. Using the back of the knife, slide it down the cut side of bean to push out all of the sticky seed pulp. If the recipe uses only the seeds and not the bean, tuck the empty bean into your vanilla extract bottle or into a container filled with granulated sugar.

Gluten Free
Espresso Macarons with Nutella Buttercream

Classic French macarons shouldn't be confused with "MA-ka-ROONS." While also delicious, the latter is a dense, almond-flavored cookie made with eggs and ground almonds. The former, also made with ground nut flour and egg whites, are small, delicate, flavored shells that are sandwiched with decadent fillings.

Making these little meringue shells is not that simple, but there are some tricks I've learned. For starters, avoid making macarons on humid days—the whites don't behave and the shells just don't dry out as much as they need to in order to make those little "pieds," or feet, around the base of the shell. And be sure to weigh your ingredients. Volume measures can fluctuate, and even a little variation can upend a batch of macarons.

For this recipe, throw out any lessons you've learned about folding ingredients into perfectly beaten egg whites. Here you'll be folding until the batter has deflated, looks glossy, and flows like lava from the spatula. Finding this perfect consistency takes some practice.

For the record, I've had bad mac days, with misshapen shells not ready for a pâtisserie window display, but even these not-so-perfect shells taste delicious.

make the shells

1 Line three large heavy baking sheets with nonstick liners. Put the espresso granules in a small ramekin and add the vanilla. Set aside.

2 Put the confectioners' sugar and almond flour in a food processor. Process until the almond flour is very fine, 45 to 60 seconds. Set a fine-mesh sieve over a medium bowl and add the confectioners' sugar mixture. Sift and discard any remaining almond bits.

3 Put the egg whites and salt in a large bowl (be sure the bowl and beater are nice and clean; see p. 41). Beat with an electric mixer fitted with the whisk attachment on medium speed until the whites are frothy and opaque, about 1 minute. Increase the speed to medium high and beat until the whites form medium-soft peaks, about 2 minutes. Continue beating while gradually sprinkling in the sugar, 1 tablespoon at a time. When all the sugar is added, increase the speed to high and whip until firm, glossy peaks form. Using a spatula, scrape down the sides of the bowl and add the espresso-vanilla mixture (be sure to scrape the ramekin to get all the flavoring) and beat just until blended, about 10 seconds.

recipe continues

FOR THE ESPRESSO MACARON SHELLS

- 1½ teaspoons instant espresso or coffee granules
- 1 teaspoon pure vanilla extract
- 1½ cups (6 ounces) confectioners' sugar
- ¾ cup (2½ ounces) almond flour
- 3 whites from large eggs, at room temperature
- Pinch of table salt
- 6 tablespoons (2⅝ ounces) granulated sugar

FOR THE NUTELLA® FILLING

- 12 tablespoons (6 ounces) unsalted butter, softened
- ¾ cup Nutella

Makes 38 sandwich cookies (76 shells)

finishing touches
Just before baking, sprinkle the tops of half of the shells with a little finely crushed cocoa nibs and use these for the tops of the macaron sandwiches.

twists
Use chocolate ganache instead of the Nutella filling. Melt 6 ounces bittersweet chocolate, finely chopped, and ½ cup heavy cream in the microwave or in a small bowl set over a pot of simmering water, stirring with a rubber spatula until smooth. Remove from the heat and set aside until cool and thick enough to spread or pipe, 1 to 2 hours.

do ahead
The shells can be made and stored, unfilled, in an airtight container for up to 1 month.

4 Add half of the confectioners' sugar-almond mixture to the meringue and, using a large rubber spatula, fold until most of the mixture is combined. Add the remaining sugar-flour mixture and continue folding until completely combined and the meringue is no longer stiff. It should be glossy and slowly flow off the spatula when lifted.

5 Using a wide plastic scraper or spatula, scoop the meringue into a large pastry bag fitted with a $\frac{1}{2}$-inch-wide plain tip (Ateco #806). Holding the pastry bag perpendicular to the lined baking sheet, pipe small flat mounds about $1\frac{1}{4}$ inches in diameter and no higher than $\frac{1}{3}$ inch onto the sheet, about $1\frac{1}{2}$ inches apart (see the photos on p. 18). Release the pressure on the bag and flick the tip away from the batter. Once the baking sheet is filled (I get 30 mounds on my sheet), firmly rap it on the counter several times to release any air bubbles and to flatten the mounds slightly. Repeat with remaining meringue and baking sheets.

6 Set the baking sheets aside until the meringue is no longer sticky when lightly pressed with a finger, 1 to 3 hours (depending on the humidity). If some meringue still sticks to your finger, continue to let them dry out before baking.

7 Position oven racks in the top and bottom thirds of the oven and heat the oven to 300°F. Slide two sheets of the meringues into the oven. Bake for 9 minutes, then rotate the sheets in the oven. Continue to bake until the shells are very pale golden brown, another 5 to 6 minutes. Move the sheets to wire racks and set aside until completely cool. Repeat with the remaining sheet of meringues.

make the filling

Put the butter in a medium bowl and, using a hand-held mixer, beat until smooth. Add the Nutella and mix on medium speed until well blended, about 1 minute. Refrigerate until the mixture is thick enough to spoon or pipe on the macarons, about 1 hour.

assemble the macarons

1 Spoon or pipe about $1\frac{1}{2}$ teaspoons of the chilled filling onto the center of the flat side of one shell, then gently press the flat side of another shell onto the filling until it is just at the edge of the shells. Repeat with remaining shells.

2 Filled macarons can be prepared and kept at room temperature for up to 1 day before serving. The longer they sit, the softer the macaron shells will be.

Espresso–Chip Fantails

The aroma of anything filled with coffee and chocolate gives me a head rush. These swoon-worthy shortbread fantails are no exception and taste even better than they smell. They don't last long in my house!

1 Position an oven rack in the center of the oven and heat the oven to 325°F. Lightly grease a 9½-inch fluted tart pan with a removable bottom. In a small ramekin, mix the vanilla and espresso granules until dissolved.

2 Put the sugar and salt in a food processor and drizzle the vanilla mixture (scraping out every last drop with a rubber spatula) evenly over the mixture. Pulse a few times until the sugar looks a bit damp. Add the flour and pulse a few more times until just blended. Scatter the cold butter pieces over the flour mixture and pulse until the mixture forms moist clumps, about 1 minute.

3 Dump the dough onto the counter or work surface and scatter the chocolate pieces over the top. Gently knead the dough a few times just until the chocolate is incorporated. Scrape into the prepared pan. Using lightly floured fingertips, press the dough into the pan to form an even layer. With the tines of a fork, prick the dough all the way through, spacing evenly around the dough. Lightly flour the tines as necessary to prevent sticking. Using a paring knife or bench scraper, score the dough all the way through, forming 16 wedges. If the dough no longer feels cool to the touch, slide the pan into the refrigerator for 10 minutes.

4 Bake until the top looks dry and pale brown, 30 to 32 minutes. Transfer the pan to a rack. Using a small knife or a bench scraper, immediately recut the wedges, using the scored lines as a guide. Let the shortbread cool completely before removing them.

finishing touches

WHITE CHOCOLATE DIP: Combine 3 ounces white chocolate, chopped, and 2 teaspoons canola or vegetable oil in a small heatproof bowl. Melt over simmering water or in a microwave. Stir until well blended. Dip about 1 inch of the points of the cooled shortbread wedges in the chocolate and arrange on a wire rack or lined cookie sheet. Sprinkle the chocolate with coarse sugar (turbinado or demerara or sugar pearls) and set aside until the chocolate firms up, about 30 minutes.

KITCHEN WISDOM ☺☺ **cutting butter into flour**

Instead of beating softened butter with flour in a mixer, I use the food processor to cut the cold butter into the flour mixture. It makes quick work of this task, and this method helps to create an even lighter, more tender-textured cookie.

---

1   teaspoon pure vanilla extract

½   teaspoon instant espresso or coffee granules

½   cup (3½ ounces) granulated sugar

½   teaspoon table salt

2   cups (9 ounces) unbleached all-purpose flour

12 tablespoons (6 ounces) unsalted butter, cut into 10 pieces and well chilled

2   ounces finely chopped bittersweet chocolate

Makes 16 wedges

twists

Instead of the instant espresso granules and chopped chocolate, use one of the following combinations: ⅓ cup (1⅔ ounces) finely chopped toasted walnuts and 1 teaspoon finely grated orange zest; or 2 ounces white chocolate, chopped, and ¼ teaspoon pure peppermint extract (add with the vanilla); or ½ cup chopped crystallized ginger and 2 teaspoons finely grated fresh ginger.

do ahead

• The shortbread can be prepared through Step 3 and refrigerated for up to 1 day or frozen for up to 1 month. If frozen, thaw in refrigerator overnight before baking.

• Layer the baked and cooled wedges between sheets of parchment or waxed paper in an airtight container. They can be stowed for up to 4 days at room temperature or for up to 6 weeks in the freezer.

FOR THE BROWNIE LAYER

6 tablespoons (3 ounces) unsalted butter, cut into pieces

$2/3$ cup ($4^5/8$ ounces) granulated sugar

$1/3$ cup (1 ounce) unsweetened natural cocoa powder, sifted if lumpy

Pinch of table salt

1 large egg, at room temperature

1 teaspoon finely grated orange zest

1 teaspoon pure vanilla extract

$1/2$ cup ($2^1/4$ ounces) unbleached all-purpose flour

FOR THE CINNAMON LAYER

$1^1/3$ cups (6 ounces) unbleached all-purpose flour

1 teaspoon ground cinnamon

$3/4$ teaspoon cream of tartar

$1/2$ teaspoon baking soda

$1/4$ teaspoon table salt

8 tablespoons (4 ounces) unsalted butter, softened

$1/3$ cup ($2^3/8$ ounces) firmly packed light brown sugar

$1/3$ cup ($2^3/8$ ounces) granulated sugar + extra for patting down the layer

1 large egg, at room temperature

1 teaspoon pure vanilla extract

Makes 24 bars

Chocolate–Cinnamon Double Deckers

One of the break-out recipes from *The Weekend Baker* continues to be the Chocolate Chip Brownie Double Deckers. Readers, reviewers, and bloggers alike love this bar cookie made from layers of brownie and chocolate chip cookie batter baked together as one. This book presented a great opportunity to create a new double decker.

This version has a hint of Mexican flavoring. The chocolate brownie layer is scented with orange zest, and the top layer is adapted from my mom's snickerdoodle recipe, with a heavy hit of ground cinnamon.

make the brownie layer

1 Arrange a rack in the center of the oven and heat the oven to 325°F. Line the bottom and sides of a 9-inch-square baking pan (I like the straight-sided kind) with foil, leaving about a 1-inch overhang on two sides (see p. 5). Lightly grease the bottom and sides of the foil.

2 Put the butter in a medium saucepan and set over medium heat, whisking until melted, about 2 minutes. Slide the pan from the heat and add the sugar, cocoa powder, and salt. Whisk until smooth, about 1 minute. Add the egg, orange zest, and vanilla and whisk until just blended. Add the flour and stir with a rubber spatula until blended. Scrape into the prepared pan and spread evenly over the bottom. Slide the pan into the refrigerator while you make the cinnamon layer.

make the cinnamon layer

1 Put the flour, cinnamon, cream of tartar, baking soda, and salt in a medium bowl. Whisk until well blended.

2 Put the butter in a large bowl. Beat with an electric mixer fitted with the paddle attachment on medium speed until well blended and smooth, about 3 minutes. Add the brown sugar and granulated sugar and beat until well blended, about 1 minute. Add the egg and vanilla and continue beating until well combined, about 2 minutes. Add the flour mixture and mix on low speed until the mixture is well blended, about 1 minute.

3 Drop the cinnamon batter by tablespoonfuls evenly over the chilled brownie batter. Dip your fingertips in the extra granulated sugar and pat the batter into an even layer. Re-sugar your fingertips as needed.

4 Bake until golden brown and a toothpick inserted in the center comes out with only a few moist crumbs clinging to it, 39 to 41 minutes. Move the pan to a wire rack and let cool completely.

5 To cut and serve, use the foil "handles" to lift the entire cookie from the pan. Carefully peel or tear away the foil and toss it out. Using a ruler as a guide (or by eye) and a serrated knife, cut crosswise into 4 equal strips and then cut each strip into 6 bars.

KITCHEN WISDOM ◎◎ **cinnamon**

Cinnamon is the dried bark of the Asian cinnamon or cassia trees. Each type has a unique color and flavor, and subtle nuances. I develop and test my recipes with store-bought brands like McCormick Gourmet® and Spice Islands® (both made with the dark red-brown and strong, sweet taste of cassia) with great results, but I encourage you to explore the different types of cinnamon and find one that you like best. A great resource is penzeys.com.

twists
- Omit the orange zest from the batter if you're not a fan of orange-flavored brownies.
- Add 3 ounces white chocolate, chopped, to the brownie batter.
- Add 1/2 cup toffee bits to the cinnamon batter along with the flour mixture.

do ahead
Cover the bars and stow at room temperature for up to 4 days or freeze for up to 1 month.

- 3⅓ cups (15 ounces) unbleached all-purpose flour
- 3 tablespoons cornstarch
- 1 teaspoon table salt
- 24 tablespoons (12 ounces) unsalted butter, softened
- 1½ cups (6 ounces) confectioners' sugar
- 1 tablespoon finely grated lemon zest
- 2 tablespoons dried lavender (be sure it's the culinary kind, not the bath salt variety)
- 1 teaspoon pure vanilla extract

Makes 45 cookies

twists

MAKE IT CINNAMON TOAST FLAVOR: Instead of using the lavender and lemon zest, add 1 teaspoon ground cinnamon to the flour mixture. Pat the dough into the pan and sprinkle 2 tablespoons granulated sugar mixed with ¾ teaspoon ground cinnamon over the top.

do ahead

- The shortbread can be prepared through Step 3 and refrigerated for 1 day or covered and frozen for up to 1 month. If frozen, thaw in refrigerator overnight before baking.
- Stow the baked and cooled cookies between sheets of parchment or waxed paper in an airtight container for up to 4 days at room temperature or for up to 6 weeks in the freezer.

Egg Free
Lemon Lavender Shortbread

Cornstarch adds a powdery texture to these shortbread bars, so I like to double up on it by using both cornstarch and confectioners' sugar (which contains cornstarch). These cookies smell like a summer morning and they taste just as good—any time of the year.

1 Lightly grease the bottom of a 9x13-inch baking pan (the straight-sided type makes for a cleaner-looking cookie). Put the flour, cornstarch, and salt in a medium bowl and whisk until well blended.

2 Put the butter and sugar into a large bowl and beat with an electric mixer fitted with the paddle attachment until smooth and creamy, about 3 minutes. Add the lemon zest, lavender, and vanilla and beat on medium until blended and fragrant, about 1 minute. Add the flour mixture and beat on low speed until the dough forms moist clumps. Dump the dough into the prepared pan. Using lightly floured fingertips, press the dough into the pan to form an even layer.

3 Using the tip of a knife or a bench scraper, score the dough all the way through, forming 1x2½-inch bars (1 inch across the short side and just a smidgen over 2½ inches on the long one.). With the tines of a fork, prick each bar twice all the way through, spacing them evenly and on the diagonal. Lightly flour the tines of the fork as necessary to prevent sticking. Slide the pan into the freezer or fridge for about 10 minutes while the oven heats.

4 Position an oven rack in the center of the oven and heat the oven to 325°F.

5 Bake the shortbread until the top looks dry and very pale brown, 30 to 34 minutes. Transfer the pan to a rack. Using a small paring knife or a bench scraper (my tool of choice), immediately recut the bars using the scored lines as a guide. Let the shortbread cool completely before removing them from the pan.

> **KITCHEN WISDOM** ☺☺ **removing citrus zest**
>
> To shave strips of zest, scrub and dry the fruit well. Using a vegetable peeler, shave off long strips of the rind (the colored part of the peel). Cut away the bitter pith (the white part) from the rind with a small sharp knife. Slice or chop the rind and discard the pith.
>
> To grate citrus, drag a Microplane® zester with small rasps over the rind in short strokes, turning the fruit as necessary to avoid the bitter white pith.

- **3** cups (13½ ounces) unbleached all-purpose flour
- **2** cups (8 ounces) confectioners' sugar + more for dusting
- **⅔** cup (2⅝ ounces) walnuts, toasted and chopped
- **2** teaspoons baking powder
- **½** teaspoon table salt
- **1** large egg, at room temperature
- **1** yolk from a large egg, at room temperature
- **1** teaspoon pure vanilla extract
- **½** teaspoon pure almond extract
- **24** tablespoons (12 ounces) unsalted butter, cut into small cubes and kept cold
- **1½** cups Spiced Pear Butter (see the recipe on the facing page)

Makes 36 bars

twists

- In place of the walnuts, use the same amount of any nut. Hazelnuts or slivered almonds are especially delicious.
- In place of the pear butter, use the same amount of apple or pumpkin butter or any flavor fruit jam.

do ahead

- These bars can be prepared through Step 4, covered, and frozen for up to 1 month before baking. Thaw in the refrigerator overnight before baking and proceeding with the recipe.
- The baked bars can be covered and stowed at room temperature for up to 2 days. Dust lightly with confectioners' sugar just before serving.

Walnut Pear Crumble Bars

Balance. It's simple to say but not always easy to accomplish in baking. This bar cookie, however, really hits the mark. It has just the right amount of sweetness, a crumbly texture with a touch of nut in every bite, and a burst of fruity flavor.

1 Position an oven rack in the center of the oven and heat the oven to 350°F. Line a 9x13-inch baking pan (I like the straight-sided kind) with foil, leaving about a 1-inch overhang on two sides (see p. 5). Lightly grease the bottom and sides of the foil.

2 Put the flour, confectioners' sugar, walnuts, baking powder, and salt in a large bowl. Mix with an electric mixer fitted with the paddle attachment on low speed until well blended, about 1 minute. Put the egg, yolk, vanilla, and almond extract in a small bowl and, using a table fork, whisk until blended.

3 Add the cold butter pieces to the flour mixture and pulse 4 or 5 times until the flour stops popping out of the bowl. Increase the speed to low and mix until the butter pieces are no bigger than small peas, 2 to 4 minutes. With the mixer on low speed, pour in the egg mixture and mix until a soft dough forms, about 1 minute. Divide the dough in half (1 pound 3½ ounces each).

4 Dump one half of the dough in the prepared pan and, using lightly floured fingertips, pat it down and into the edges and sides to make an even layer. Spread the pear butter evenly over the dough. Break off small chunks of the remaining dough (you'll need floured fingertips for this) and scatter evenly over the butter. It won't cover the butter completely but will come close.

5 Bake until golden brown and the pear butter is bubbling, 49 to 51 minutes. Move the pan to a wire rack and let cool completely.

6 To cut and serve, use the foil "handles" to lift the entire cookie from the pan. Carefully peel or tear away the foil and toss it out. Using a ruler as a guide (or by eye) and a serrated knife, cut crosswise into 4 equal strips and then cut each strip into 9 bars. I use a gentle sawing motion to break through the top crust and then firmly push down on the knife. Dust lightly with confectioners' sugar just before serving.

spiced pear butter

1 Cut the pears into 1-inch chunks. Put the cut-up fruit and the cider in a very large pot (at least 14 cups). Bring to a boil over high heat. Once boiling, reduce the temperature to medium low and simmer, stirring frequently, until the fruit is very tender when pierced with a knife, 20 to 30 minutes. Some pear varieties will break down completely while others will hold their shape even when very tender. Slide the pot from the heat.

2 Set a food mill over a large bowl, making sure it's stable and secure. Purée the fruit in small batches, discarding seeds and skins and changing bowls when necessary.

3 Wipe out any remaining seeds and/or peels from the pot (no need to wash) and pour in the purée. Add the maple syrup, brown sugar, cinnamon, cloves, and salt. Stir until well blended.

4 Bring to a boil over high heat, then reduce the heat to low or medium low to maintain a simmer. Using a large spoon, skim off most of the foam that rises to the surface during the initial simmering.

5 Continue simmering, stirring often with an angled spatula, making sure to scrape the bottom, corners, and sides of the pot, until the purée becomes thick and dark and the bubbling becomes slow and laborious (more like volcanic burps), 1 hour to 1¾ hours. Be sure to stir often toward the end of cooking to avoid scorching. To test for doneness, spoon a dollop of the butter onto a small plate and refrigerate for a minute or two. It should hold its shape with no water separating out around its edge.

6 Slide the pot from the heat and add the lemon juice and vanilla, stirring until well blended. Transfer the pear butter to a container, let cool to room temperature, and then store, covered, in the refrigerator for up to 2 weeks.

3 pounds firm-ripe pears, rinsed and dried (don't peel)

1½ cups pear (or apple) cider

⅔ cup pure maple syrup (preferably grade B)

¼ cup (1¾ ounces) firmly packed light brown sugar

¾ teaspoon ground cinnamon

⅛ teaspoon ground cloves

Pinch of table salt

1½ teaspoons freshly squeezed lemon juice

¾ teaspoon pure vanilla extract

Makes about 2¾ cups

Orange Cardamom Slice 'n Bakes

The thing I like best about this slice 'n bake cookie is its versatility. It morphs easily from an orange-cardamom-poppyseed to a double chocolate peppermint, which is great for the holidays. All variations are loaded with flavor and will fill your house with incredible aromas. Come holiday time, I bake both varieties, divide them into piles, and wrap 'em up to give as hostess or teacher gifts (my mailman likes them, too).

make the dough

1 In a medium bowl, whisk the flour, poppyseeds, cardamom, baking powder, and salt until well blended. Put the butter and sugar in a large bowl and beat with an electric mixer fitted with the paddle attachment until smooth and creamy, about 3 minutes. Add the egg, orange zest, and vanilla to the sugar mixture and beat on medium until blended and fragrant, about 1 minute. Add the flour mixture and beat on low speed until the dough begins to form moist clumps, about 1 minute.

2 Dump the dough onto a large piece of plastic wrap.

3 Using the plastic as a guide, gently knead into a smooth dough. Shape into a 14-inch-long square or round log and wrap well in the plastic. (The square is easiest to shape, but the round is more traditional. If you're going for a round shape, make sure to rotate the log often while it begins to chill.) Refrigerate until chilled and very firm, about 4 hours.

bake the cookies

1 Position an oven rack in the center of the oven and heat the oven to 350°F. Line two (or more if you have them) cookie sheets with parchment or nonstick liners.

2 Using a thin-bladed knife, cut the dough into slices about ¼ inch thick. Arrange the slices about 1 inch apart on the prepared sheets. Bake, one sheet at a time, until the tops look dry and the edges are golden brown, 11 to 13 minutes. Move the sheet to a wire rack and let sit for 5 minutes, then transfer the cookies to a wire rack and let cool completely. Repeat with the remaining dough, using cookie sheets that are completely cold.

2¼ cups (10⅛ ounces) unbleached all-purpose flour

3 tablespoons poppyseeds

1½ teaspoons ground cardamom

½ teaspoon baking powder

¼ teaspoon table salt

12 tablespoons (6 ounces) unsalted butter, softened

1 cup (7 ounces) granulated sugar

1 large egg, at room temperature

4 teaspoons finely grated orange zest

1 teaspoon pure vanilla extract

Makes about 70 cookies

twists

MAKE IT DOUBLE CHOCOLATE-PEPPERMINT: Instead of using the poppyseeds, cardamom, and orange zest, substitute ⅔ cup (2 ounces) unsweetened cocoa powder for ½ cup (2¼ ounces) of the unbleached all-purpose flour. Add ¼ teaspoon pure peppermint extract to the butter mixture along with the egg. Add 3 ounces white or bittersweet chocolate, finely chopped, to the dough along with the flour mixture.

do ahead

• The dough can be prepared through Step 2 and refrigerated for up to 3 days or frozen for up to 1 month before proceeding with the recipe. If frozen, thaw in the fridge overnight before baking.

• Layer the baked and cooled cookies between sheets of parchment or waxed paper in an airtight container. These cookies can be stowed for up to 5 days at room temperature or for up to 3 months in the freezer.

2 cups (9 ounces) unbleached all-purpose flour

1 tablespoon ground ginger

1¾ teaspoons baking powder

¼ teaspoon table salt

Scant ⅛ teaspoon freshly ground black pepper

⅓ cup turbinado sugar (Sugar in the Raw®)

8 tablespoons (4 ounces) unsalted butter, at room temperature

1¼ cups (8¾ ounces) firmly packed dark brown sugar

1 large egg, at room temperature

1 yolk from a large egg, at room temperature

¼ cup finely chopped crystallized ginger

2 teaspoons finely grated fresh ginger

Makes 36 cookies

finishing touches
Before baking, gently press a sliver of crystallized ginger into the center of each cookie.

twists
Add ½ cup (2 ounces) finely chopped, toasted walnuts to the batter along with the crystallized ginger.

Coat the knife with cooking spray to easily cut crystallized ginger or dried fruit.

3X Ginger Sparklers

My favorite accent ingredient by far is ginger—the flavor is big, bold, and filled with citrus and floral tones, plus a bit of spicy heat. Fresh, ground, or crystallized, I love it all, and I use it a lot.

All three types of ginger flavor these soft, moist cookies, turning an ordinary cookie into one that's sensational. The fresh ginger gives each bite a bright, clean flavor, making it a perfect match for spring and summer as well as fall and holiday time. After all, three's a charm.

1 Position an oven rack in the center of the oven and heat the oven to 350°F. Line two cookie sheets with parchment or nonstick liners.

2 Whisk the flour, ground ginger, baking powder, salt, and pepper in a medium bowl until well blended. Put the turbinado sugar in a small bowl. Put the butter and brown sugar in a large bowl and beat with an electric mixer fitted with the paddle attachment until smooth and creamy, about 3 minutes. Add the egg, egg yolk, crystallized ginger, and fresh ginger to the brown sugar mixture and beat on medium until blended and fragrant, about 1 minute. Add the flour mixture and beat on low speed until the dough is just blended, about 1 minute.

3 Using a 1-tablespoon mini scoop, shape the dough into balls, roll the tops in the turbinado sugar, and arrange, sugar side up, about 1½ inches apart on the prepared cookie sheets. Using your fingers, flatten each dough mound slightly.

4 Bake, one sheet at a time, until the cookies are puffed and crackled but still moist looking, about 11 minutes. Move the sheet to a wire rack and let the cookies cool for 5 minutes. Using a spatula, transfer the cookies to a wire rack until completely cooled.

do ahead
• The dough can be made, shaped, rolled in sugar (through Step 3), and put into an airtight container (arrange the balls close together—touching is just fine) and refrigerated for up to 3 days or frozen for up to 1 month before baking. If frozen, thaw on the cookie sheets while the oven heats up and bake as directed.

• Layer the baked and cooled cookies between parchment or waxed paper in an airtight container. They can be stowed for up to 5 days at room temperature or up to 3 months in the freezer. There's almost no thawing necessary—they're delicious even when very cold!

Chunky, Chewy Brownie Drops

I love brownies that are deeply chocolaty and fudgy, but there are times that I want (need!) that big chocolate flavor and chewy texture faster than it takes to cook and cool a panful. These little cookies hold the key to satisfying that craving fast.

The baked cookies measure only a scant 2 inches, making them a perfect two-biter. That said, if you like your cookies a bit heftier, use a 2-tablespoon mini scoop instead of the 1 tablespoon and bake them a touch longer.

1 Position an oven rack in the center of the oven and heat the oven to 350°F. Line three cookie sheets with parchment or nonstick liners.

2 Put the butter in a medium saucepan and set over medium heat, stirring occasionally, until melted. Slide the pan from the heat and add the cocoa powder, brown sugar, and granulated sugar. Whisk until no lumps remain. Set aside to cool, about 5 minutes. In a medium bowl, whisk the flour, baking soda, and salt until well blended. Once the butter mixture has cooled, add the egg and vanilla and whisk until blended. Pour in the flour mixture and stir with a rubber spatula until blended. Stir in the chopped chocolate.

3 Using a 1-tablespoon mini scoop, shape into balls and arrange about 1½ inches apart on the prepared baking sheets. Using slightly dampened fingers, flatten each dough mound slightly, re-wetting your fingers as needed. Bake, one sheet at a time, until the tops look a bit dry but still glisten with moisture, 9 to 11 minutes (if the cookies are overbaked, they won't come out chewy). Move the sheet to a wire rack and let the cookies sit for 10 minutes and then transfer them to a rack to cool completely.

8   tablespoons (4 ounces) unsalted butter, cut into 4 pieces

⅓   cup (1 ounce) unsweetened natural cocoa powder, sifted if lumpy

½   cup (3½ ounces) firmly packed light brown sugar

¼   cup (1¾ ounces) granulated sugar

1¼ cups (5½ ounces) unbleached all-purpose flour

½   teaspoon baking soda

¼   teaspoon table salt

1   large egg, at room temperature

¾   teaspoon pure vanilla extract

6   ounces semisweet or bittersweet chocolate, chopped

Makes 32 cookies

twists

• Add ½ cup (2 ounces) chopped walnuts or pecans along with the chopped chocolate.

• Instead of using semi- or bittersweet chocolate, sub in the same amount of white chocolate, butterscotch, milk chocolate, or peanut butter chips, or use a combination of some or all of them and pair the nuts accordingly. I like using semisweet chocolate and peanut butter chips paired with ½ cup (2½ ounces) lightly salted peanuts.

do ahead

Layer the baked and cooled cookies between parchment or waxed paper in an airtight container. They can be stowed for up to 5 days at room temperature or for up to 3 months in the freezer. There's almost no thawing necessary—they're delicious even when very cold.

FOR THE FILLING

8   ounces cream cheese, softened

4   ounces bittersweet chocolate, melted (see p. 7)

1   yolk from a large egg, at room temperature

2   tablespoons brewed coffee, coffee liqueur, or water, at room temperature

½   teaspoon pure vanilla extract

Pinch of table salt

FOR THE BROWNIE LAYERS

1⅓ cups (6 ounces) unbleached all-purpose flour

½   cup (1½ ounces) unsweetened natural cocoa powder, sifted if lumpy

¼   teaspoon baking powder

½   teaspoon table salt

16 tablespoons (8 ounces) unsalted butter, softened

1¾ cups (12 ounces) granulated sugar

3   large eggs, at room temperature

1½ teaspoons pure vanilla extract

FOR THE GLAZE

5   ounces semisweet chocolate, chopped

4   tablespoons (2 ounces) unsalted butter, cut into 3 pieces

½   cup (2½ ounces) pistachios, lightly toasted and chopped (optional)

Makes 54 small squares

Triple-Threat Chocolate Squares

Like my love affair with all things ginger, I am obsessed with chocolate of all kinds. This cookie speaks volumes about the depth of my love. Riding the line between brownie and cake, it's packed with cocoa and bittersweet and semisweet chocolates. Add cream cheese, butter, and a few other supporting characters and you've baked up a superstar dessert that will satisfy a crowd. I know you'll be tempted to cut these into larger bars but don't—the small two-bite version is just the right amount of chocolaty richness to cure whatever ails you.

make the filling

Put the cream cheese in a medium bowl. Beat with an electric mixer (hand held is fine for this job) until smooth, about 2 minutes. Add the melted chocolate, yolk, coffee, vanilla, and salt. Beat until just blended.

make the brownie layers

1   Position an oven rack in the center of the oven and heat the oven to 350°F. Line a 9x13-inch baking pan (I like the straight-sided kind) with foil, leaving about a 1-inch overhang on two sides (see p. 5). Lightly grease the bottom and sides of the foil.

2   Whisk the flour, cocoa powder, baking powder, and salt in a medium bowl until well blended and no lumps remain. Put the butter and sugar in a large bowl. Beat with an electric mixer fitted with the paddle attachment on medium speed until well blended and smooth, about 3 minutes. Add the eggs, one at a time, beating until just blended between additions. Add the vanilla with the last egg. Add the flour mixture to the sugar mixture and mix on low speed until a soft dough forms, about 1 minute. Divide the dough in half (each half weighs 1 pound, but eyeballing it is fine).

3   Scrape one half of the dough into the prepared pan and, using an offset spatula, spread evenly. Drop spoonfuls of the filling evenly over the batter and spread evenly. If the filling is still soft, pop the pan into the freezer for a few minutes until it's firmer; this will make it easier to spread the top layer. Drop small chunks of the remaining dough evenly over the filling and carefully spread evenly. Bake until a toothpick inserted in the center comes out almost clean (a few crumbs sticking is good), 27 to 29 minutes. Move the pan to a wire rack and let cool completely.

recipe continues

finishing touches

Top each square with a chocolate-covered espresso bean or a candied violet.

do ahead

These bars can be prepared and baked, then covered and frozen for up to 1 month before glazing and serving. Thaw in the refrigerator overnight before proceeding with the recipe.

make the glaze, cut, and serve

1 Melt the chocolate and butter in the microwave or in a small bowl set over a pot of simmering water, stirring with a rubber spatula until smooth. Remove from the heat and set aside. Scrape the glaze onto the top of the brownie and, using an offset spatula, spread evenly. Sprinkle the pistachios (if using) evenly over the chocolate. Slide the baking pan into the refrigerator until the glaze is set, about 20 minutes.

2 Use the foil "handles" to lift the entire brownie from the pan onto a cutting board. Carefully peel or tear away the foil and toss it out. Using a ruler as a guide (or by eye) and a large knife, cut crosswise into 6 equal strips and then cut each strip into 9 pieces. Cover and stow in the refrigerator for up to 3 days. Serve slightly chilled.

Five-Spice Honey Cutouts

Why is it that we only pull out our cookie cutters around the winter holidays? I believe this cookie will break that pattern and make cutouts a year-round treat. The five-spice honey flavor pairing is aromatic and sophisticated, and the cookies are not overly sweet. They're delicious served as is but can also be dressed up to serve at parties and festive occasions (see Finishing Touches at right for ideas).

Take special note of the doneness test here, as the crispness and depth of flavor depend on the proper cooking time.

make the dough

1 Put the flour, five-spice powder, baking soda, and salt in a medium bowl. Whisk until well blended.

2 Put the butter and sugar in a large bowl. Beat with an electric mixer fitted with the paddle attachment on medium speed until well blended and smooth, about 3 minutes. Add the honey, egg, and vanilla and continue beating until well combined, about 2 minutes. Add the flour mixture and mix on low speed until the mixture is completely blended and forms moist clumps, about 1 minute.

3 Scrape the dough onto the counter or work surface and divide into two equal piles (they don't need to be perfectly equal) on two pieces of plastic wrap. Using the plastic as a guide, gently knead each pile into a smooth dough. Shape into flat, 5-inch disks and wrap well in the plastic. Refrigerate until chilled and firm enough to roll, about 15 minutes.

roll and bake the cookies

1 Position an oven rack in the center of the oven and heat the oven to 350°F. Line two to four large cookie sheets with parchment or nonstick liners.

2 Set the dough on the counter to soften enough to roll, about 15 minutes. Working with one piece of dough at a time on lightly floured parchment, roll out the dough to about 3/16-inch thickness (see Roll Like a Pro on p. 5). Dust with additional flour as needed. Using a 2½-inch cookie cutter in any shape, cut out the cookies. Arrange them about 1 inch apart on the lined cookie sheets. Stack the scraps and gently press together; reroll and cut. Repeat with remaining dough.

3 Bake, one sheet at a time, until the edges (about ¼ inch into the cookie) are light brown, 11 to 13 minutes. Move the sheet to a wire rack and let cool for 10 minutes. Carefully remove the cookies from the sheet, set them on a wire rack, and let cool completely. Repeat until all cookies are baked and cooled.

3 cups (13½ ounces) unbleached all-purpose flour

¼ teaspoon five-spice powder

¼ teaspoon baking soda

½ teaspoon table salt

16 tablespoons (8 ounces) unsalted butter, softened

¾ cup (5¼ ounces) granulated sugar

¼ cup honey, preferably one with full, deep flavor (lavender, wildflower, or clover are nice)

1 large egg, at room temperature

1 teaspoon pure vanilla extract

Makes 4 dozen 2½-inch-round cookies

finishing touches
• Before baking, brush the tops of the cutouts with egg wash and sprinkle with demerara sugar.

• Dust the tops of the cooled cookies with a little confectioners' sugar.

twists
MAKE 'EM CARDAMOM: Instead of the five-spice powder, use ¾ teaspoon ground cardamom.

do ahead
• The dough can be wrapped in plastic and/or stowed in a zip-top bag in the refrigerator for up to 3 days or in the freezer for up to 1 month. If frozen, thaw in the refrigerator overnight before proceeding with the recipe.

• The unbaked cutouts can be layered between waxed paper or parchment and frozen for up to 1 month. To thaw, set them on a cookie sheet at room temperature while the oven heats up.

• The baked cookies can be covered in plastic and stowed at room temperature for up to 5 days before serving.

FOR THE MERINGUE SHELLS

¼ cup (1¾ ounces) granulated sugar

⅔ cup (2⅝ ounces) confectioners' sugar

Pinch of table salt

2 whites from large eggs, at room temperature

¼ teaspoon cream of tartar

¼ teaspoon pure vanilla extract

¼ teaspoon pure lemon extract

¼ cup (1¼ ounces) finely crushed gingersnap cookies

FOR THE LEMON CURD FILLING

6 tablespoons (3 ounces) unsalted butter

½ cup (3½ ounces) granulated sugar

⅓ cup freshly squeezed lemon juice

2 tablespoons finely grated lemon zest

Pinch of table salt

6 yolks from large eggs, at room temperature

Makes 40 sandwich cookies (80 shells)

twists

• Substitute 1 cup store-bought lemon or orange curd for the homemade.

• Substitute the same amount of crushed graham crackers or chocolate graham crackers for the gingersnaps.

• Substitute 3 large eggs for the 6 yolks for a less rich (but still delicious) curd.

Gluten Free

Lemon Meringue Pie Poppers

The inspiration for this one-bite cookie needs little explanation. I've topped crisp meringue "buttons" with a sprinkling of finely crushed gingersnap crumbs to give a hint of "crust" and sandwiched them with a tart lemon curd, a.k.a. the "filling." Be sure to tell your guests that these are one-bite poppers—they'll love how the flavors explode in their mouth.

The curd is deliberately tart to balance the high-sugar meringues. If you use this curd for a filling for a less-sweet cookie, you may want to increase the sugar to ⅔ cup.

make the meringues

1 Position oven racks in the top and bottom thirds of the oven and heat the oven to 175°F. Line two large heavy baking sheets with parchment (*do not* use a nonstick liner). Put the sugar in a food processor and process until the sugar is very fine, about 45 seconds. Add the confectioners' sugar and salt. Pulse until well blended, about 15 seconds.

2 In a very clean large bowl (see the sidebar on the facing page), combine the egg whites and cream of tartar and beat with an electric mixer fitted with the wire whisk attachment. Begin mixing on medium-low speed until frothy. Increase the speed to medium high and beat until the whites form soft peaks. Continue beating while gradually sprinkling in the processed sugar mixture. When all of the sugar is added, increase the speed to high and whip until firm, glossy peaks form. Add the vanilla and lemon extracts and beat just until blended, about 10 seconds.

3 Using a wide plastic scraper or spatula, scrape about half of the meringue into a large pastry bag fitted with a ¼-inch-wide plain tip (Ateco #803). Holding the pastry bag perpendicular to the lined baking sheet, pipe small flat mounds about 1¼ inches in diameter and no higher than ¼ inch onto the prepared baking sheets about ½ inch apart. The trick is to keep the tip down in the meringue and let it spread out rather than lifting the tip up as you pipe. Sprinkle the finely crushed cookies evenly over the tops of the meringues. Don't worry if crumbs fall off. Using a fingertip, lightly press down on the crumbs to tap down any meringue peaks.

4 Bake the meringues until dried and crisp but not browned, about 2½ hours. Turn off the oven (leave the door shut) and let the meringues sit in the oven until cool, about 1 hour. Remove the baking sheets from the oven and gently lift the meringues off the parchment.

make the lemon curd

1 Put the butter in a large saucepan and melt over medium heat. Slide the pan from the heat and whisk in the sugar, lemon juice, lemon zest, and salt. Whisk in the yolks until well blended. Cook over medium-low heat, whisking constantly, until the mixture is thick enough to coat a spatula and hold a line drawn through it with a finger, 4 to 6 minutes. Don't let the mixture boil.

2 Set a fine-mesh sieve over a small bowl, strain the curd, discard the zest, and cover the surface directly with plastic wrap. Let cool at room temperature, then refrigerate until chilled or for up to 3 weeks.

assemble the cookies

1 Spread or pipe about 1 teaspoon of the chilled lemon curd on the flat side of one meringue, then gently press another meringue, flat side down, onto the curd.

2 Serve immediately or keep at room temperature for up to 2 hours before serving. The longer the poppers sit, the softer the meringues will become.

do ahead

The meringue "buttons" can be stored, unfilled, in an airtight container for up to 1 month.

KITCHEN WISDOM ☺☺
why a clean bowl and beaters matter

To make sure you get the maximum volume from beaten egg whites, you need to start with a very clean bowl and beaters without any trances of grease. Put the whisk into the bowl, add a good splash of white vinegar, and fill with some warm water. Swirl the bowl to coat the whisk and the inside of the bowl. Pour out the vinegar water, rinse with fresh cold water, and dry thoroughly with a clean towel.

1²/₃ cups (7½ ounces) unbleached all-purpose flour

¾ cup (2 ounces) old-fashioned rolled oats (I use Quaker®)

⅓ cup (1⅞ ounces) shredded sweetened coconut

1 teaspoon baking soda

½ teaspoon table salt

12 tablespoons (6 ounces) unsalted butter, at room temperature

½ cup (3½ ounces) granulated sugar

½ cup (3½ ounces) firmly packed light brown sugar

1 large egg

1½ teaspoons pure vanilla extract

¼ to ½ teaspoon pure almond extract

6 ounces bittersweet or semisweet chocolate, chopped

½ cup (2 ounces) slivered almonds, toasted

Makes 15 cookies

do ahead

These cookies can be baked, cooled, covered, and frozen for up to 1 month before thawing and serving.

twists

- In place of the chocolate chips, use one or more of the following to equal 1 cup: white chocolate chips, butterscotch chips, peanut butter chips, raisins, dried chopped cherries, dried cranberries, dried chopped apricots.

- In place of the almond extract, use finely grated lemon zest (1 to 2 teaspoons) or finely grated orange zest (2 to 3 teaspoons).

- In place of the slivered almonds, use pecans, toasted and chopped (½ cup) or walnuts, toasted and chopped (½ cup).

Almond–Oatmeal "Giants"

I remember when I tasted my first homemade oatmeal cookie like it was yesterday. Something about that cookie's tender, chewy texture and its heady buttery-vanilla taste sent me straight to cookie heaven. What happened next could be considered my first culinary epiphany. It dawned on me that the cookie could be even better by adding some extras into the batter and swapping out some other ingredients. It proved to be the beginning of my love for "twists" and "switch-ins"!

I was a sassy kid of 12, so the first move I made was to swap out the raisins and add chocolate chips (the nuts came later). Over the years, this recipe has morphed into what I think of as the best of the best in oatmeal cookie land.

As the title suggests, these cookies are big. In fact, they are about 4½ inches of goodness. They make a great picnic dessert and also make for great ice cream sandwiches.

1 Position an oven rack in the center of the oven and heat the oven to 350°F. Line three large cookie sheets with parchment or nonstick liners.

2 Whisk the flour, oats, coconut, baking soda, and salt in a medium bowl until well blended.

3 Put the butter in a large bowl. Beat with an electric mixer fitted with the paddle attachment on medium speed until well blended and smooth, about 3 minutes. Add the granulated and brown sugars and continue beating until well combined, about 2 minutes. Add the egg, vanilla, and almond extract and beat until just blended. Add the flour mixture and mix on low speed until just blended, about 1 minute. Add the chocolate and nuts and mix until they are just incorporated.

4 Using a 3-tablespoon mini scoop, shape the dough into balls and arrange about 2½ inches apart on the prepared cookie sheets. Lightly dampen your fingers and press down on each dough mound to flatten to a ½-inch thickness.

5 Bake, one sheet at a time, until the cookies are golden brown, 13 to 15 minutes. Move the sheet to a wire rack for 5 minutes and then transfer the cookies to a wire rack and let cool completely. Repeat with the remaining cookie dough using cooled cookie sheets and liners.

6 Serve the cookies warm or at room temperature.

Coconut Caramel Macadamia Squares

This recipe can be a bit tricky and time-consuming, but it's worth the effort. Simply put aside some time and set up your *mise en place* (French kitchen-speak for having all ingredients measured out before you start the recipe). Be sure you have an accurate candy thermometer (see p. 5), follow the directions, and pay close attention to the doneness tests for the crust and the caramel. In the end, you will have made a sinfully good cookie, and your friends and family will love you forever.

make the crust

1 Line a 9-inch-square baking pan (I like the straight-sided kind) with foil, leaving about a 1-inch overhang on two sides (see p. 5). Lightly grease the bottom and sides of the foil.

2 Put the flour, sugar, and salt in a food processor. Process until blended, about 2 seconds. Scatter the chilled butter pieces over the flour mixture and pulse until the mixture forms coarse crumbs. Sprinkle the water over the flour mixture, then pulse just until the dough forms moist crumbs, about 10 seconds. Scatter the dough in the prepared pan. Using lightly floured fingertips, pat the dough to make an even layer (or as close to even you can get) on the bottom and about ½ inch up the sides of the pan. Refrigerate the pan while the oven heats.

3 Position an oven rack in the center of the oven and heat the oven to 350°F. Bake until the crust is pale golden brown, 24 to 26 minutes. Don't overbake the crust or it will be too crumbly. Move the pan to a wire rack.

make the topping

1 Sprinkle the nuts and coconut evenly over the crust. Put the sugar and water in a medium heavy saucepan. Cook, stirring, over medium-low heat until the sugar dissolves, about 5 minutes. Increase the heat to high and bring to a boil. Boil, without stirring, until the sugar begins to color around the edges of the pan, about 5 minutes. Swirl the pan over the heat until the caramel is an evenly deep amber, about another 2 minutes.

2 Slide the pan off the heat and add the cream and butter. Be careful—it will bubble up, and the steam is super hot. Whisk until well blended and smooth. (If the caramel

recipe continues

FOR THE CRUST

- 1¼ cups (5½ ounces) unbleached all-purpose flour
- ⅓ cup (1⅓ ounces) confectioners' sugar
- ¼ teaspoon table salt
- 10 tablespoons (5 ounces) unsalted butter, cut into 10 pieces and chilled
- 1 tablespoon cold water

FOR THE TOPPING

- 2 cups (10 ounces) unsalted macadamia nuts, toasted and coarsely chopped
- ½ cup (1¼ ounces) shredded coconut, toasted
- 1¼ cups (8¾ ounces) granulated sugar
- ⅔ cup water
- ½ cup heavy cream, at room temperature
- 4 tablespoons (2 ounces) unsalted butter, cut into 2 pieces and softened
- 1 teaspoon pure vanilla extract
- ¼ teaspoon table salt

Makes thirty-six 1½-inch squares

do ahead

Prepare the cookie through Step 2 in Make the Topping and cover and refrigerate for up to 5 days before cutting into squares and serving.

twists

- Instead of the macadamia nuts, use toasted walnuts or whole blanched almonds.

- **ADD A LAYER OF CHOCOLATE:** Melt 8 ounces bittersweet chocolate and 1/3 cup cream in a small heatproof bowl. (I use the microwave, but an improvised double boiler works just fine.) Whisk until well blended and smooth. Spoon 3 tablespoons of the ganache into one corner of a small zip-top plastic bag and set aside. Spread the remaining ganache evenly over the baked crust (through Step 3 in Make the Crust) and freeze while making the caramel filling. Once the caramel is ready, quickly sprinkle the nuts and coconut over the ganache and continue with the recipe. When the caramel is set and chilled, remove the foil from the pan and peel away. Pop the remaining ganache in the zip-top bag in the microwave to remelt, about 30 seconds. Snip off a tiny bit of one corner and drizzle the ganache over the caramel in a random zigzag pattern. Refrigerate until chilled.

clumps, put the pan over low heat and whisk until smooth.) Bring to a boil over medium-high heat and boil, without stirring, until a candy thermometer registers 240°F, about another 2 to 4 minutes. Slide the pan from the heat and whisk in the vanilla and salt. Pour the caramel evenly over the nuts and coconut to cover completely. Gently wiggle the tart pan to settle the caramel. Set aside to cool completely, about 3 hours, then refrigerate until ready to serve or for up to 5 days.

3 To cut and serve, use the foil "handles" to lift the entire cookie from the pan. Carefully peel or tear away the foil and toss it out. Using a ruler as a guide (or by eye) and a sharp, long knife, cut crosswise into 6 equal strips and then cut each strip into 6 bars. Cover and stow in the refrigerator for up to 2 days. These are best when served slightly chilled.

> **KITCHEN WISDOM** ◎◎ **cleaning up when making caramel**
>
> Pots and utensils used to make caramel can be a real drag to clean because of the sticky remnants. The easiest cleanup is simply to fill the pot with water, set it on the stove, and bring it to a boil over high heat. Once boiling, add the utensils and boil until the caramel left in the pot is dissolved, about 5 minutes. Keep an eye on any utensils with wooden handles, as they can scorch. Drain the water and clean the pot and utensils with soapy water.

- 8 tablespoons (4 ounces) unsalted butter, softened
- ⅓ cup (2⅜ ounces) firmly packed light or dark brown sugar
- ¾ teaspoon pure vanilla extract
- ¼ teaspoon table salt
- 2¼ cups (10⅛ ounces) unbleached all-purpose flour
- ½ cup (2 ounces) finely chopped lightly toasted pecans

FOR THE CARAMEL TOPPING:

- 11 small caramels (I use Kraft® brand), unwrapped
- 1 tablespoon + 1½ teaspoons heavy cream

Makes 19 cookies

twists

In place of the caramel, spoon Nutella, dulce de leche, or fruit preserves into the wells of the baked and cooled cookies.

finishing touches

Drizzle the tops of the filled cookies with milk chocolate (see p. 14).

Pecan Caramel Thumbprints

My mom used the word "smart" to describe a well-dressed, chic woman. She'd say something like this: "Oh Abby, did you see Princess Grace on the news? Didn't she look smart?" So many years later, I find myself using that exact same term and not only for the glam and the chic. I like my cookies to be "smart," too. Sometimes this means they are attractive, sometimes they are ridiculously easy to make, and other times their flavor is sophisticated. In this cookie's case, all three superlatives apply. This is one "smart" cookie.

make the cookies

1 Position an oven rack in the center of the oven and heat the oven to 350°F. Line two cookie sheets with parchment or nonstick liners.

2 Put the butter, brown sugar, vanilla, and salt in a large bowl. Beat with an electric mixer fitted with the paddle attachment on medium speed until well blended and smooth, about 3 minutes. Add the flour and mix on low speed until a soft dough forms, about 1 minute.

3 Put the pecans in a small bowl. Using a 1-tablespoon mini scoop, shape the dough into balls and, using your palms, roll into smooth balls. Roll the dough balls in the pecans, pressing lightly so the nuts stick. Arrange the balls about 1½ inches apart on the prepared cookie sheets. Using a round ½-teaspoon measuring spoon, press down into the middle of each mound to make a well that is almost as deep as the dough ball. If the dough sticks to the measuring spoon, dip the bottom of the spoon in a little flour as needed. If the edges crack or break open, pinch the dough together: The finished cookies will look better and hold the caramel without leaking.

4 Bake, one sheet at a time, until the tops look dry and the edges are golden brown, 15 to 17 minutes. Move the sheet to a wire rack and let the cookies sit for 5 minutes, then transfer them to a wire rack and let cool completely.

make the caramel topping and assemble

1 In a small saucepan, combine the unwrapped caramels and heavy cream. Set the pan over very low heat and cook, stirring constantly, until the caramels have melted and the mixture is smooth, about 2 minutes. (This can also be done in the microwave.)

2 Arrange the cooled cookies on a cookie sheet or sheet pan. Using a small spoon (I use a pointed grapefruit spoon) drizzle the warm caramel into each indentation, filling just to the rim but not to overflowing. Let cool completely before stowing or serving.

do ahead

- The cookies can be prepared through Step 4 in Make the Cookies. Layer the baked and cooled (but not filled) cookies between sheets of parchment or waxed paper in an airtight container. These cookies can be stowed for up to 5 days at room temperature or for up to 3 months in the freezer.

- The caramel topping can be prepared though Step 1 in Make the Caramel and stored in the refrigerator for up to 2 weeks. Gently reheat in the microwave or on top of the stove and fill the cookies while the caramel is still warm.

- The filled cookies can be stored at room temperature for up to 3 days. To keep the cookies looking their best, arrange them on a jelly roll pan in a single layer and cover the pan tightly (avoiding the cookie tops) with plastic.

Spiced Raspberry Linzers

This is a soft, moist, cake-like cookie that's loaded with cinnamon and cloves. Like many traditional Linzer torte recipes, cocoa powder is the secret ingredient. The chocolate flavor is subtle and blends with the spices for a deep, sophisticated flavor.

1 Position an oven rack in the center of the oven and heat the oven to 325°F. Line a 9x13-inch baking pan (I like the straight-sided kind) with foil, leaving about a 1-inch overhang on two sides (see p. 5). Lightly grease the bottom and sides of the foil.

2 Whisk the flour, hazelnuts, cocoa powder, cinnamon, cloves, and salt in a medium bowl until well blended. Put the butter and brown sugar in a large bowl. Beat with an electric mixer fitted with the paddle attachment on medium speed until well blended and smooth, about 3 minutes. Add the eggs, one at a time, beating until just blended between additions. Add the vanilla with the last egg. Add the flour mixture to the sugar mixture and mix on low speed until a soft dough forms, about 1 minute.

3 Scoop out about a third of the dough (1⅓ cups or 12¾ ounces) and set aside. Scrape the remaining dough into the prepared pan. Using lightly floured fingers, pat the dough into an even layer, flouring your fingers as needed. Using an offset spatula, spread the preserves evenly over the dough. Using two small spoons, drop ½-tablespoon scoops of the reserved dough over the preserves, spacing them evenly. (Alternatively, you can fill a heavy-duty zip-top bag with the remaining dough, snip about ¾ inch off one corner, and gently squeeze the bag to drop the batter over the preserves.) Using lightly floured fingertips, press the dough to flatten. It will not completely cover the preserves.

4 Bake until a toothpick inserted in the center comes out almost clean (it should still have a few moist crumbs clinging to it), 40 to 42 minutes. Move the pan to a wire rack and let cool completely. Use the foil "handles" to lift the entire tart from the pan onto a cutting board. Carefully peel or tear away the foil and toss it out. Using a ruler as a guide (or by eye) and a large knife, cut crosswise into 4 equal strips and then cut each strip into 9 pieces.

2⅓ cups (10½ ounces) unbleached all-purpose flour

1 cup (5 ounces) whole, blanched hazelnuts, finely ground

2 tablespoons unsweetened natural cocoa powder, sifted if lumpy

1 teaspoon ground cinnamon

¾ teaspoon ground cloves

½ teaspoon table salt

16 tablespoons (8 ounces) unsalted butter, at room temperature

1½ cups (10½ ounces) firmly packed light brown sugar

2 large eggs, at room temperature

1 teaspoon pure vanilla extract

1 cup raspberry preserves (I prefer the seedless variety)

Makes about 36 bars

finishing touches
Just before serving, lightly dust the tops of the bars with confectioners' sugar.

do ahead
The Linzers can be stored at room temperature for up to 5 days.

·2·

Mini Pies & Slab Pies

....

TARTS, TURNOVERS & PIES
PERFECT FOR EATING OUT OF HAND

FOR THE CHOCOLATE DOUGH

- 8 tablespoons (4 ounces) unsalted butter, chilled
- 1 yolk from a large egg
- 3 tablespoons water
- 1⅓ cups (6 ounces) unbleached all-purpose flour
- ½ cup (3½ ounces) granulated sugar
- ⅓ cup (1 ounce) unsweetened natural cocoa powder, sifted if lumpy
- ¼ teaspoon table salt

FOR THE FILLING AND ASSEMBLING

- 1 large egg
- 1 tablespoon milk, heavy cream, or water
- ¾ cup (7¾ ounces) Nutella
- 3 tablespoons demerara or turbinado sugar (Sugar in the Raw)

Makes 8 hand tarts

Nutella–Chocolate Hand Tarts

Chocolate "everything" intrigues me, including the store-bought chocolate toaster pastries. You know the ones I'm talking about. I even tried them once just to satisfy my curiosity. These hand tarts are the result of that taste test. The crust from these homemade tarts is rich and chocolaty, and just to make sure you get an extra dose of chocolate, I've sandwiched them with Nutella. When warmed in the toaster oven, they're gooey and oh so good.

make the chocolate dough

1 Cut the butter in half lengthwise, cut each half lengthwise again and then cut each strip into 6 pieces. Pile the butter onto a plate and slide it into the freezer until ready to use. Put the yolk and water in a small bowl and, using a fork, mix until blended.

2 Whisk the flour, sugar, cocoa powder, and salt in a large bowl until well blended. Add the cold butter pieces and, using a pastry blender or two knives, cut the butter into the flour mixture until the pieces are pea-sized, about 3 minutes. (You can also do this in a food processor using short pulses; scrape the blended mixture into a large bowl before proceeding.)

3 Pour the egg-water mixture over the flour and, using a rubber spatula, stir and fold until it forms a shaggy, moist dough with some floury bits remaining. (If you don't mind getting your hands dirty, use one hand to mix the dough and hold the spatula in the other.) Scrape the dough and any remaining floury bits onto the counter and knead (see Kitchen Wisdom on facing page) a few times until the dough is evenly moist and holds together. Divide the dough into two equal pieces (about 7 ounces each) and shape each into a 5-inch square; wrap each square in plastic and refrigerate until well chilled, about 2 hours.

assemble and bake

1 Position an oven rack in the center of the oven and heat the oven to 400°F. Line a cookie sheet with parchment or a nonstick liner. Put the egg and milk in a small bowl and, using a fork, mix until well blended.

2 Working with one piece of dough at a time (if it's very cold, set it out at room temperature until it's pliable enough to roll) on lightly floured parchment, roll out the dough to a square slightly larger than 9 inches, lightly dusting with flour as needed (see Roll Like a Pro, p. 5). Using a sharp paring knife and a ruler, trim the edges to get a neat 9-inch square and then cut it into 2¼x4½-inch rectangles (for a total of 8 rectangles). (If the dough is soft, slide the dough onto a cookie sheet and into the

fridge until chilled, about 20 minutes, before proceeding). Arrange the pastry rectangles about 2 inches apart on the prepared cookie sheet, cover with plastic wrap, and chill. Roll out and cut the second piece of dough as you did the first one and chill the rectangles on another cookie sheet (or the two can be stacked on the one sheet).

3   Uncover the dough on the cookie sheet and spoon about 1½ tablespoons of the Nutella onto the center of eight of the rectangles and spread, leaving a ½-inch border at the edges. Using a small pastry brush, brush the edges of each rectangle with egg wash. Lay the remaining rectangles over the filling, pressing firmly on the edges to seal.

4   Using the tines of a fork (dip in flour if necessary), press (or crimp) the pastry edges to seal (see the bottom photo on p. 56). Lightly brush the top of each tart with egg wash. Using the tip of a small sharp knife, cut 2 or 3 small slits in the top of each tart to let steam escape. Sprinkle the tops evenly with the demerara sugar.

5   Bake until the tarts are puffed and dark around the edges, 15 to 17 minutes. Move the sheet to a wire rack and let cool for 10 minutes. Carefully remove the tarts from the sheet, set them on a wire rack, and let cool completely. The tarts are best when served the same day but can be reheated in a toaster oven.

do ahead
The dough can be made and stowed in the fridge for up to 2 days or frozen for up to a month.

twists
Instead of Nutella, use the same amount of strawberry jam, raspberry jam, or apricot jam.

KITCHEN WISDOM ෙෙ
fraisage

Fraisage is the French term for a style of kneading a delicate pastry dough to keep it from being overworked and tough. Whenever the recipe says to "knead" the dough, use this technique: Dump the dough on the counter or work surface, then lightly smear the ingredients together by pushing them away from you with the heel of your hand and then gathering the dough together. Repeat one or two times until the dough holds together and proceed with the recipe.

Peach–Rosemary Mini Hand Tarts

Have you ever made a pastry dough in a saucepan? That's exactly how you'll make this brown butter crust. The dough is soft, supple, and easy to roll between pieces of parchment, making it amazingly easy to handle—a real bonus for beginning bakers. The inspiration for this dough came from the wafers for the Brown Butter Ice Cream Sandwiches (see p. 154).

For the filling, I mixed chopped fresh rosemary with store-bought peach preserves. I like to add savory herbs to my baked goods for the earthy quality they provide as well as the higher level of sophistication. Feel free to play around with the filling flavors and substitute other preserves and herbs.

make the brown butter dough

1 Put the butter in a large saucepan. Cook, stirring, over medium heat until nutty brown and the milk solids are dark brown, 6 to 7 minutes. Slide the pan from the heat and add the brown sugar, salt, and five-spice powder, if using. Stir until the sugar is almost dissolved, then set aside for 5 minutes to cool slightly. Using your fingertip, check the temperature of the batter—it should be warm but not hot. If it's hot, set the pan aside for a few more minutes before continuing with the recipe.

2 Add the eggs and vanilla and stir until well blended. Add the flour and stir until a smooth, soft dough forms.

3 Arrange two pieces of plastic wrap on the counter and scrape the dough onto the center of one. Divide the dough in half (about 14¾ ounces each) and put half on the second piece of plastic wrap. Using the plastic as a guide, shape both into 5-inch squares. Wrap in the plastic and set aside at room temperature until firm enough to roll, about 3 hours. (You can pop the dough rectangles into the refrigerator for a hour or so, but you don't want the dough to be too chilled. It would be impossible to roll.)

make the filling

Put the preserves, rosemary, and salt in a small bowl. Using a fork, stir until well blended. Taste the preserves and add more rosemary, if you like.

recipe continues

FOR THE BROWN BUTTER DOUGH

16 tablespoons (8 ounces) unsalted butter, cut into 1-inch pieces

1 cup (7 ounces) firmly packed light brown sugar

½ teaspoon table salt

⅛ teaspoon five-spice powder (optional)

2 large eggs, at room temperature

1 teaspoon pure vanilla extract

3 cups (13½ ounces) unbleached all-purpose flour

FOR THE FILLING

10 tablespoons peach preserves

1 teaspoon finely chopped fresh rosemary; more to taste

Pinch of table salt

FOR ASSEMBLY

1 large egg

1 tablespoon water

Confectioners' sugar, for serving

Makes 18 mini hand tarts

do ahead

The hand tarts can be assembled, covered in plastic, and stowed in the refrigerator for up to 1 day before baking.

twists

• Instead of peach preserves, use the same amount of strawberry or apricot preserves.

• **MAKE 'EM APPLE:** Instead of peach preserves, use the apple filling from Cinnamon–Sugar Apple Phyllo Triangles (see p. 77).

• **MAKE 'EM BIGGER:** Follow the directions for making and rolling the dough but instead of cutting into 3x2½-inch rectangles, cut into 3x5-inch rectangles. Use about 1 rounded tablespoon of the filling for each and proceed as directed. This twist will make 9 hand tarts.

Spoon the filling onto each rectangle.

Spread the filling to within ½ inch of the edge of the dough.

Crimp the edges of the pastry rectangles with a fork.

assemble and bake

1   Line two cookie sheets with parchment or nonstick liners. Put the egg and water in a small bowl and, using a fork, mix until well blended.

2   Working with one piece of dough at a time on a lightly floured piece of parchment (this dough is soft, so the parchment is a must for successful rolling), roll out to a rectangle slightly larger than 9x15 inches (see Roll Like a Pro, p. 5). Using a sharp paring knife or a fluted roller and a ruler, trim the edges to get a neat 9x15-inch rectangle, then cut into 3x2½-inch rectangles (for a total of 18 rectangles). Arrange the pastry rectangles about 2 inches apart on the prepared cookie sheets and cover with plastic. Roll out and cut the second piece of dough as you did the first one.

3   Uncover the dough on one of the cookie sheets. Spoon 1½ teaspoons of the filling onto the center of each rectangle and spread, leaving a ½-inch border at the edges. Using a small pastry brush, brush the edges of each rectangle with egg wash. Lay the remaining rectangles over the filling. Using the tines of a fork, press (or crimp) the pastry edges to seal (see the photo below left). Lightly brush the top of each hand tart with egg wash. Using the tip of a small sharp knife, cut 2 small slits in the top of each hand tart to let steam escape. Slide the cookie sheets into the fridge while the oven heats up.

4   Position an oven rack in the center of the oven and heat the oven to 375°F.

5   Bake, one sheet at a time, until the tarts are dark brown on the edges, 20 to 23 minutes. Move the sheet to a wire rack and let cool for 10 minutes. Carefully remove the tarts from the sheet and set them on a wire rack and let cool completely. Just before serving, lightly dust the tops with confectioners' sugar. The tarts are best when served the same day.

finishing touches

• After brushing the tops of the hand tarts with the egg wash, sprinkle with turbinado sugar.

• **ADD VANILLA DRIZZLE:** Instead of adding turbinado sugar, add a drizzle.

>   1 cup (4 ounces) confectioners' sugar
>   2 to 3 tablespoons heavy cream
>   ¼ teaspoon pure vanilla extract
>   ¼ teaspoon ground cinnamon (optional)

Put the confectioners' sugar, heavy cream, vanilla, and cinnamon (if using) in a small bowl. Using a spoon, stir until well blended and smooth. Continue stirring until smooth and shiny. Spoon the mixture into a heavy-duty zip-top bag and seal tightly. Snip off about ½ inch from one corner and, squeezing gently, move the bag evenly over the top of the completely cooled hand tarts in a zigzag pattern to form a ribbon.

Brown Sugar–Ginger–Pear Turnovers

These turnovers make a flavorful splash on a dessert table and also are a perfect afternoon treat. But I've also been known to double this recipe and keep a few aside so I can reheat them for a heavenly breakfast the next morning. A toaster oven is perfect for this task as all that's needed is about 10 minutes at a moderate temperature—just enough time to crisp the pastry and warm the fruit filling. If you're feeding more than just yourself, assemble the pastries, cover, and stow them unbaked in the fridge so they are ready to bake up in the morning.

I've filled these classic-sized turnovers with two of my favorite flavors of fall: ginger and ripe pears, but if your pears aren't ripe or you'd like smaller, bite-sized turnovers, check out the Twists on p. 58. All the Twists are fall-worthy—and delicious.

make the filling

Cut the pears into ½-inch pieces. Put the butter in a medium skillet and cook, stirring, over medium-low heat until melted. Add the pears, brown sugar, flour, and salt. Cook over medium heat, stirring, until the pears are tender and most of the liquid is evaporated and a little thick syrup remains, 7 to 9 minutes. Add the brandy, if using, and lemon juice (be careful—it will steam up) and cook, stirring frequently, over low heat until the liquid is evaporated, 1 to 2 minutes. Slide the pan from the heat, stir in the crystallized ginger, and set aside to cool completely. You'll have about 1 firmly packed cup of cooked filling.

assemble and bake

1 Position an oven rack in the center of the oven and heat the oven to 425°F. Line a cookie sheet with parchment or a nonstick liner. Put the egg and water in a small bowl and, using a fork, mix until well blended.

2 Unfold the puff pastry and on a lightly floured surface, roll out the dough to a square slightly larger than 12 inches. (I don't use parchment for rolling this store-bought dough). Using a sharp paring knife and a ruler, trim the edges to get a neat 12-inch square and then cut into four 6-inch squares.

3 Spoon about a quarter of the filling onto the center of each square and spread down the middle, leaving a ¾-inch border of dough. Using a small pastry brush, brush

recipe continues

FOR THE FILLING

- 2 (1 pound total) firm-ripe pears (Anjou, Comice, or Bartlett are my favorites), peeled and cored
- 2 tablespoons unsalted butter
- 3 tablespoons firmly packed light brown sugar
- ½ teaspoon unbleached all-purpose flour

Pinch of table salt

- 1 tablespoon brandy (optional)
- 1 teaspoon freshly squeezed lemon juice
- 2 tablespoons finely chopped crystallized ginger

FOR ASSEMBLY

- 1 large egg
- 1 teaspoon water
- 1 sheet (about 9 ounces) frozen puff pastry, thawed
- 2 tablespoons demerara or turbinado sugar (Sugar in the Raw)

Makes 4 turnovers

do ahead

- The filling can be made and stowed in the refrigerator for up to 2 days before using.

- The turnovers can be assembled, covered in plastic, and stowed in the refrigerator for up to 1 day before adding the egg wash and demerara sugar and baking.

twists

- Instead of pears, use the same amount of apples or a combination of the two.
- Instead of brandy, stir in, off the heat, one of the following: $1/2$ teaspoon finely grated lemon zest or $1/4$ teaspoon pure almond extract or $3/4$ teaspoon pure vanilla extract or $1/2$ teaspoon ground cinnamon.
- Instead of the demerara sugar topping, substitute a sugar-nut topping. Just before baking, evenly sprinkle the tops of the glazed turnovers with 2 tablespoons granulated sugar and $1/3$ cup ($1 3/8$ ounces) sliced almonds.
- Instead of using frozen puff pastry, use a half-recipe of the Rough Puff Pastry (see p. 62)
- Top the cooled turnovers with Honey Ribbon Glaze (see p. 68) or Vanilla Drizzle (see p. 56)
- **MAKE 'EM SMALLER:** Roll the pastry as directed and cut into nine 4-inch squares. Portion the filling evenly among the squares and proceed as directed, baking for 20 to 22 minutes.

the edges of each square with egg wash (be careful not to let the egg dribble over the edge or the pastry won't puff). Fold the dough over the filling to form triangles. Using the tines of a fork, gently press (or crimp) the pastry edges to seal (see the bottom photo on p. 56).

4 Arrange the turnovers about 2 inches apart on the prepared cookie sheet. Lightly brush the top of each turnover with egg wash and sprinkle evenly with the demerara sugar. Using the tip of a small sharp knife, cut 2 or 3 small slits in the top of each turnover to let steam escape.

5 Bake until the turnovers are deep golden brown, 23 to 25 minutes. Move the sheet to a wire rack and let cool for 10 minutes. Carefully remove the turnovers from the sheet, set them on a wire rack, and let cool completely. The turnovers are best when served the same day and can be warmed slightly in a 300°F oven, if you like.

Elderberry–Blueberry Turnovers

I think of this dough as a hybrid of my favorite crusts. Cream cheese, cornmeal, and vanilla added to a traditional pie dough bakes into a tender, flaky, sweet crust with a hint of cornmeal texture. The dough is a bit soft and, therefore, a bit more challenging to work with, so I urge you to do as I do and roll it between sheets of parchment (see Roll Like a Pro, p. 5).

This dough is just about perfect for turnovers filled with any fruit, but fresh blueberries mixed with a hint of elderberry liqueur really say "summertime" to me and my family.

make the dough

1 Cut the butter in half lengthwise, cut each half lengthwise again, and then cut each strip into 8 pieces. Cut the cream cheese into 3/4-inch pieces. Pile the butter and cream cheese onto a plate and slide into the freezer until ready to use. Measure the water in a 1-cup glass measure or a small bowl; add the vanilla and keep in the fridge until ready to use.

2 Whisk the flour, cornmeal, sugar, and salt in a large bowl until well blended. Add the cold butter and cream cheese pieces and, using a pastry blender or two knives, cut the butter and cream cheese into the flour mixture until the pieces are pea-sized, about 3 minutes. (You can also do this in a food processor using short pulses, scraping the blended mixture into the large bowl before proceeding.)

3 Pour the water mixture over the flour and, using a rubber spatula, stir and fold until it forms a shaggy, moist dough with some floury bits remaining (If you don't mind getting your hands dirty, use one hand to mix the dough and the spatula in the other.) Scrape the dough and any remaining floury bits onto the counter and knead (see Kitchen Wisdom on p. 53) a few times until the dough is evenly moist and holds together. Divide the dough into two equal pieces (about 14 ounces each) and shape each into a 4x6-inch rectangle; wrap in plastic and refrigerate until well chilled, about 2 hours.

make the filling

Put the blueberries, sugar, flour, liqueur, and salt in a medium bowl. Using a fork, toss to blend while lightly crushing the berries.

recipe continues

FOR THE DOUGH

- 14 tablespoons (7 ounces) unsalted butter, chilled
- 4 ounces cream cheese, chilled
- 1/2 cup very cold water
- 1/2 teaspoon pure vanilla extract
- 2 1/4 cups (10 1/8 ounces) unbleached all-purpose flour
- 1/2 cup (2 1/4 ounces) coarse yellow cornmeal
- 1/4 cup (1 3/4 ounces) granulated sugar
- 1/4 teaspoon table salt

FOR THE FILLING

- 2 cups (10 ounces) fresh blueberries, picked over and rinsed
- 3 tablespoons granulated sugar
- 2 tablespoons unbleached all-purpose flour
- 2 teaspoons elderberry liqueur

Pinch of table salt

FOR ASSEMBLY

- 1 large egg
- 1 teaspoon water
- 3 tablespoons demerara or turbinado sugar (Sugar in the Raw)

Makes 16 turnovers

do ahead

- The dough can be made and stowed in the refrigerator for up to 2 days before using or frozen for up to 1 month. Thaw overnight in the refrigerator before rolling.

- The turnovers can be assembled, covered in plastic, and stowed in the refrigerator for up to 1 day before baking.

twists

- Instead of blueberries, use the same amount of raspberries or a combination of raspberries and blueberries.
- Instead of elderberry liqueur, use one of the following: 1/2 teaspoon finely grated lemon zest or 1/4 teaspoon pure almond extract or 3/4 teaspoon pure vanilla extract or 1/2 teaspoon ground cinnamon.
- Instead of the demerara sugar topping, substitute a sugar-nut topping. Just before baking, evenly sprinkle the tops of the turnovers with 2 tablespoons granulated sugar and 1/3 cup (1 3/8 ounces) sliced almonds.
- **MAKE 'EM TRIANGLES:** For a more traditional turnover shape, fold the dough over the filling to bring the points together.

assemble and bake

1 Position an oven rack in the center of the oven and heat the oven to 400°F. Line two cookie sheets with parchment or nonstick liners. Put the egg and water in a small bowl and, using a fork, mix until well blended.

2 Working with one piece of dough at a time on a lightly floured piece of parchment (this dough is soft so the parchment is a must for successful rolling), roll out the dough to a rectangle slightly larger than 8x16 inches (see Roll Like a Pro, p. 5). Using a sharp paring knife and a ruler, trim the edges to get a neat 8x16-inch rectangle and cut into 4-inch squares (for a total of 8 squares). Roll out and cut the second piece of dough as you did the first one.

3 Spoon 1 rounded tablespoon of the filling onto the center of each square and spread down the center, leaving a 1/2-inch border at the edges. Using a small pastry brush, brush the edges of each square with the egg wash. Fold the dough over the filling to form rectangles. Using the tines of a fork, press (or crimp) the pastry edges to seal (see the bottom photo on p. 56).

4 Arrange the turnovers about 2 inches apart on the prepared cookie sheets. Lightly brush the top of each turnover with egg wash and sprinkle evenly with the demerara sugar. Using the tip of a small sharp knife, cut 2 or 3 small slits in the top of each turnover to let steam escape.

5 Bake, one sheet at a time (if your kitchen is hot, loosely cover the second sheet with plastic and stow in the fridge until ready to bake), until the turnovers are deep golden brown, 28 to 30 minutes. Move the sheet to a wire rack and let cool for 10 minutes. Carefully remove the turnovers from the sheet and set them on a wire rack and let cool completely. The turnovers are best when served the same day and can be warmed slightly in a 300°F oven, if you like.

FOR THE ROUGH PUFF PASTRY
(makes 1¼ pounds of dough)

- 2 cups (9 ounces) unbleached all-purpose flour
- ½ teaspoon table salt
- 8 ounces (16 tablespoons) unsalted butter, cut into 16 pieces and well chilled
- ½ cup water, well chilled

FOR THE FILLING

- ½ cup (2 ounces) slivered almonds, toasted
- ¼ cup (1¾ ounces) granulated sugar
- 1 large egg
- 4 tablespoons (2 ounces) unsalted butter, softened
- ½ teaspoon pure vanilla extract

FOR ASSEMBLY

- 2 firm-ripe, medium-sized pears, peeled, cored, and sliced ¼-inch thick
- 2 teaspoons granulated sugar
- ⅛ teaspoon ground cinnamon

Serves 8 to 10

finishing touches
Just before serving, sprinkle the pie with 3 tablespoons slivered almonds, chopped and toasted.

twists
- Instead of pears, use the same amount of apples, peaches, plums, or apricots.

do ahead
- The rough puff pastry can be made and stowed in the refrigerator for up to 2 days before using, or it can be frozen up to 1 month. Thaw overnight in the refrigerator before rolling.
- The tart shell can be assembled, covered in plastic, and stowed in the refrigerator for up to 1 day before filling and baking.

Pear Almond Frangipane Slab Pie

Rough puff pastry is one of those pastry miracles/culinary leaps of faith that I like to talk about. The first time you make this recipe, you won't believe that such a scraggly, messy dough could ever become a buttery, flaky, melt-in-your-mouth pastry, but it does. Trust me, have some faith and follow my directions, and I promise that you will end up with a gorgeous dough and feel like a modern-day pastry genius. Sure, when pressed for time, you can buy ready-made frozen puff pastry at the grocery store and have good results, but once you try this easy recipe and taste the outstanding results, you'll never look at the premade the same way.

The flavor pairing of this tart—pear and almond frangipane—is a personal favorite and one that always reminds me of France. When I first moved there, I was a young culinary student eager to try everything that each pâtisserie had to offer. And try I did. Everything. As many desserts as I sampled, however, it was always the pear-almond frangipane tarts that I chose for my Sunday afternoon treat. The texture is comforting, almost pudding-like, and the flavors smell and taste like sunshine.

make the rough puff pastry

1 Whisk the flour and salt in a large bowl until blended. Add the butter and toss to coat with flour. Using a pastry blender or two table knives, cut the butter into the flour until the mixture is dry and rough with ½- to ¾-inch chunks of butter. Add the ½ cup very cold water and continue cutting until you get a shaggy dough that barely hangs together. Scrape the dough out onto a lightly floured counter or work surface and, using your hands, shape into a rectangle. Using a rolling pin, roll into a 6x18-inch rectangle, scraping the rolling pin and lightly flouring the dough as necessary. The dough will be ragged at first.

2 With a metal bench scraper, fold both short ends toward each other so they meet in the middle. Fold one half over the other half to make a 4x6-inch rectangle. Turn the dough so that the seam is on the right. Using the rolling pin, roll into a 6x18-inch rectangle and repeat the folding technique. Wrap in plastic; chill for 20 minutes.

3 Position the dough so the seam is on the right. Roll into a 6x18-inch rectangle and fold the dough again as directed above, flouring lightly if needed. It should be smooth with visible flecks of butter. Divide the puff pastry crosswise into 2 rectangles, one about ¾ inch longer than the other. Wrap in plastic and refrigerate until well chilled, about 2 hours or overnight.

make the filling and assemble the pie

1 Arrange an oven rack in the center of the oven and heat the oven to 425°F. Line a cookie sheet with parchment or a nonstick liner.

2 Put the almonds and sugar in a food processor. Pulse until the nuts are finely chopped. Add the egg, butter, and vanilla and process until creamy. Chill until the dough is rolled out.

3 On a lightly floured surface, roll out the smaller pastry rectangle to a rectangle roughly 9x14 inches. Gently roll it around the pin and arrange on the prepared sheet. Using a sharp paring knife and a ruler, trim the edges to get a neat rectangle 8x13 inches. Cover loosely with plastic wrap.

4 Roll out the larger pastry rectangle to roughly 11½x14 inches and, using a sharp paring knife and a ruler, trim the edges to get a neat rectangle 11x13 inches. Cut this rectangle into four 13x¾-inch strips and four 8x¾-inch strips. (You'll have leftover dough, which can be refrigerated or frozen for another use.)

5 Using a small pastry brush, brush a little water over two of the shorter strips and lay them, wet side down, along the short sides of the smaller rectangle. Brush a little water over two of the longer strips and lay them, wet side down, along the longer sides of the rectangle, overlapping the shorter strips at the corners. Repeat with the remaining four strips, stacking them on the first set of strips to make a double-high edge.

6 Spread the almond filling evenly over the bottom of the tart crust, up to the edges. Arrange the sliced pears in a shingled crosswise pattern over the filling, alternating directions with each row. Combine the sugar and cinnamon in a small bowl and stir until blended. Sprinkle the cinnamon sugar over the fruit.

7 Bake until the crust is puffed and well browned and the fruit is tender, 23 to 26 minutes. Using a spatula, lift one corner of the pastry to check that the bottom is nicely browned. If not, bake a few minutes longer. Move the pan to a wire rack to cool for at least 15 minutes. Using a bench scraper or a knife, cut the pie in half lengthwise and then cut each strip into four pieces. Serve warm or at room temperature.

FOLDING ROUGH PUFF PASTRY

Use a bench scraper to lift and fold the short ends of the dough.

Cut the finished dough into two pieces, with one slightly larger than the other.

½ cup lightly salted mixed nuts,
    coarsely chopped

⅓ cup store-bought dulce de leche

FOR ASSEMBLY

1 large egg

1 teaspoon water

FOR THE DOUGH

1 sheet (about 9 ounces) frozen
   puff pastry, thawed

Makes 8 dumplings

Nutty Dulce de Leche Dumplings

This four-ingredient dessert is just the thing you need when last-minute guests drop in or when you're pressed for time and need a fabulous dessert fast. The baked dumplings, or turnovers, are flaky and bursting with a slightly salty, nutty, caramel filling.

I've tested many types of store-bought dulce de leches and prefer La Salamandra® (though I'm still sampling). It's rich and flavorful and behaves well when mixed with lightly salted nuts (don't use dry roasted) and baked up in store-bought puff pastry.

make the filling

Put the nuts and dulce de leche in a small bowl and stir until blended. You'll have about ½ firmly packed cup of filling.

assemble and bake

1 Position an oven rack in the center of the oven and heat the oven to 425°F. Line a cookie sheet with parchment or a nonstick liner. Put the egg and water in a small bowl and, using a fork, mix until well blended.

2 Unfold the puff pastry and, on a lightly floured surface, roll out the dough to a 10-inch square (no need for perfection here as you are cutting out rounds from the dough). Using a 4-inch round cookie cutter, cut out 6 rounds. Stack the scraps (because it's puff pastry, you want to stack—not gather—to preserve the layers as much as possible), roll out to a ⅛-inch thickness, and cut another 2 rounds for a total of 8 rounds of dough.

3 Spoon about 1 tablespoon of the filling onto the center of each round. Using a small pastry brush, brush the edges of each round with egg wash (be careful not to let the egg dribble over the edge or the pastry won't puff). Put one round in your palm, cupping it to bring the edges together; pinch the edges to seal and place on the prepared sheet. Do the same with the other rounds, arranging them about 2 inches apart on the cookie sheet.

4 Using the tines of a fork, gently press (or crimp) the pastry edges to seal (see the bottom photo on p. 56). Lightly brush the top of each dumpling with egg wash. Using the tip of a small sharp knife, cut 2 or 3 small slits in the top of each dumpling to let steam escape.

5 Bake until the dumplings are puffed and deep golden brown, 19 to 21 minutes. Move the sheet to a wire rack and let cool for 10 minutes. Carefully remove the dumplings from the sheet, set them on a wire rack, and let cool completely. The dumplings are best when served the same day and can be warmed slightly in a 300°F oven, if you like.

KITCHEN WISDOM ☺☺ dulce de leche

Dulce de leche is a very thick, sweet milk sauce that is similar in taste to caramel. Widely available in cans and jars, it's also easy to make at home. Pour 1 can (14 or 14½ ounces) sweetened condensed milk (not evaporated) into a medium saucepan. Cook, stirring frequently, over low heat until golden brown, creamy, and very thick, about 22 minutes. Off the heat, stir in ¼ teaspoon pure vanilla extract and a pinch of table salt or fleur de sel. Let cool completely before using or cover and refrigerate for up to 1 week.

finishing touches
• Before baking, sprinkle the tops of the egg-glazed dumplings with demerara sugar.
• Dust the tops of the warm or cool dumplings with a little confectioners' sugar.

twists
• Instead of mixed nuts, use the same amount of any one nut or combination of nuts.
• Instead of frozen puff pastry, use a half-recipe of the Rough Puff Pastry (see p. 62).

do ahead
The dumplings can be assembled, covered in plastic, and stowed in the refrigerator for up to 1 day before baking.

FOR THE DOUGH

1   package (7 ounces) premade
    pie dough

FOR THE FILLING

¾   cup (3¾ ounces) chopped
    pistachios, toasted

⅓   cup (2⅜ ounces) granulated
    sugar

6   tablespoons (3 ounces) unsalted
    butter, softened and cut into
    6 pieces

2   teaspoons dark rum

Pinch of table salt

1   large egg

6   small, ripe apricots, trimmed
    and quartered

Chopped pistachios, toasted, for
    serving

Confectioners' sugar, for serving

Makes 24 mini tarts

finishing touches

ADD MORE APRICOT FLAVOR: In a
small ramekin, heat 3 tablespoons
apricot preserves or jelly in the
microwave until melted. Using
a small pastry brush, glaze the
tops of the fruit and filling
before topping with the chopped
pistachios.

twists

• Instead of premade pie dough,
  use 24 frozen mini tarts (Dufour®
  is my brand of choice), baked and
  cooled according to the package
  directions.

• Instead of rum, use 1 teaspoon
  pure vanilla extract.

• Instead of apricots, use 6 small
  ripe figs, trimmed and quartered,
  or ½ pint blueberries, rinsed
  and dried.

Two-Bite Apricot–Pistachio Tarts

When I'm in the mood for a quick dessert that's not too sweet, this is the recipe
I turn to. Made with pistachios, the frangipane filling is sweet without being
cloying and, when baked with ripe apricots, it's bursting with flavor.

As with all the recipes, I've given you plenty of alternatives in case ripe apricots
aren't available or pistachios aren't your thing (see Twists, below left).

line the tart pans

1   Lightly grease 24 mini-sized (scant 2-inch diameter) muffin cups.

2   Unroll the pie dough on a very lightly floured surface. Using a 2⅛-inch round
cookie cutter, cut out 18 rounds. Gather up the scraps, roll out to a ⅛-inch thickness,
and cut another 4 rounds. Reroll and cut 2 more rounds for a total of 24 rounds
of dough.

3   Working with one round at a time, use your fingers to gently press the dough into
the prepared muffin cups, making sure that there are no air bubbles in the bottom
and that the dough is pressed firmly and evenly up the side up to the top of the cup.
Slide the tins into the refrigerator.

make the filling

Put the pistachios and granulated sugar in a food processor and process until finely
ground. Add the butter, rum, and salt and process until well blended. Add the egg and
process just until blended.

fill and bake the tarts

1   Position an oven rack in the lower third of the oven and heat the oven to 375°F.

2   Evenly spoon the filling (about 2½ teaspoons) into the tart crusts (they will be
two-thirds to three-quarters full). Press one of the apricot quarters, skin side down,
into the filling. Bake until the crusts are golden brown and the filling is puffed and
browned, 19 to 21 minutes.

3   Move the muffin tins to a wire rack and let cool for 10 minutes. Using a thin,
metal spatula or the tip of a paring knife, carefully remove the tarts from the muffin
cups and set them on a wire rack. The mini tarts can be served warm or at room
temperature. Just before serving, sprinkle with toasted chopped pistachios and lightly
dust with confectioners' sugar.

Streusel-Topped Double Cherry Slab Pie

I like my fruit fillings for tarts and pies to be intensely flavored. For this open-faced hand tart, I used a combination of dried and fresh fruit and simmered them to concentrate their flavors before filling and baking the tart. Although it's an extra step, it will reward you with a richly flavored dessert.

Rosé wine is one of my summertime favorites for sipping as well as for cooking. I like to simmer the cherry compote in a cup of Triennes (2010), a lovely French rosé, but any floral, dry rosé will work, too.

make the dough

1 Cut the butter in half lengthwise, cut each half lengthwise again, and then cut each strip into 8 pieces. Pile the butter onto a plate and slide it into the freezer until ready to use. Combine the water and lemon juice and keep in the refrigerator until ready to use.

2 Whisk the flour, brown sugar, and salt in a large bowl until well blended. Add the cold butter pieces and, using a pastry blender or two knives, cut the butter into the flour mixture until the pieces are pea-sized, about 3 minutes. (You can also do this in a food processor using short pulses, scraping the blended mixture into a large bowl before proceeding.)

3 Pour the water over the flour and, using a rubber spatula, stir and fold until it forms a shaggy, moist dough with some floury bits remaining (If you don't mind getting your hands dirty, use one hand to mix the dough and the spatula in the other.) Scrape the dough and any remaining floury bits onto the counter and knead (see Kitchen Wisdom on p. 53) a few times until the dough is evenly moist and holds together. Shape the dough into a 4x6-inch rectangle, wrap in plastic, and refrigerate until well chilled, about 2 hours.

make the compote

1 Put the dried cherries, sugar, wine, and orange and lemon zests in a medium saucepan. Bring to a boil over high heat. Reduce the heat to low and simmer, stirring frequently, until the cherries are very plump and almost breaking apart and the liquid is reduced, 15 to 17 minutes.

recipe continues

FOR THE DOUGH

- 10 tablespoons (5 ounces) unsalted butter, chilled
- ¼ cup very cold water
- 1 teaspoon freshly squeezed lemon juice
- 1⅔ cups (7½ ounces) unbleached all-purpose flour
- 3 tablespoons firmly packed light brown sugar
- ¼ teaspoon table salt

FOR THE COMPOTE

- 1 cup (6 ounces) dried cherries, coarsely chopped
- ½ cup (3½ ounces) granulated sugar
- 1 cup dry rosé
- 2 strips of orange zest (see the sidebar on p. 28)
- 2 strips of lemon zest (see the sidebar on p. 28)
- 12 ounces fresh sweet cherries, pitted and halved
- ⅓ cup water
- 2 tablespoons freshly squeezed lemon juice
- Pinch of table salt
- 1 tablespoon cherry- or orange-flavored liqueur

FOR THE STREUSEL TOPPING

- ⅓ cup (1½ ounces) unbleached all-purpose flour
- ⅓ cup (2⅜ ounces) firmly packed light brown sugar
- ½ teaspoon ground cinnamon
- 2 tablespoons (1 ounce) unsalted butter, melted
- ¼ cup (1 ounce) slivered almonds, lightly toasted

FOR ASSEMBLY

- 1 large egg
- 2 teaspoons water

Serves 10

finishing touches

Let cool completely and drizzle with
HONEY RIBBON GLAZE:

> 2 ounces cream cheese,
> softened
>
> 4 to 5 tablespoons heavy cream
>
> 2 tablespoons honey
> (lavender or orange blossom)

Put the cream cheese, 2 tablespoons of the heavy cream, and
the honey in a small bowl. Using
a hand-held mixer, beat on low
speed until well blended. Increase
the speed to medium and continue
beating until smooth and shiny.
The glaze should be thick but fluid
enough to fall from the spoon and
form a soft dollop. If it isn't, add
more heavy cream, 1 teaspoon at a
time. Spoon the honey mixture into
a heavy-duty zip-top bag and seal
tightly. Snip off about 1/2 inch from
one corner and, squeezing gently,
move the bag evenly over the top
of the cooled pie in a zigzag pattern
to form a thick ribbon.

twists

Instead of using dried and fresh
cherries, substitute an equal
amount of dried and fresh
peaches. Coarsely chop the dried
peaches and cut the fresh peaches
into 3/4-inch chunks. Use orange-
flavored liqueur or brandy instead
of the cherry-flavored liqueur.

do ahead

- The dough can be made and
  stowed in the refrigerator for up
  to 2 days before using or frozen
  for up to 1 month. Thaw overnight
  in the refrigerator before rolling.

- The compote can be made and
  stowed, covered, in the refrigerator for up to 2 days before using.

2 Add the fresh cherries, water, lemon juice, and salt. Simmer, stirring occasionally,
until the cherries are very tender and the liquid is reduced to a very thick syrup (you'll
have about 3 or 4 tablespoons), 20 to 25 minutes. Slide the pan from the heat and
pick out and discard the orange and lemon zest. Add the liqueur and stir until well
blended. Set aside, stirring occasionally, until cooled to room temperature.

make the streusel

In a small bowl, combine the flour, brown sugar, and cinnamon. Drizzle the melted
butter over the top and, using a fork (or your fingers), mix the ingredients until well
blended and they form small crumbs. Add the almonds and stir. Pop in the fridge
while you assemble the pie.

assemble and bake

1 Arrange an oven rack in the center of the oven and heat the oven to 375°F. Line a
cookie sheet with parchment or a nonstick liner. Put the egg and water in a small bowl
or ramekin and, using a fork, mix until well blended.

2 On a lightly floured surface, roll the dough into a rectangle slightly larger than
7x18 inches. Using a sharp paring knife and a ruler, trim the edges to get a neat
rectangle that measures 7x18 inches. Gently roll the dough around the pin and
arrange on the center of the prepared cookie sheet. The two short ends will hang over
the edges of the cookie sheet.

3 Spoon the cooled filling down the length of the dough on the cookie sheet, leaving
about a 1½-inch border on the long sides and a 1-inch border on the two short sides.
Fold the dough border over the filling, pressing firmly on the overlapping corners.
Using a small pastry brush, brush the dough border with egg wash. Scatter the
streusel evenly over the filling and the dough border.

4 Bake until the crust and streusel are well browned, 41 to 43 minutes. Move the
sheet to a wire rack and let cool for 15 to 20 minutes. Using two long offset spatulas,
move the pie from the cookie sheet onto a wire rack and let cool completely. The pie is
best when served the same day.

KITCHEN WISDOM ୨୧ pitting cherries

Pitting cherries is messy business, as the red juice can stain clothes, fingers, and
counters. To keep things clean, I recommend using a pitter that has an enclosed
container to catch the cherries as they're pitted. Even then, you might want to wear
an apron and do this task outside or in the sink.

FOR THE DOUGH

- 7 tablespoons (3½ ounces) unsalted butter, chilled
- 2 ounces cream cheese, chilled
- ¼ cup very cold water
- ¼ teaspoon pure vanilla extract
- 1 cup + 1 tablespoon (5 ounces) unbleached all-purpose flour
- ¼ cup (1⅛ ounces) coarse yellow cornmeal
- 2 tablespoons granulated sugar
- ⅛ teaspoon table salt

FOR THE FILLING

- 14 ounces ripe figs, trimmed and quartered
- ¼ cup (1¾ ounces) firmly packed light brown sugar
- 2 tablespoons unbleached all-purpose flour
- 1 teaspoon finely grated orange zest
- 1 tablespoon orange liqueur or brandy

Pinch of table salt

FOR ASSEMBLY

- 1 large egg
- 1 teaspoon water
- 3 tablespoons demerara or turbinado sugar (Sugar in the Raw; optional)

Serves 12 to 14

Fresh "Big Mountain" Slab Pie

Fig Newtons have always held a warm and tasty spot in my heart as well as my belly. I loved them when I was little, especially when Mom served them with a little cup of warm Bigelow® Constant Comment tea. When I became a mom, I was delighted that my little boy shared my love of these soft, slightly sweet cookies. Whenever I asked what kind of cookie he'd like for a snack, Alex would sing out "Big Mountain please," which, to a very young boy, was the same thing as "Fig Newton".

This Big Mountain slab pie is my fresh take on the store-bought cookie. The crust is less cakey than the original and, instead, is tender, buttery, and flaky with a hint of cornmeal for texture. And because I love fresh figs unadorned, I've kept the filling very straightforward, with only a little sweetener and flavor to keep the fig flavor right up front and delicious.

Unlike most of my baked pies, I bake this slab pie on a jelly roll pan because the figs are especially juicy and have a tendency to run onto the pan. The short sides of the pan keep the juices from running onto the oven floor.

make the dough

1 Cut the butter in half lengthwise, cut each half lengthwise again, and the cut each strip into 8 pieces. Cut the cream cheese into ¾-inch pieces. Pile the butter and cream cheese onto a plate and slide into the freezer until ready to use. Measure the water in a 1-cup glass measure or small bowl; add the vanilla and keep in the fridge until ready to use.

2 Whisk the flour, cornmeal, sugar, and salt in a large bowl until well blended. Add the cold butter and cream cheese pieces and, using a pastry blender or two knives, cut the butter and cream cheese into the flour mixture until the pieces are pea-sized, about 3 minutes. (You can also do this in a food processor, omitting the cornmeal, using short pulses, scraping the blended mixture into the large bowl before adding the cornmeal and proceeding.)

3 Pour the water mixture over the flour and, using a rubber spatula, stir and fold until it forms a shaggy, moist dough with some floury bits remaining. (If you don't mind getting your hands dirty, use one hand to mix the dough and hold the spatula in the other.) Scrape the dough and any remaining floury bits onto the counter and knead (see Kitchen Wisdom on p. 53) a few times until the dough is evenly moist and holds together. Divide the dough into two equal pieces (about 7 ounces each); shape each piece into a 3x5-inch rectangle, wrap in plastic, and refrigerate until well chilled, about 2 hours.

make the filling

Put the figs, sugar, flour, orange zest, liqueur, and salt in a medium bowl. Using a rubber spatula, toss until the figs are evenly covered. Set aside.

assemble and bake

1 Position an oven rack in the center of the oven and heat the oven to 375°F. Line a flat jelly roll pan with parchment or a nonstick liner. Put the egg and water in a small bowl and, using a fork, mix until well blended.

2 Working with one piece of dough at a time, on a lightly floured surface, roll out the dough to a rectangle slightly larger than 4x12 inches (see Roll Like a Pro, p. 5). Using a sharp paring knife and a ruler, trim the edges to get a neat 4x12-inch rectangle. Gently roll it around the pin, arrange on the center of the prepared pan, and cover loosely with plastic wrap. Repeat with the remaining dough, rolling in into a rectangle that's slightly larger than 4½x12 inches. Using a sharp paring knife and a ruler, trim the edges to get a neat 4½x12-inch rectangle.

3 Remove the plastic wrap from the smaller bottom rectangle on the pan. Spoon the filling down the center of the bottom rectangle and spread out, leaving a ½-inch border of dough. Using a small pastry brush, brush the edges with egg wash.

4 Lay the remaining rectangle over the filling, pressing firmly on the edges to seal. Using the tines of a fork, press (or crimp) the pastry edges to seal (see the bottom photo on p. 56). Lightly brush the top with egg wash and sprinkle evenly with the demerara sugar, if using. Using the tip of a small sharp knife, cut 4 or 5 small slits in the top to let steam escape.

5 Bake (if your kitchen is hot, loosely cover the pastry with plastic and stow in the fridge while the oven heats), until the pie is deep golden brown, 32 to 34 minutes. Move the sheet to a wire rack and let cool for 10 minutes. Using a long offset spatula, carefully remove the pie from the sheet, set on a wire rack, and let cool completely. The slab pie is best when served the same day and can be warmed slightly in a 300°F oven, if you like.

twists

Instead of using orange zest in the filling, use one of the following: ¾ teaspoon finely grated lemon zest, or ¼ teaspoon pure almond extract, or 1 teaspoon pure vanilla extract, or ¾ teaspoon ground cinnamon.

do ahead

The dough can be made and stowed in the refrigerator for up to 2 days or frozen for up to 1 month. Thaw overnight in the refrigerator before rolling.

16 tablespoons (8 ounces) unsalted
   butter, chilled

⅓ cup + 1 tablespoon very cold
   water

2½ cups (11¼ ounces) unbleached
   all-purpose flour

3 tablespoons granulated sugar

½ teaspoon table salt

FOR THE FILLING

1 cup strawberry jam

FOR ASSEMBLY

1 large egg

1 teaspoon water

Makes 8 tarts

finishing touches

• Before baking, sprinkle the tops
  of the egg-glazed triangles with
  demerara sugar.

• Dust the tops of the warm or
  cooled triangles with a little
  confectioners' sugar.

Jam-Filled Triangle Hand Pies

If you've ever wondered what else you can make with homemade pie dough, look no further than this recipe. My dough is an all-butter version (no lard) with just a hint of sugar for sweetness and extra browning ability. Baked up, this dough is tender, a bit flaky, and just sweet enough to make it perfect for any one- or two-crust pie or for these triangle-shaped hand pies.

If you're especially time-pressed, use premade pie dough for the bottom layer of dough but for the top, use frozen puff pastry (thawed, of course). It's lighter and flakier than pie dough and it adds a buttery sweetness to the triangles.

I like to fill these hand pies with homemade strawberry jam made by my friend Ann, but if you aren't lucky enough to have some homemade jam in your pantry, feel free to use your favorite flavor and brand of store-bought jam or preserves.

make the dough

1 Cut the butter in half lengthwise, cut each half lengthwise again, and then cut each strip into 8 pieces. Pile the butter onto a plate and slide into the freezer until ready to use. Measure the water into a 1-cup glass measure or small bowl and keep in the fridge until ready to use.

2 Whisk the flour, sugar, and salt in a large bowl until well blended. Add the cold butter pieces and, using a pastry blender or two knives, cut the butter into the flour mixture until the pieces are pea-sized, about 3 minutes. (You can also do this in a food processor, using short pulses, scraping the blended mixture into a large bowl before proceeding.)

3 Pour the water over the flour and, using a rubber spatula, stir and fold until it forms a shaggy, moist dough with some floury bits remaining. (If you don't mind getting your hands dirty, use one hand to mix the dough and hold the spatula in the other.) Scrape the dough and any remaining floury bits onto the counter and knead (see Kitchen Wisdom on p. 53) a few times until the dough is evenly moist and holds together. Divide the dough into two equal pieces (about 10½ ounces each) and shape each into a 5-inch disk. Wrap in plastic and refrigerate until well chilled, about 2 hours.

assemble and bake

1 Position an oven rack in the center of the oven and heat the oven to 400°F. Line a cookie sheet with parchment or a nonstick liner. Put the egg and water in a small bowl and, using a fork, mix until well blended.

2 Set the dough on the counter to soften enough to roll, about 15 minutes. Working with one piece of dough at a time, on lightly floured parchment, roll out the dough to a round slightly larger than 12½ inches (see Roll Like a Pro, p. 5). Using a sharp paring knife and a ruler (I use the lid to one of my larger pots as a guide), trim the edges to get a neat 12½-inch round. Using a large knife or a pizza wheel, cut the round into 8 equal triangles, arrange about 2 inches apart on the prepared cookie sheet, and cover loosely with plastic wrap. Repeat with the remaining dough and leave on the work surface, covered with plastic wrap.

3 Spoon about 2 tablespoons of the jam onto the center of each triangle on the cookie sheet and spread it with an offset spatula, leaving a ½-inch border at the edges. Using a small pastry brush, brush the edges of each triangle with egg wash. Lay the remaining triangles over the jam-covered triangles, pressing firmly on the edges to seal. Some preserves might leak out; this is fine.

4 Using the tines of a fork, gently press (or crimp) the pastry edges to seal (see the bottom photo on p. 56). Lightly brush the top of each triangle with egg wash. Using the tip of a small sharp knife, cut 2 or 3 small slits in the top of each triangle to let steam escape.

5 Bake until the triangles are deep golden brown, 22 to 24 minutes. Move the sheet to a wire rack and let cool for 10 minutes. Carefully remove the triangles from the sheet, set them on a wire rack, and let cool completely. The triangles are best when served the same day and can be warmed slightly in a 300°F oven, if you like.

twists

Instead of strawberry jam, use the same amount of any jam or preserve.

do ahead

- The dough can be made and stowed in the refrigerator for up to 2 days or frozen for up to 1 month. Thaw in the refrigerator overnight before using.

- The triangles can be assembled, covered in plastic, and stowed in the fridge for up to 1 day before baking.

Poppyseed–Lemon Hand Tarts

Key lime tart is coveted by all the Dodges, me included. In fact, I like it even more when I make it with fresh lemon juice; the texture is rich and creamy with just the right amount of tangy tartness. My challenge for this book was to recreate the same flavors you'd find in a tart in a hand-held treat.

The crust is a sweet, cookie-like dough laced with poppyseeds. Even in small amounts, poppyseeds are pretty, and they add a lovely, nubby texture to the baked crust. But the filling was a bit more challenging. It took more than a few testing rounds to get the ratio of creaminess to tang just right, but it was well worth the effort, or so says my son, Alex, my primary taste tester for this dessert.

make the dough

1 Cut the butter in half lengthwise, cut each half lengthwise again, and then cut each strip into 8 pieces. Pile the butter onto a plate and slide it into the freezer until ready to use. Measure the water in a 1-cup glass measure or small bowl; add the yolks and vanilla. Using a table fork, mix until well blended and keep in the fridge until ready to use.

2 Put the flour, sugar, and salt in a food processor and pulse until well blended. Add the cold butter pieces and pulse to cut the butter into the flour mixture until the pieces are pea-sized, about 1 minute. Pour the egg-water mixture over the flour mixture and pulse until the dough forms moist, small clumps.

3 Dump the dough onto the counter and sprinkle evenly with the poppyseeds. Knead (see Kitchen Wisdom on p. 53) a few times until the dough is evenly moist and holds together. Divide the dough into two pieces (they don't need to be exactly even), shape each into a flat disk, wrap in plastic, and refrigerate until well chilled, about 2 hours.

make the cream cheese filling

Put the cream cheese and confectioners' sugar in a small bowl. Using a whisk or a hand-held mixer, mix until well blended and smooth. Add the yolk, vanilla, and salt and whisk until just blended. Cover and set aside.

recipe continues

FOR THE DOUGH

- 16 tablespoons (8 ounces) unsalted butter, chilled
- ¼ cup cold water
- 2 yolks from large eggs
- 1½ teaspoons pure vanilla extract
- 3 cups (13½ ounces) unbleached all-purpose flour
- ½ cup (3½ ounces) granulated sugar
- ½ teaspoon table salt
- 2 tablespoons poppyseeds

FOR THE CREAM CHEESE FILLING

- 3 ounces cream cheese, softened
- ¼ cup (1 ounce) confectioners' sugar
- 1 yolk from large egg
- ¾ teaspoon pure vanilla extract
- Pinch of table salt

FOR THE LEMON FILLING

- ¾ cup lemon curd, homemade (see p. 100) or store-bought

FOR ASSEMBLY

- 1 large egg
- 1 teaspoon water

Makes 12 hand tarts

finishing touches

After brushing with the egg wash, sprinkle the tops with additional poppyseeds.

do ahead

- The dough can be made ahead and stowed in the refrigerator for up to 2 days frozen for up to 1 month. Thaw overnight in the refrigerator before rolling.
- The tarts can be assembled, covered in plastic, and stowed in the refrigerator for up to 1 day before baking.

twists

- Instead of lemon curd, use the same amount of orange or grapefruit curd.
- For a lemony crust, add 1½ teaspoons finely grated lemon zest to the dough along with the egg-water mixture.

assemble and bake

1 Line two cookie sheets with parchment or nonstick liners. Put the egg and water in a small bowl and, using a fork, mix until well blended.

2 Working with one piece of dough at a time, on a lightly floured surface, roll out the dough until it's about 3/16 inch thick (see Roll Like a Pro, p. 5). Using a 4-inch round cookie cutter with a scalloped edge, cut out rounds. Gather the scraps, reroll, and cut more rounds. Do the same with the other piece of dough. You should have 24 rounds total (12 bottoms and 12 tops). Arrange 6 rounds on each cookie sheet.

3 Spoon 2 teaspoons of the cream cheese filling onto the center of each of the 12 rounds on the cookie sheets. Using an offset spatula, spread in an even layer, leaving a ½-inch border of dough. Spoon 1 tablespoon of the lemon curd onto the center (no need to spread). Using a small pastry brush, brush the edges with egg wash. Lay the remaining rounds on top, pressing firmly on the edges to seal.

4 Lightly brush the tops with egg wash. Using the tip of a small sharp knife, cut a small X into the center of the top crusts to let steam escape. Slide the cookie sheets into the fridge while the oven heats up.

5 Position an oven rack in the center of the oven and heat the oven to 375°F.

6 Bake, one sheet at a time, until the tarts are golden brown, 31 to 33 minutes. Move the sheet to a wire rack and let cool for 10 minutes. Carefully remove the hand tarts from the sheet, set them on a wire rack, and let cool completely. The hand tarts are best when served the same day.

Cinnamon–Sugar Apple Phyllo Triangles

These little triangles have a crunchy, sugary outside and a buttery caramelized apple center. Come fall, I make a ton of these—sometimes even quadrupling the recipe—and stow them, unbaked, in the freezer. This way, I can pull out the exact number I need for an afternoon snack, dessert, or even, dare I say, a sweet breakfast treat.

make the filling

Cut the apples into ½-inch pieces. Put the butter in a medium skillet and cook, stirring, over medium low heat until melted. Add the apples, honey, and salt and cook, stirring, until the apples are tender and caramelized, 10 to 12 minutes. Add the calvados (be careful—it will steam up) and, cook, stirring frequently, over low heat until the liquid is evaporated, 1 to 2 minutes. Remove from the heat and set aside to cool completely. You'll have about 1 firmly packed cup of cooked filling.

assemble and bake the triangles

1 Position an oven rack in the center of the oven and heat the oven to 375°F. Line two cookie sheets with parchment or nonstick liners. Put the sugar, walnuts, and cinnamon in a small bowl and stir until well blended.

2 Unroll the phyllo and lay it flat on a clean, dry surface. Cover completely with plastic wrap or a damp (not wet) dishtowel. Working with one sheet of phyllo at a time, and keeping the rest covered to prevent it from drying out, place a sheet with one long side in front of you on a cutting board. Brush with the melted butter, sprinkle with 2½ tablespoons of the cinnamon-walnut-sugar mixture, and cover with another sheet of phyllo. Press lightly on the top sheet. Using a pizza wheel or a sharp knife, cut the phyllo lengthwise into equal 2¾- to 3-inch-wide strips.

3 Spoon 1 tablespoon of the cooled apple filling on the short end of each strip, pushing it slightly to one corner. Fold the phyllo on the diagonal over the filling to make a triangle. Continue the folding to the end of the phyllo strips just as you would fold a flag, alternating the direction of folding. Arrange on the prepared cookie sheets about 1 inch apart, with the phyllo edges under the triangle, and cover with plastic. Repeat with the rest of the phyllo and filling, for a total of 12 triangles.

recipe continues

FOR THE APPLE FILLING

- 2 apples (8 ounces each), peeled and cored (firm-fleshed, crisp-tart apples are best)
- 3 tablespoons (1½ ounces) unsalted butter
- 3 to 4 tablespoons honey
- Pinch of table salt
- 2 tablespoons calvados, Applejack® brandy, or apple cider

FOR ASSEMBLY

- ⅔ cup (4⅝ ounces) granulated sugar
- ⅓ cup (1⅜ ounces) finely chopped toasted walnuts
- 2 teaspoons ground cinnamon
- ½ package (8 ounces) frozen phyllo dough (one roll from a twin pack), thawed
- 8 tablespoons (4 ounces) unsalted butter, melted and cooled slightly

Makes 12 triangles

do ahead

- The apple filling can be prepared and refrigerated for up to 3 days before assembling the triangles.
- Unbaked phyllo triangles without the butter and cinnamon-walnut-sugar topping can be frozen for up to 1 month. Freeze the triangles on a baking sheet. When frozen, transfer them to an airtight container, setting parchment or plastic wrap between layers if needed, and return to the freezer. To bake, arrange the frozen triangles (do not thaw) on prepared cookie sheets, brush with melted butter, and sprinkle with cinnamon-walnut-sugar topping. Bake until browned, 20 to 25 minutes.

twists

Instead of the apples, use the same amount of firm-ripe pears.

4 Brush the tops of the triangles with some of the remaining melted butter and sprinkle with the remaining cinnamon-walnut-sugar mixture. Bake, one sheet at a time, until crisp and brown, 15 to 17 minutes. Transfer the cookie sheet to a rack to cool for about 5 minutes. Serve the triangles warm or let cool completely, cover, and stow at room temperature for up to 3 days.

ASSEMBLING THE TRIANGLES

Trim the edges of dough with a pastry wheel guided by a ruler.

Add filling in one corner and fold up the edge of the dough to cover.

Fold the dough like a flag to make the triangles.

Continue to fold until you've reached the end of the dough strip.

FOR THE FILLING

¼ cup (1¾ ounces) firmly packed light brown sugar

1½ teaspoons unbleached all-purpose flour

½ teaspoon ground cinnamon

⅛ teaspoon ground nutmeg

Pinch of ground cloves

Pinch of table salt

1 apple (8 ounces), peeled and cored (use a firm-fleshed, tart variety like Golden Delicious; see Kitchen Wisdom on p. 78)

2 firm-ripe pears (5 to 6 ounces each), peeled and cored (I like Bosc or Bartlett)

3 tablespoons (1½ ounces) unsalted butter

½ teaspoon pure vanilla extract

FOR THE STREUSEL TOPPING

½ cup (1⅓ ounces) quick-cooking oats

¼ cup (1¾ ounces) firmly packed light brown sugar

¼ cup (1⅛ ounces) unbleached all-purpose flour

¼ teaspoon ground ginger

¼ teaspoon ground cinnamon

Pinch of table salt

4 tablespoons unsalted butter, cut into 4 pieces and softened

¼ cup (1 ounce) slivered almonds, lightly toasted

FOR THE DOUGH

1 package (7 ounces) premade pie dough

Makes 10 mini tarts

Mini Apple–Pear Tarts with Oatmeal-Almond Streusel

When I was young, I would pick off the streusel topping from my pie slices and eat it like it was a separate dessert. I'll admit that I still find those sweet little crumbles irresistible—so much so that I added extra streusel to this recipe just in case you have a nibbler in your group.

While I love the topper for these little pies, the filling is equally captivating. You'll love the spiced buttery flavor of the apple-pear filling. Combined with the topping, this may just be my favorite go-to fall dessert.

make the filling

1 Put the brown sugar, flour, cinnamon, nutmeg, cloves, and salt in a ramekin or small bowl and, using a table fork, mix until well blended.

2 Cut the apple and pears into ½-inch pieces. Put the butter in a medium skillet and cook, stirring, over medium-low heat until melted. Add the apples and pears and cook, stirring, until tender, 8 to 10 minutes. Add the brown sugar mixture and, cook, stirring frequently, over low heat until the sugar is melted and the fruit is evenly coated, 1 to 2 minutes. Remove from the heat and stir in the vanilla. Set aside to cool completely.

3 Position an oven rack in the lower third of the oven and heat the oven to 375°F.

make the streusel

Put the oats, brown sugar, flour, ginger, cinnamon, and salt in a small bowl and stir until well blended. Add the butter and, using a fork (or your fingers), mix and mash until the ingredients are well blended and form small crumbs. Stir in the almonds. Pop in the fridge while you assemble the tarts.

line the tart pans

1 Lightly grease ten regular-sized (2¾-inch diameter) muffin cups.

2 Unroll the pie dough on a very lightly floured surface. Using a 3½-inch round cookie cutter, cut out 8 rounds. Gather up the scraps, reroll to a ⅛-inch thickness, and cut another round. Reroll and cut one more round for a total of 10 rounds of dough.

3 Working with one round at a time, use your fingers to gently press the dough into a prepared muffin cup, making sure there are no air bubbles in the bottom and the dough is pressed firmly and evenly up the side to within ¼ inch of the top of the cup. Repeat with the remaining dough rounds.

fill and bake the tarts

1 Evenly spoon the cooled fruit filling into the lined muffin cups. Scatter the streusel evenly over the filling. Bake until the crusts and streusel are golden brown, 22 to 25 minutes.

2 Move the muffin tin to a wire rack and let cool for 10 minutes. Using a thin, metal spatula or the tip of a paring knife, carefully remove the tarts from the muffin cups and set them on a wire rack. Serve warm or at room temperature.

finishing touches

Warm the tarts first if they're at room temperature and, just before serving, top with a small scoop of Hard Sauce.

HARD SAUCE
Makes ⅔ cup

    8 tablespoons (4 ounces) unsalted butter, softened
    1 cup (4 ounces) confectioners' sugar
    1 tablespoon brandy
    ½ teaspoon pure vanilla extract

Put the butter and confectioners' sugar in a medium bowl and beat with an electric mixer until smooth and fluffy, about 2 minutes. Add the brandy and vanilla and beat until well blended. Serve immediately or cover and refrigerate up to 1 week.

twists

- Add 1 teaspoon finely grated lemon zest to the filling along with the vanilla.

- Instead of the vanilla extract in the filling, use 1 tablespoon Applejack brandy.

- Instead of the almonds in the streusel, use the same amount of walnuts or pecans.

- Instead of premade pie dough, use a half-recipe of the dough for Jam-Filled Triangle Hand Pies (p. 72).

do ahead

The tarts can be filled, covered in plastic, and stowed in the refrigerator for up to 2 days before baking.

FOR THE FILLING

- 1 cup pure pumpkin purée
- 1/2 cup pure maple syrup (preferably grade B)
- 3/4 teaspoon ground cinnamon
- 1/4 teaspoon ground nutmeg
- 1/4 teaspoon ground ginger
- Pinch of ground cloves
- Pinch of table salt
- 1 large egg
- 1/2 teaspoon pure vanilla extract

FOR THE DOUGH

- 1 package (7 ounces) premade pie dough

FOR THE TOASTED PECAN STREUSEL

- 1/2 cup (2 ounces) toasted pecans, chopped
- 2 tablespoons firmly packed light brown sugar
- 1/2 teaspoon ground cinnamon

Makes 10 mini tarts

finishing touches

Before sprinkling the tarts with the pecan streusel, drop a small dollop of sweetened whipped cream onto the center of the tarts.

Mini Pumpkin–Maple Tarts with Toasted Pecan Streusel

I am a bit of a pumpkin pie fiend. While I love to eat it, I also really love to toy with the recipe—always tweaking it until it's just perfect or unique thanks to a new ingredient. Here's this year's take on the classic pumpkin pie filling, and the star ingredient is pure maple syrup. You'll recognize the classic spices (cinnamon, nutmeg, ginger, and cloves) but also taste sweetness thanks to the maple syrup. You'll get the deepest maple flavor from grade B, but if it's not available, use the darkest grade A that you can find.

Just before serving, I sprinkle the tarts with Toasted Pecan Streusel. Unlike traditional streusel that's made with butter and flour and then baked on top of pies, this streusel is an easy-to-make, flavorful combination of toasted nuts, sugar, and cinnamon. It's not baked with the tarts, so technically it's not a streusel. But it adds an earthy flavor and nice crunch to the tarts—a perfect partner to the soft, custardy filling.

Position an oven rack in the lower third of the oven and heat the oven to 375°F.

make the filling

Put the pumpkin purée, maple syrup, cinnamon, nutmeg, ginger, cloves, and salt in a medium bowl or 4-cup measure (this makes it easy to fill the tarts). Whisk until well blended and smooth. Add the egg and vanilla and whisk until just blended.

line the tart pans

1 Lightly grease ten regular-sized (2 3/4-inch diameter) muffin cups.

2 Unroll the pie dough on a very lightly floured surface. Using a 3 1/2-inch round cookie cutter, cut out 8 rounds. Gather up the scraps, reroll to a 1/8-inch thickness, and cut another round. Reroll and cut one more round for a total of 10 rounds of dough.

3 Working with one round at a time, use your finger to gently press the dough into a prepared muffin cup, making sure that there are no air bubbles in the bottom and that the dough is pressed firmly and evenly up the side to within 1/4 inch of the top of the cup. Repeat with the remaining dough rounds.

fill and bake the tarts

1 Evenly spoon (or pour if you're using a 4-cup measure) the filling into the lined muffin cups. Bake until the crusts are golden brown and the centers jiggle slightly when the pan is nudged, 27 to 29 minutes.

2 While the tarts are baking, make the streusel topping. Put the pecans, brown sugar, and cinnamon in a food processor and pulse until the nuts are finely ground.

3 Move the muffin tin to a wire rack and let cool for 10 minutes. Using a thin, metal spatula or the tip of a paring knife, carefully remove the tarts from the muffin cups and set them on a wire rack. Serve warm or at room temperature. Just before serving, sprinkle the tops with some of the pecan streusel.

KITCHEN WISDOM ⌒⌒ working with pumpkin purée

It's my experience that canned, organic pumpkin purée tends to be a bit more watery than the traditional store-bought variety. It's absolutely fine to use in this recipe and any other that calls for pumpkin purée, but I'd suggest you strain off some of the water before using it. To do so, set a fine-mesh sieve over a small or medium bowl and line the inside of the sieve with 2 layers of cheesecloth. Scrape the purée into the sieve and let sit for 2 to 3 hours before proceeding with the recipe.

---

twists

• Instead of pumpkin purée, use the same amount of butternut squash purée.

• Instead of premade pie dough, use a half-recipe of the dough for Jam-Filled Triangle Hand Pies (p. 72).

• Instead of pecans in the streusel, use the same amount of walnuts.

do ahead

The tarts can be filled, covered in plastic, and stowed in the refrigerator for up to 1 day before baking.

FOR THE FILLING

- 2 ounces bittersweet chocolate, chopped
- 2 tablespoons (1 ounce) unsalted butter
- 1/3 cup Lyle's Golden Syrup
- 1/3 cup (2 3/8 ounces) firmly packed light brown sugar
- 1/3 cup heavy cream
- Pinch of table salt
- 1 large egg, at room temperature
- 1/2 teaspoon pure vanilla extract
- 2/3 cup (2 5/8 ounces) chopped pecans, lightly toasted

FOR THE DOUGH

- 1 package (7 ounces) premade pie dough

Makes 10 mini tarts

finishing touches
Just before serving, dust the tops with a little confectioners' sugar.

twists
- Add 2 teaspoons finely grated orange zest to the filling along with the vanilla.
- Instead of the vanilla extract, use 1 tablespoon brandy.
- Instead of premade pie dough, use a half-recipe of dough for Jam-Filled Triangle Hand Pies (p. 72).

do ahead
The tarts can be filled, covered in plastic, and stowed in the fridge for up to 2 days before baking.

KITCHEN WISDOM ◎◎
Lyle's Golden Syrup

Also known as pale treacle, Lyle's is a form of inverted sugar syrup made by evaporating sugar cane juice until it's thick and syrupy. Light corn syrup can be substituted.

Mini Chocolate–Pecan Tarts

My very first chocolate-pecan pie recipe came from Marion Cunningham's iconic cookbook *Fannie Farmer Baking Book*. I made it for Thanksgiving dinner in 1979 (or thereabout) and it was love at first bite. Over the years, I've tinkered with the recipe, adding a touch of cream to the sweet, buttery custard filling. The cream mellows the sweetness of the cane syrup and marries the chocolate flavor with the pecans. To me, it's still the perfect finale to a Thanksgiving feast. With these mini tarts, you don't need the excuse of a holiday to enjoy the same goodness year-round.

Position an oven rack in the lower third of the oven and heat the oven to 350°F.

make the filling
Melt the bittersweet chocolate and butter in a medium heatproof bowl or 4-cup measure (this makes it easy to fill the tarts). I use the microwave but an improvised double boiler works just fine. Whisk until well blended. Add the golden syrup, brown sugar, heavy cream, and salt; whisk until well blended and smooth. Add the egg and vanilla and whisk until just blended.

line the tart pans
1 Lightly grease ten regular-sized (2 3/4-inch diameter) muffin cups.

2 Unroll the pie dough on a very lightly floured surface. Using a 3 1/2-inch round cookie cutter, cut out 8 rounds. Gather up the scraps, reroll to a 1/8-inch thickness, and cut another round. Reroll and cut one more round for a total of 10 rounds of dough.

3 Working with one round at a time, use your fingers to gently press the dough into a prepared muffin cup, making sure that there are no air bubbles in the bottom and that the dough is pressed firmly and evenly up the side to within 1/4 inch of the top of the cup. Repeat with the remaining dough rounds.

fill and bake the tarts
1 Evenly spoon (or pour if you're using a 4-cup measure) the filling into the lined muffin cups. Scatter the pecans evenly over the filling. Bake until the crusts are golden brown and the centers are puffed and jiggle slightly when the pan is nudged, 26 to 28 minutes.

2 Move the muffin tin to a wire rack and let cool for 10 minutes. Using a thin, metal spatula or the tip of a paring knife, carefully remove the tarts from the muffin cups and set them on a wire rack. They can be served warm or at room temperature.

Mini Strawberry–Rhubarb Pies

Here in New England, the winters can be cold, harsh, and long, so when the first fruits of summer—strawberries and rhubarb—start showing up at the markets, it's time to fire up the ovens and bake some pie—mini pies, that is. I've jazzed up this classic fruit combo with a splash of lemon and fresh ginger. By no means does this addition overwhelm the stars of this dessert—it only makes 'em shine a bit brighter.

Position an oven rack in the lower third of the oven and heat the oven to 375°F.

make the filling
Put the butter in a small skillet and cook over low heat until melted. Add the rhubarb, increase the heat to medium, and cook, stirring constantly, until very tender and beginning to break apart, 6 to 8 minutes. Slide the skillet from the heat and add the chopped strawberries, sugar, flour, lemon zest, ginger, and salt. Stir until well blended. Set aside to cool.

line the tart pans
1 Lightly grease ten regular-sized (2¾-inch diameter) muffin cups.

2 Unroll the pie dough on a very lightly floured surface. Using a 3½-inch round cookie cutter, cut out 8 rounds. Gather up the scraps, reroll to a ⅛-inch thickness, and cut another round. Reroll and cut one more round for a total of 10 rounds of dough.

3 Working with one round at a time, use your fingers to gently press the dough into a prepared muffin cup, making sure that there are no air bubbles in the bottom and that the dough is pressed firmly and evenly up the side to within ¼ inch of the top of the cup. Repeat with the remaining dough rounds.

fill and bake the tarts
1 Evenly spoon the filling into the lined muffin cups. Bake until the crusts are golden brown and the filling is bubbling, 23 to 25 minutes.

2 Move the muffin tin to a wire rack and let cool for 10 minutes. Using a thin, metal spatula or the tip of a paring knife, carefully remove the tarts from the muffin cups and set them on a wire rack. Serve warm or at room temperature. Just before serving, lightly dust with confectioners' sugar.

FOR THE FILLING
1 tablespoon unsalted butter

⅔ cup (2 ounces) chopped fresh rhubarb

1⅔ cups (8 ounces) chopped fresh strawberries

¼ cup (1¾ ounces) granulated sugar

1 tablespoon unbleached all-purpose flour

¼ teaspoon finely grated lemon zest

¼ teaspoon finely grated fresh ginger

Pinch of table salt

FOR THE DOUGH
1 package (7 ounces) premade pie dough

Confectioners' sugar, for serving

Makes 10 mini pies

finishing touches
ADD MORE STRAWBERRY PUNCH:
In a small ramekin, heat 3 tablespoons seedless strawberry preserves or jelly in the microwave until melted. Using a small pastry brush, glaze the tops of the filling before serving the tarts.

Spoon a small dollop of sweetened whipped cream onto the center of the tarts.

twists
• Instead of lemon zest and ginger, use ½ teaspoon finely grated orange zest and ½ teaspoon pure vanilla extract.

• Instead of premade pie dough, use a half-recipe of the dough for Jam-Filled Triangle Hand Pies (p. 72).

• Before serving, top the tarts with streusel topping (p. 82).

·3·
Whoopie Pies, Cake Bites & Mini Cakes

MOIST AND FLAVORFUL CAKES
OF ALL SHAPES & SIZES

FOR THE CUPCAKES

1²⁄₃ cups (7½ ounces) unbleached all-purpose flour

1½ teaspoons baking powder

1 teaspoon ground cinnamon

¼ teaspoon table salt

8 tablespoons (4 ounces) unsalted butter, softened

½ cup (3½ ounces) granulated sugar

½ cup (3½ ounces) firmly packed light brown sugar

2 large eggs, at room temperature

1 teaspoon pure vanilla extract

²⁄₃ cup buttermilk

FOR THE FROSTING

½ cup half-and-half or whole milk

½ cup (2 ounces) finely chopped walnuts, toasted

1 tablespoon unbleached all-purpose flour

²⁄₃ cup (4²⁄₃ ounces) firmly packed light brown sugar

16 tablespoons (8 ounces) unsalted butter, softened

1 teaspoon pure vanilla extract

Pinch of table salt

Makes 12 cupcakes

Cinnamon Cupcakes with Toasted Walnut Buttercream

For me, recipe development is a combination of solid science, a touch of trial and error, a dash of intuition, and a smidgen of luck. This frosting recipe is a perfect example of my method—if you can call it that. For this spiced cupcake, I had in mind a rich, thick, smooth frosting infused with toasted walnuts, so I began by infusing the milk with the toasted nuts. I had meant to strain the nuts from the milk before adding the flour and cooking until thick, but as luck would have it, I added the flour directly to the milk-nut mixture. Instead of chucking the lot and starting again, I continued to improvise by melting the brown sugar in the walnut mixture. This helped eliminate the raw taste that some butter-sugar frostings can take on. Once the mixture was cool, I beat it into softened butter. That's how this intensely flavored, nutty yet silky frosting was born.

And by the way, it's days and recipes like this one that remind me how much I love my job.

make the cupcakes

1 Position an oven rack in the center of the oven and heat oven to 350°F. Line 12 regular-sized (2³⁄₄-inch diameter) muffin cups with paper or foil liners.

2 Whisk the flour, baking powder, cinnamon, and salt in a medium bowl until well blended. Put the butter in a large bowl. Beat with an electric mixer fitted with the paddle attachment on medium speed until well blended and smooth, about 1 minute. Add the granulated sugar and brown sugar and beat on medium-high speed until well blended, about 2 minutes. Add the eggs, one at a time, beating well after each addition. Add the vanilla with the last egg. Stop to scrape down the bowl and the beater as needed. Add half of the flour mixture and mix on low speed until just blended. Add the buttermilk and mix until just blended. Add the remaining flour mixture and mix on low speed until just blended.

3 Portion the batter evenly among the prepared muffin cups (a scant ¼ cup of batter per cup will be about two-thirds of the way full). Bake until a toothpick inserted in the center comes out clean, 20 to 22 minutes. Move to a wire rack and let cool for 15 minutes. Carefully remove the cupcakes from the pan, set them on a wire rack, and let cool completely.

make the frosting

1 While the cupcakes are cooling, make the frosting. Put the half-and-half or milk, walnuts, and flour in a small saucepan. Cook, whisking constantly, over medium heat until boiling, then continue to boil, whisking constantly, until thick, 1 minute. Slide the pan from the heat, add the brown sugar, and whisk until the sugar is dissolved. Set aside to cool completely.

2 Put the butter in a large bowl. Beat with an electric mixer fitted with the paddle attachment on medium speed until well blended and smooth, about 1 minute. Add the cooled walnut-sugar mixture, vanilla, and salt and beat on medium-high speed until light and fluffy, about 2 minutes.

assemble the cupcakes

Portion the frosting evenly among the cooled cupcakes (about 2 tablespoons per cupcake). Using a small metal spatula, mound and swirl the frosting on top of the cupcakes, leaving a border of cake around each one. Serve immediately or chill for 30 minutes. The cupcakes are best when served slightly chilled.

finishing touches
- Sprinkle the tops with additional toasted walnuts.

- Fit a large round tip (I use an Ateco #5) into a pastry bag and fill with the frosting (see the sidebar on p. 18). Evenly pipe the frosting onto the cooled cupcakes, leaving a border of cake around each one.

twists
Substitute the same amount of pecans for the walnuts.

do ahead
- The cupcakes can be prepared through Step 3 in Make the Cupcakes, covered, and stowed at room temperature for up to 1 day before frosting.

- The frosted cupcakes can be stowed in the refrigerator for up to 2 days.

FOR THE CUPCAKES

1½ cups (6¾ ounces) unbleached all-purpose flour

2 teaspoons baking powder

½ teaspoon baking soda

1¾ teaspoons ground ginger

¾ teaspoon ground cinnamon

¼ teaspoon ground nutmeg

¼ teaspoon table salt

8 tablespoons (4 ounces) unsalted butter, softened

½ cup (3½ ounces) firmly packed dark brown sugar

2 large eggs, at room temperature

1 teaspoon freshly squeezed lemon juice

½ cup buttermilk, at room temperature

¼ cup dark molasses

FOR THE FROSTING

¾ cup heavy cream

⅓ cup mascarpone

3 tablespoons firmly packed dark or light brown sugar

Pinch of table salt

2 to 3 teaspoons brandy

Makes 12 cupcakes

do ahead

- The cupcakes can be prepared through Step 3 in Make the Cupcakes, covered, and stowed at room temperature for up to 1 day before frosting.

- The frosted cupcakes can be stowed in the refrigerator for up to 2 days.

Gingerbread Cupcakes with Brown Sugar Whipped Cream

These cupcakes are a nod to my brother Tim and his love of gingerbread. Growing up, Mom would bake up a square pan of old-fashioned, dark-style gingerbread cake just for him. She served it warm, with a big bowl of lightly sweetened, freshly whipped cream alongside. As it was "his" dessert, Tim would get first pick on which piece to choose. His selection was always the same—the center square—which was fine by me since I liked the corner pieces with their slightly chewy edges.

With these cupcakes, I've taken a few liberties with my mom's recipe. The flavor is gingery for sure, but the cake isn't the same molasses-ladened classic; instead, the texture is lighter and more cakelike. For the whipped cream topping, I've added a touch of mascarpone to keep it firm and stabilized, as well as a touch of brandy for a more complex flavor.

make the cupcakes

1 Position an oven rack in the center of the oven and heat the oven to 350°F. Line 12 regular-sized (2¾-inch diameter) muffin cups with paper or foil liners.

2 Whisk the flour, baking powder, baking soda, ginger, cinnamon, nutmeg, and salt in a medium bowl until well blended. Put the butter and brown sugar in a large bowl. Beat with an electric mixer fitted with the paddle attachment on medium speed until well blended and smooth, about 3 minutes. Add the eggs, one at a time, beating until just blended between additions. Add the lemon juice with the last egg. Stop to scrape down the bowl and the beater as needed. Add a third of the flour mixture and mix on low speed until just blended. Add the buttermilk and mix until just blended. Add another third of the flour mixture and mix until just blended. Add the molasses and mix until blended. Add the remaining flour mixture and mix on low speed until just blended.

3 Portion the batter evenly among the prepared muffin cups (about 3 tablespoons batter per cup will be about two-thirds of the way full). Bake until a toothpick inserted in the center comes out clean, 16 to 18 minutes. (The tops will only be slightly domed.) Move to a wire rack and let cool for 15 minutes. Carefully remove the cupcakes from the pan, set them on a wire rack, and let cool completely.

make the frosting

Put the heavy cream and mascarpone in a large bowl. Beat with an electric mixer fitted with the whip attachment on medium-low speed until well blended and smooth, about 1 minute. Add the brown sugar and salt. Beat on medium-high speed until thick enough to hold firm peaks when the beater is lifted, about 2 minutes. Add the brandy and beat on medium speed until well blended.

assemble the cupcakes

Portion the frosting evenly among the cooled cupcakes (about 2 tablespoons per cupcake). Using a small metal spatula, mound and swirl the frosting on top of the cupcakes, leaving a border of cake around each one. Serve immediately or chill for 30 minutes. The cupcakes are best when served slightly chilled.

finishing touches

Top each frosted cupcake with finely chopped crystallized ginger.

twists

- **USE CHOCOLATE FROSTING:** Instead of the whipped cream frosting, top the cupcakes with one of the chocolate frostings (see pp. 107 and 118).

- **FLAVOR THE FROSTING:** Instead of the brandy, add ¼ teaspoon ground cinnamon or 1 teaspoon pure vanilla extract to the frosting.

Chocolate-Covered Banana Cake Bites

I'm often asked about where I find inspiration for my recipes. The answer is easy. I find it everywhere. In the case of these mouthwatering cake bites, I have combined my family's love of chocolate and banana with my overwhelming urge to make the now-trendy cake pops from scratch instead of with the store-bought ingredients those recipes call for. These from-scratch cake bites are easy to make with fresh ingredients and are even more adorable than the ones made with packaged mixes. They're a cross between a bite of cake and a rich truffle—the best of both worlds.

make the cake

1 Position an oven rack in the center of the oven and heat the oven to 350°F. Lightly grease and flour the bottom and sides of a 9-inch round cake pan.

2 Whisk the flour, baking powder, baking soda, and salt in a medium bowl until well blended.

3 Put the butter in a large bowl. Beat with an electric mixer fitted with the paddle attachment on medium speed until well blended and smooth, about 1 minute. Add the brown sugar and beat on medium-high speed until well blended, about 2 minutes. Add the eggs, one at a time, beating well after each addition. Add the vanilla with the last egg. Stop to scrape down the bowl and the beater as needed. Add a third of the flour mixture and mix on low speed until just blended. Add the bananas and mix until just blended. Add another third of the flour mixture and mix briefly until blended. Add the sour cream and mix until just blended. Add the remaining flour mixture and mix on low speed until just blended.

4 Scrape the batter into the prepared pan and, using an offset spatula, spread evenly. Bake until a toothpick inserted in the center comes out clean, 31 to 33 minutes. Move to a wire rack and let cool for 20 minutes. Run a small knife between the cake and the pan and invert onto a wire rack. Set aside until completely cool.

make the frosting and assemble the cake bites

1 Line a large cookie sheet with parchment or a nonstick liner and make room in the refrigerator so the baking sheet will be level. (I arrange dairy containers that are the same height so the sheet can sit on top.) Put the butter in a large bowl. Beat with an electric mixer fitted with the paddle attachment on medium speed until well blended and smooth, about 1 minute. Add the confectioners' sugar, vanilla, and salt and beat on medium-high speed until light and fluffy, about 2 minutes.

FOR THE BANANA CAKE

1⅓ cups (6 ounces) unbleached all-purpose flour

1 teaspoon baking powder

¼ teaspoon baking soda

¼ teaspoon table salt

8 tablespoons (4 ounces) unsalted butter, softened

1 cup (7 ounces) firmly packed light brown sugar

2 large eggs, at room temperature

1 teaspoon pure vanilla extract

2 medium, very ripe bananas (8 ounces each, with peels), peeled and mashed

⅓ cup sour cream, at room temperature

FOR THE FROSTING

8 tablespoons (4 ounces) unsalted butter, softened

1¼ cups (5 ounces) confectioners' sugar

1 teaspoon pure vanilla extract

Pinch of table salt

FOR THE GLAZE

10 ounces bittersweet chocolate, chopped

2 tablespoons vegetable or canola oil

½ cup (2 ounces) finely chopped, toasted walnuts

Makes 54 cake bites

twists

- **MAKE IT ORANGE:** Add 2 tea-spoons finely grated orange zest to the cake batter along with the vanilla extract.
- **MAKE IT COLORFUL:** Substitute the same amount of colored sprinkles for the walnuts.

do ahead

- The cake can be prepared through Step 4 in Make the Cake, covered, and stowed at room temperature for up to 1 day before continuing with the recipe.
- The cake bites can be prepared through Step 2 in Make the Frosting, covered, and stowed at room temperature for up to 1 day before glazing.
- The finished cake bites can be arranged in a plastic container separated with layers of waxed paper or parchment and stowed in the refrigerator for up to 3 days.

2 Cut or gently break the cooled cake into about 1-inch pieces and add to the bowl with the frosting. Mix on low speed until the cake is broken into crumbs and completely combined with the frosting, about 1 or 2 minutes. Using a 1-tablespoon mini scoop, shape into balls and lightly roll them in your palms to smooth the edges. Arrange close together on the prepared cookie sheet and refrigerate until very cold and firm, about 4 hours.

make the glaze and finish the cake bites

1 Have ready a cookie sheet lined with parchment or a nonstick liner and a table fork (I like to use a lobster fork or fondue fork). Melt the chocolate and oil in the microwave or in a small deep bowl set over a pot of simmering water, stirring with a rubber spatula until smooth. Remove from the heat and set on a heatproof surface.

2 Put the nuts in a ramekin. Working with 8 to 10 cake bites at a time (keep the rest in the fridge), put the bite on the fork tines. Dip the bite into the chocolate to cover completely and tap the fork gently on the side of the bowl so that the excess chocolate drips off and back into the bowl. Arrange the bite on the prepared cookie sheet and sprinkle with a little of the chopped walnuts. Continue dipping and sprinkling with the remaining bites.

3 Refrigerate the chocolate-covered bites until the chocolate is set, about 1 hour. Serve immediately, slightly chilled.

Make sure the chocolate completely covers the cake bite before sprinkling with nuts.

Toasted Coconut Snowball Cupcakes

These coconut cupcakes and their frosting get their full-on coconut flavor from coconut milk that's reduced to intensify its flavor. Most grocery stores will sell both shredded and flaked coconut. For my recipes, either variety may be used as long as it's "sweetened," but I prefer the longer, elegant shreds.

make the condensed coconut milk

Give the coconut milk cans a shake before opening, pour into a large saucepan, and bring to a boil over medium heat. Boil, stirring occasionally, until reduced to 1½ cups, 15 to 20 minutes. Set aside to cool completely. (The milk settles a bit as it cools. You will need 1 cup for the cupcakes and ⅓ cup for the frosting.)

make the cupcakes

1 Position an oven rack in the center of the oven and heat the oven to 350°F. Line 18 regular-sized (2¾-inch diameter) muffin cups with paper or foil liners.

2 Whisk the flour, baking powder, and salt in a medium bowl until well blended. Put the butter in a large bowl. Beat with an electric mixer fitted with the paddle attachment on medium speed until well blended and smooth, about 1 minute. Add the granulated sugar and beat on medium-high speed until well blended, about 2 minutes. Add the eggs, one at a time, beating well after each addition. Add the vanilla with the last egg. Stop to scrape down the bowl and the beater as needed. Add half of the flour mixture to the sugar mixture and mix on low speed until just blended. Add 1 cup of the cooled condensed coconut milk and mix just until blended. Add the remaining flour mixture and mix on low speed until just blended.

3 Portion the batter evenly among the prepared muffin cups (a scant ¼ cup of batter per cup will be about two-thirds of the way full). Bake until a toothpick inserted in the center comes out clean, 18 to 20 minutes. Move to a wire rack and let cool for 15 minutes. Carefully remove the cupcakes from the pan and set them on a wire rack and let cool completely.

recipe continues

FOR THE CONDENSED COCONUT MILK

2 cans (13½ ounces each) coconut milk

FOR THE CUPCAKES

2½ cups (11¼ ounces) unbleached all-purpose flour

2½ teaspoons baking powder

½ teaspoon table salt

12 tablespoons (6 ounces) unsalted butter, softened

1⅓ cups granulated sugar

3 large eggs, at room temperature

1½ teaspoons pure vanilla extract

FOR THE FROSTING

16 tablespoons (8 ounces) unsalted butter, at room temperature

2½ cups (10 ounces) confectioners' sugar

1½ teaspoons pure vanilla extract

¼ teaspoon table salt

TO SERVE

2 cups sweetened shredded coconut, toasted

Makes 18 cupcakes

finishing touches

Fit a large star tip (I use an Ateco #6) into a pastry bag and fill with the frosting (see the sidebar on p. 18). Evenly pipe the frosting onto the cooled cupcakes, leaving a border of cake around each one. Sprinkle with some of the toasted coconut (save the remaining coconut for another use).

twists

ADD LEMON CURD: Just before frosting the cooled cupcakes, use a small sharp knife to cut a 1-inch circle into the center of each cupcake. Continue cutting, on an angle, into the cake until you reach the middle. Carefully pull out the cake center (it will be shaped a bit like a cone), cut off and reserve the top, and snack on the inside. Spoon about 2 teaspoons lemon curd (see p. 100) into each cupcake, replace the tops, and frost as directed.

Cut and pull out the cake center to fill the cupcake, if you like.

do ahead

- The coconut milk can be prepared and stowed in the refrigerator up to 5 days ahead. Bring to room temperature and stir before using. I pop mine in the microwave for about 30 seconds.
- The cupcakes can be prepared through Step 3, covered, and stowed at room temperature for up to 1 day before frosting.
- The frosted cupcakes can be covered and refrigerated for up to 2 days. Bring to room temperature before serving.

make the frosting

While the cupcakes are cooling, make the frosting. Put the butter in a large bowl. Beat with an electric mixer fitted with the paddle attachment on medium speed until well blended and smooth, about 1 minute. Add the confectioners' sugar, the remaining $1/3$ cup of the cooled condensed coconut milk, the vanilla, and salt. Beat on medium-low speed until the sugar is combined. Scrape down the sides of the bowl and the beater. Increase the speed to medium high and beat until light and fluffy.

assemble the cupcakes

Portion the frosting evenly among the cooled cupcakes (about 2 tablespoons per cupcake). Using a small metal spatula, mound and swirl the frosting on top of the cupcakes, leaving a border of cake around each one. Sprinkle each cupcake generously with the toasted coconut. Serve immediately; the cupcakes are best served at room temperature.

1½ cups (6¾ ounces) unbleached all-purpose flour

1½ teaspoons baking powder

¼ teaspoon table salt

8 tablespoons (4 ounces) unsalted butter, softened

⅔ cup (4⅝ ounces) firmly packed light brown sugar

2 large eggs, at room temperature

1 teaspoon pure vanilla extract

¼ cup store-bought dulce de leche

¼ cup whole milk, at room temperature

FOR THE DULCE DE LECHE FROSTING

1⅓ cups dulce de leche (store-bought or homemade, see p. 65)

Pinch of table salt

FOR THE GLAZE

12 ounces white chocolate, chopped

5½ teaspoons vegetable or canola oil

2 tablespoons Caramel Dust (recipe on facing page; optional)

Makes 56 cake bites

twists

Omit the Caramel Dust from the glaze and sprinkle ½ cup chocolate-covered toffee bits or ⅓ cup finely chopped toasted pecans on the just-dipped cake bites.

Dulce de Leche Cake Bites

This recipe owes much of its stunning flavor and texture to the "Caramel Dust" added to the white chocolate glaze. For that bit of genius, I must send a shout-out to the wonderful "chocolaholic" blogger Districtofchocolate. I met Victoria on Twitter a while back, and I've been fascinated by the depth and breadth of her chocolate knowledge along with her willingness to share it. She is simply inspiring.

When I was working on this recipe, I was struggling with the white chocolate coating—it was overwhelming the heavenly dulce de leche cake filling. I took my struggle to the Twitter world and asked if anyone had any idea how to impart a caramel flavor into a white chocolate coating. Victoria told me about a white chocolate bar she had tasted that contained pulverized caramel fleck; so was born Caramel Dust. Thanks, Victoria, for collaborating with me and sharing your visions.

make the cake

1 Position an oven rack in the center of the oven and heat the oven to 350°F. Lightly grease and flour the bottom and sides of a 9-inch round cake pan.

2 Put the flour, baking powder, and salt in a medium bowl and whisk until well blended. Put the butter in a large bowl. Beat with an electric mixer fitted with the paddle attachment on medium speed until well blended and smooth, about 1 minute. Add the brown sugar and beat on medium-high speed until well blended, about 2 minutes. Add the eggs, one at a time, beating well after each addition. Add the vanilla with the last egg. Stop to scrape down the bowl and the beater as needed. Add the dulce de leche and mix until blended. Add half of the flour mixture and mix on low speed until just blended. Add the milk and mix until just blended. Add the remaining flour mixture and mix on low until just blended.

3 Scrape the batter into the prepared pan and, using an offset spatula, spread evenly. Bake until a toothpick inserted in the center comes out clean, 25 to 27 minutes. Move to a wire rack and let cool for 20 minutes. Run a small knife between the cake and the pan, invert onto a wire rack, and set aside until completely cool.

make the frosting and assemble the cake bites

1 Line a large cookie sheet with parchment or a nonstick liner and make room in the refrigerator so the baking sheet will be level. (I arrange dairy containers that are the same height so that the sheet can sit on top.)

2 Put the dulce de leche and salt in a large bowl. Beat with an electric mixer fitted with the paddle attachment on medium speed until well blended and smooth, about 30 seconds.

3 Cut or gently break the cake into about 1-inch pieces and add to the large bowl with the dulce de leche frosting. Mix on low speed until the cake is broken into crumbs and completely combined with the dulce de leche, about 1 or 2 minutes. Using a 1-tablespoon mini scoop, shape the mixture into balls and lightly roll them in your palms to smooth the edges. Arrange the balls close together on the prepared cookie sheet and freeze until very cold and firm, 1 to 2 hours.

make the glaze and finish the cake bites

1 Have ready a cookie sheet lined with parchment or a nonstick liner and a table fork (I like to use a lobster fork or fondue fork). Melt the white chocolate and oil in the microwave or in a small deep bowl set over a pot of simmering water, stirring with a rubber spatula until smooth. Remove from the heat and set on a heatproof surface. Stir in the Caramel Dust, if using.

2 Working with 8 to 10 cake bites at a time (keep the rest in the fridge), put the bite on the fork tines. Dip the bite into the white chocolate to cover completely and tap the fork gently on the side of the bowl so that the excess chocolate drips off and back into the bowl. Arrange the bite on the prepared cookie sheet. Continue dipping with the remaining bites.

3 Refrigerate the chocolate-covered bites until the chocolate is set, about 1 hour. Serve immediately, slightly chilled.

do ahead

- The cake can be prepared through Step 3 in Make the Cake, covered, and stowed at room temperature for up to 1 day before continuing with the recipe.

- The cake bites can be prepared through Step 3 in Make the Frosting, covered, and stowed at room temperature for up to 1 day before glazing.

- The finished cake bites can be arranged in a plastic container separated with layers of waxed paper or parchment and stowed in the refrigerator for up to 3 days.

caramel dust

1 Line a cookie sheet with a nonstick liner (parchment won't work for this recipe).

2 Put the sugar and water in a small heavy saucepan. Cook, stirring, over medium-low heat until the sugar dissolves. Increase the heat to high and bring to a boil. Boil, without stirring, until the sugar begins to color around the edges of the pan, about 5 minutes. Swirl the pan over the heat until the caramel is an even deep amber, about another 1 to 3 minutes.

3 Carefully pour the mixture onto the prepared baking sheet. It will spread some, but there's no need to encourage it. Set aside at room temperature until completely cool, about 2 hours. Break into small pieces and put in a food processor. Whiz until the caramel is very finely ground. Stow in an airtight container for up to 1 week.

Makes about ½ cup

½ cup (3½ ounces) granulated sugar

3 tablespoons water

FOR THE LEMON CAKE

1⅓ cups (6 ounces) unbleached all-purpose flour

2 teaspoons baking powder

¼ teaspoon table salt

3 whites from large eggs, at room temperature

8 tablespoons (4 ounces) unsalted butter, softened

⅔ cup (4⅝ ounces) + 2 tablespoons granulated sugar, divided

2 teaspoons finely grated lemon zest

½ teaspoon pure vanilla extract

½ cup whole milk, at room temperature

FOR THE LEMON CURD

8 tablespoons (4 ounces) unsalted butter

½ cup (3½ ounces) granulated sugar

½ cup freshly squeezed lemon juice

1 tablespoon finely grated lemon zest

Pinch of table salt

2 large eggs, at room temperature

2 yolks from large eggs, at room temperature

FOR THE GLAZE

12 ounces white chocolate, chopped

4½ teaspoons vegetable or canola oil

1 teaspoon pure lemon extract or pure lemon oil

½ cup colored sprinkles

Makes 56 cake bites

Zesty Lemon Cake Bites

Don't wait until springtime to make these bites, as their vibrant, zesty flavor and sunny appearance will brighten any day, any time of the year. This is the "no-fork" version of my favorite lemon layer cake—the perfect complement to any meal.

make the cake

1 Position an oven rack in the center of the oven and heat the oven to 350°F. Lightly grease and flour the bottom and sides of a 9-inch round cake pan.

2 Sift the flour, baking powder, and salt onto a paper plate or into a medium bowl. Put the egg whites in a clean, medium bowl (see the sidebar on p. 41). Set aside.

3 Put the butter in a large bowl. Beat with an electric mixer fitted with the paddle attachment on medium speed until well blended and smooth, about 1 minute. Add the ⅔ cup sugar, the lemon zest, and vanilla and beat on medium-high speed until well blended, about 2 minutes. Stop to scrape down the bowl and the beater as needed. Add a third of the flour mixture and mix on low speed until just blended. Add half of the milk and mix until just blended. Add another third of the flour mixture and mix on low speed until just blended. Add the remaining milk and mix until just blended. Add the remaining flour mixture and mix on low until just blended.

4 Beat the egg whites with an electric mixer fitted with the whisk attachment until soft peaks form when the beater is lifted, about 2 minutes. Increase the speed to high and gradually add the remaining 2 tablespoons sugar. Continue beating until the whites form medium-firm peaks.

5 Using a rubber spatula, add about one-third of the whites to the batter and stir gently to lighten the mixture. Add the remaining whites and fold gently until just blended.

6 Scrape the batter into the prepared pan and, using an offset spatula, spread evenly. Bake until a toothpick inserted in the center comes out clean, 26 to 28 minutes. Move to a wire rack and let cool for 20 minutes. Run a small knife between the cake and the pan, invert onto a wire rack, and set aside until completely cool.

make the lemon curd

1 Put the butter in a medium saucepan and melt over medium heat. Slide the pan from the heat and whisk in the sugar, lemon juice, zest, and salt. Add the eggs and yolks and whisk until well blended. Cook over medium-low heat, whisking constantly, until the mixture is thick enough to coat a spatula and hold a line drawn through it with a finger, 4 to 6 minutes. Don't let the mixture boil.

2 Using a fine-mesh sieve, strain the curd into a clean bowl, discard the zest, and cover the surface directly with plastic wrap. Let cool at room temperature.

assemble the cake bites

1 Line a large cookie sheet with parchment or a nonstick liner and make room in your refrigerator so the baking sheet will be level. (I arrange dairy containers that are the same height so that the sheet can sit on top.)

2 Cut or gently break the cooled cake into 1-inch pieces and add to a large bowl with the lemon curd. Mix on low speed until the cake is broken into crumbs and completely combined with the lemon curd, 1 to 2 minutes. Using a 1-tablespoon mini scoop, shape the mixture into balls and lightly roll them in your palms to smooth the edges. Arrange the balls close together on the prepared cookie sheet and refrigerate until very cold and firm, about 4 hours.

make the glaze and finish the cake bites

1 Have ready a cookie sheet lined with parchment or a nonstick liner and a table fork (I like to use a lobster fork or fondue fork). Melt the chocolate and vegetable oil in the microwave or in a small deep bowl set over a pot of simmering water, add the extract, and stir with a rubber spatula until smooth. Remove from the heat and set on a heatproof surface.

2 Working with 8 to 10 cake bites at a time (keep the rest in the fridge), put the bite on the fork tines. Dip the bite into the chocolate to cover completely and tap the fork gently on the side of the bowl so that the excess chocolate drips off and back into the bowl. Arrange the bite on the prepared cookie sheet and sprinkle with a few of the sprinkles. Continue dipping and sprinkling with the remaining bites.

3 Refrigerate the chocolate-covered bites until the chocolate is set, about 1 hour. Serve immediately, slightly chilled.

> ### KITCHEN WISDOM ◎◎ adding oils and extracts
> Don't be tempted to add more of the lemon extract or oil than listed because you think that "more" will be better. In fact, adding too much of any kind of oil (peppermint, orange, and lemon, for example) will make your cake bites taste medicinal.

twists
Substitute 2 tablespoons finely grated lemon zest for the colored sprinkles; sprinkle a pinch on each cake bite.

do ahead
• The cake can be prepared through Step 6 in Make the Cake, covered, and stowed at room temperature for up to 1 day before continuing with the recipe.

• The curd can be made and refrigerated for up to 2 days before using.

• The cake bites can be prepared through Step 2 in Assemble the Cake Bites, covered, and stowed at room temperature for up to 1 day before glazing.

• The finished cake bites can be arranged in a plastic container separated with layers of waxed paper or parchment and stowed in the refrigerator for up to 3 days.

Mini Red Velvet Whoopie Pies with Marshmallow Filling

My daughter, Tierney (a.k.a. T), goes to college in Maine. On her birthday this past year, her roommate gave her a giant (it was at least 12 inches in diameter) red velvet whoopie pie from the landmark Lewiston bakery, Labadie's Bakery. As all good Mainers know, the whoopie pie is the state's official treat (not to be confused with the state dessert, which is blueberry pie). Apparently, the thing got devoured in record time by T's dorm mates. My version is smaller and more manageable for those of us without a college-sized appetite.

make the whoopies

1 Position an oven rack in the center of the oven and heat the oven to 350°F. Line three cookie sheets with parchment or nonstick liners.

2 Whisk the flour, cocoa powder, baking powder, baking soda, and salt in a medium bowl until well blended and no lumps remain. Put the butter and granulated sugar in a large bowl. Beat with an electric mixer fitted with the paddle attachment on medium speed until well blended and smooth, about 3 minutes. Add the eggs, one at a time, beating until just blended between additions. Add the vanilla and food coloring with the last egg. Stop to scrape down the bowl and the beater as needed. Add half of the flour mixture and mix on low speed until just blended. Add the sour cream and mix just until blended. Add the remaining flour mixture and mix on low speed until just blended.

3 Using a 1-tablespoon mini scoop, shape the dough into balls and arrange about 1½ inches apart on the prepared cookie sheets. Bake, one sheet at a time, until a toothpick inserted in the center of one whoopie comes out clean, 10 to 12 minutes. Move the sheet to a wire rack, let the whoopies sit for 10 minutes, and then transfer them to a wire rack to cool completely.

recipe continues

FOR THE WHOOPIES

- 1½ cups (6¾ ounces) unbleached all-purpose flour
- ½ cup (1½ ounces) unsweetened natural cocoa powder, sifted if lumpy
- 1 teaspoon baking powder
- ½ teaspoon baking soda
- ½ teaspoon table salt
- 6 tablespoons (3 ounces) unsalted butter, softened
- 1 cup (7 ounces) granulated sugar
- 2 large eggs, at room temperature
- 1½ teaspoons pure vanilla extract
- ½ teaspoon red food coloring paste (or 1 tablespoon liquid food coloring)
- 1 cup (8 ounces) sour cream, at room temperature

FOR THE FILLING

- 16 tablespoons (8 ounces) unsalted butter, at room temperature
- 1 jar (7 ounces) Marshmallow Fluff®
- ½ cup (2 ounces) confectioners' sugar
- 1½ teaspoons pure vanilla paste or seeds scraped from 1 large vanilla bean (see the sidebar on p. 21)
- ¼ teaspoon table salt

Colored sprinkles, for garnish (optional)

Makes 28 filled whoopie pies

finishing touches

Before filling, pipe a small swirl of Orange–White Chocolate Drizzle (see p. 12) over the domed side of half of the whoopies and use these as the tops. Fit a large round or star tip (I use an Ateco #6) into a pastry bag and fill with the frosting (see p. 18). Evenly pipe the frosting onto half of the cooled whoopies and continue as directed in Assemble the Whoopie Pies.

twists

• Substitute Brown Sugar Cream Cheese Frosting (see p. 109) for the filling instead of Fluff.

• Use toasted sweetened shredded coconut or chopped, toasted nuts instead of the sprinkles.

do ahead

• The whoopies can be prepared through Step 3 in Make the Whoopies, covered, and stowed at room temperature for up to 1 day before filling.

• Filled whoopies can be stowed in the refrigerator for up to 2 days. Serve at room temperature.

make the filling

Put the butter and Fluff in a large bowl. Beat with an electric mixer fitted with the whisk attachment on medium speed until well blended and smooth, about 2 minutes. Add the confectioners' sugar, vanilla, and salt. Continue beating until smooth and fluffy, about 2 minutes.

assemble the whoopie pies

Turn over half of the cooled whoopies so they are flat side up. Spoon a slightly rounded 1 tablespoon of the filling onto the center of each whoopie. Top with the remaining whoopies, flat side down. Press gently on each top to spread the filling almost to the edge. Roll the edges in the sprinkles, if using, to coat the frosting. Serve immediately or chill for 30 minutes. Whoopie pies are best when served at room temperature.

Double Espresso Whoopie Pies

I'm not a coffee drinker—not even a drop. This surprises many people because I create a lot of coffee-flavored desserts. Think of it this way: If I were to order a coffee, I would ask for it "light and sweet" (Dunkin' Donuts® speak for "lots of cream and sugar, please"), much like a serving of hot coffee ice cream.

These whoopies are a perfect example of my food-crush with coffee. The brown sugar–sweetened cakes are flavored with instant espresso granules and coffee liqueur and sandwiched with a buttery, creamy coffee filling. Double espresso served up my way!

make the whoopies

1 Position an oven rack in the center of the oven and heat the oven to 350°F. Line three cookie sheets with parchment or nonstick liners.

2 Put the milk and instant espresso in a small ramekin and stir occasionally until the espresso is dissolved.

3 Whisk the flour, baking powder, baking soda, and salt in a medium bowl until well blended and no lumps remain. Put the butter in a large bowl. Beat with an electric mixer fitted with the paddle attachment on medium speed until well blended and smooth, about 3 minutes. Add the granulated and brown sugars and beat on medium speed until fluffy, about 2 minutes. Add the eggs, one at a time, beating until just blended between additions. Add the coffee liqueur (if using) and vanilla with the last egg. Stop to scrape down the bowl and the beater as needed. Add half of the flour mixture and mix on low speed until just blended. Add the milk mixture and mix just until blended. Add the remaining flour mixture and mix on low speed until just blended.

4 Using a 1-tablespoon mini scoop, shape the dough into balls and arrange about 1½ inches apart on the prepared cookie sheets. Bake, one sheet at a time, until a toothpick inserted in the center of one whoopie comes out clean, 9 to 11 minutes. Move the sheet to a wire rack, let the whoopies sit for 10 minutes, and then transfer them to a wire rack to cool completely.

recipe continues

FOR THE WHOOPIES

- ½ cup whole milk
- 4 teaspoons instant espresso granules
- 2 cups (9 ounces) unbleached all-purpose flour
- 2 teaspoons baking powder
- ¼ teaspoon baking soda
- ½ teaspoon table salt
- 6 tablespoons (3 ounces) unsalted butter, softened
- ½ cup (3½ ounces) granulated sugar
- ½ cup (3½ ounces) firmly packed light brown sugar
- 2 large eggs, at room temperature
- 1 tablespoon coffee liqueur, such as Kahlúa® (optional)
- 1 teaspoon pure vanilla extract

FOR THE FILLING

- 2 tablespoons heavy cream
- 1 tablespoon coffee liqueur, such as Kahlúa
- 1 tablespoon instant espresso granules
- 8 tablespoons (4 ounces) unsalted butter, at room temperature
- 2 cups (8 ounces) confectioners' sugar

Pinch of table salt

Makes 22 filled whoopie pies

finishing touches

- Before baking, sprinkle the tops of half of the whoopies with crushed cocoa nibs. Bake and let cool as directed and, when assembling the pies, use the cocoa nib–coated whoopies as the tops.

  OR

  Just before serving, dust the tops with a little confectioners' sugar.

- Fit a large round or star tip (I use an Ateco #6) into a pastry bag and fill with the frosting (see the sidebar on p. 18). Evenly pipe the frosting onto half of the cooled whoopies and continue as directed.

twists

Omit the coffee liqueur in the filling and use an additional 1 tablespoon of heavy cream.

do ahead

- The whoopies can be baked, cooled, covered, and stowed at room temperature for up to 1 day before filling.

- The filled whoopies can be stowed in the refrigerator for up to 2 days. Serve at room temperature.

make the filling

1 Put the heavy cream, coffee liqueur, and instant espresso in a small ramekin and stir occasionally until the espresso is dissolved.

2 Put the butter and confectioners' sugar in a large bowl. Beat with an electric mixer fitted with the whisk attachment on medium speed until well blended and smooth, about 2 minutes. Add the heavy cream mixture and salt. Continue beating until smooth and fluffy, about 2 minutes.

assemble the whoopies

Turn half of the cooled whoopies over so they are flat side up. Spoon 1 tablespoon of the filling onto the center of each whoopie. Top with the remaining whoopies, flat side down. Press gently on each top to spread the filling almost to the edge. Serve immediately or chill for 30 minutes. Whoopie pies are best when served at room temperature.

Double-Trouble Chocolate Cupcakes

My kids call these cupcake "double trouble" because both the cake and frosting are so deadly—but in a good way, of course. If you're not in the mood for "double trouble," feel free to use another frosting, like the Brown Sugar Cream Cheese (p. 109).

make the cupcakes

1 Position an oven rack in the center of the oven and heat the oven to 350°F. Line 12 regular-sized (2³/₄-inch diameter) muffin cups with paper or foil liners.

2 Whisk the flour, cocoa powder, baking soda, and salt in a medium bowl until well blended and no lumps remain. Put the butter, granulated sugar, and brown sugar in a large bowl. Beat with an electric mixer fitted with the paddle attachment on medium speed until well blended and smooth, about 3 minutes. Add the egg, beating until just blended. Add the yolk and vanilla. Stop to scrape down the bowl and the beater as needed. Add half of the flour mixture and mix on low speed until just blended. Add the buttermilk and mix until just blended. Add the remaining flour mixture and mix on low speed until just blended.

3 Portion the batter evenly among the prepared muffin cups (a scant 3 tablespoons of batter per cup will be about halfway full). Bake until a toothpick inserted in the center comes out clean, 16 to 18 minutes. Move to a wire rack and let cool for 15 minutes. Carefully remove the cupcakes from the pan, set them on a wire rack, and let cool completely.

make the frosting

1 Melt the chocolate in the microwave or in a large bowl set over a pot of simmering water, stirring with a rubber spatula until smooth. Remove from the heat and set aside until cool. For faster cooling, set the bowl over a larger bowl filled with ice and water and stir until cool.

2 Add the butter, vanilla, and salt to the cooled chocolate. Beat with an electric mixer fitted with the whip attachment on medium speed until well blended and smooth, about 2 minutes.

recipe continues

FOR THE CUPCAKES

- 1 cup (4¹/₂ ounces) unbleached all-purpose flour
- ¹/₂ cup (1¹/₂ ounces) unsweetened natural cocoa powder, sifted if lumpy
- ¹/₂ teaspoon baking soda
- ¹/₄ teaspoon table salt
- 8 tablespoons (4 ounces) unsalted butter, softened
- ¹/₂ cup (3¹/₂ ounces) granulated sugar
- ¹/₄ cup (1³/₄ ounces) firmly packed light brown sugar
- 1 large egg, at room temperature
- 1 yolk from a large egg, at room temperature
- 1 teaspoon pure vanilla extract
- ¹/₂ cup buttermilk, at room temperature

FOR THE FROSTING

- 6 ounces bittersweet chocolate, chopped
- 16 tablespoons (8 ounces) unsalted butter, softened
- 1 teaspoon pure vanilla extract
- Pinch of table salt

Makes 12 cupcakes

finishing touches

Top each cupcake with crushed cocoa nibs or chocolate shavings.

do ahead

• The cupcakes can be prepared through Step 3, covered, and stowed at room temperature for up to 1 day before frosting.

• The frosted cupcakes can be covered and stowed at room temperature for up to 2 days.

assemble the cupcakes

Portion the frosting evenly among the cooled cupcakes (about 2 tablespoons per cupcake). Using a small metal spatula, mound and swirl the frosting on top of the cupcakes, leaving a border of cake around each one. Serve immediately; the cupcakes are best served at room temperature.

twists

• **FLAVOR THE FROSTING:** Add ½ teaspoon ground cinnamon or ¼ teaspoon peppermint extract to the frosting along with the vanilla extract, or 2 teaspoons instant espresso granules dissolved in the vanilla.

• **USE A PASTRY BAG FOR A FANCY FINISH:** Fit a large star tip (I use an Ateco #6) into a pastry bag and fill with the frosting (see the sidebar on p. 18). Evenly pipe frosting onto the cooled cupcakes, leaving a border of cake around each one.

Carrot Cake Cone Cakes with Brown Sugar Cream Cheese Frosting

I first learned about cone cakes—cupcake batter baked into flat-bottomed ice cream cones—when I was working on a kids' party story at *Woman's Day* magazine. Having spent most of the previous years working in French kitchens, this was my first look at this charming cupcake varietal. Since then, I've produced a number of cupcake recipes with the batter baked directly in the cones, and each one is more adorable than the next.

And here's the news flash: Cone cakes aren't just for kids—especially this carrot cake version, with its traditional, not-too-sweet cake and brown sugar cream cheese frosting that has the perfect balance of sweet and tangy. If you're out of cones (or not inclined to try them), I've given directions for baking the batter in traditional cupcake liners. Either way, this is a must-try, classic carrot cake.

Position an oven rack in the center of the oven and heat the oven to 350°F. Arrange the cones in the cups of a mini (scant 2-inch diameter) muffin tin.

make the cake

1 Whisk the flour, cinnamon, baking soda, salt, nutmeg, and ginger in a medium bowl until well blended. Put the carrots, brown sugar, eggs, oil, and vanilla in a large bowl. Beat with an electric mixer fitted with the paddle attachment on medium speed until well blended, about 2 minutes. Add the dry ingredients and mix on low speed until just blended, about 1 minute.

2 Portion the batter evenly among the prepared cones; they'll be about three-quarters full. Bake until the top of the cake springs back when lightly pressed and a toothpick inserted in the center comes out clean, 25 to 27 minutes. Move the muffin tin to a wire rack and let the cone cakes cool completely.

make the frosting

Put the cream cheese and butter in a large bowl. Beat with an electric mixer fitted with the whisk attachment on medium speed until well blended and smooth, about 2 minutes. Add the brown sugar, vanilla, and salt. Continue beating until smooth and fluffy, about 1 minute.

recipe continues

12 flat-bottomed ice cream cones

FOR THE CAKE

1   cup (4½ ounces) unbleached all-purpose flour
1   teaspoon ground cinnamon
¾   teaspoon baking soda
½   teaspoon table salt
¼   teaspoon ground nutmeg
¼   teaspoon ground ginger
1   cup (3¾ ounces) finely grated carrots
1   cup (7 ounces) firmly packed light brown sugar
2   large eggs, at room temperature
½   cup canola, corn, or vegetable oil
1   teaspoon pure vanilla extract

FOR THE FROSTING

5   ounces cream cheese
4   tablespoons (2 ounces) unsalted butter, at room temperature
½   cup (3½ ounces) firmly packed light brown sugar
¾   teaspoon pure vanilla extract
Pinch of table salt

Makes 12 cone cakes

finishing touches

Scatter some toasted, chopped walnuts onto the frosting. You'll need about ⅓ cup.

do ahead

- The cupcakes can be baked, cooled, covered, and stowed at room temperature for up to 1 day before frosting.
- The frosted cupcakes can be covered and refrigerated for up to 2 days. Serve at room temperature.

assemble the cone cakes

Portion the frosting evenly among the cooled cone cakes (about 2 tablespoons per cake). Using a small metal spatula, mound and swirl the frosting on top of the cupcakes, leaving a border of cake around each one. Serve immediately.

twists

- **ADD SOMETHING EXTRA:** Add ¼ cup currants or raisins to the batter. If you use raisins, chop them coarsely before adding them; otherwise, they'll sink to the bottom of the cone.
- **ADD A DIFFERENT FLAVOR:** Add 2 teaspoons finely grated orange zest or 1 teaspoon finely grated lemon zest to the batter.
- **MAKE 'EM CUPCAKES:** Instead of using ice cream cones, line 10 regular-sized (2¾-inch-diameter) muffin cups with paper or foil liners and bake for 18 to 20 minutes. Continue with the recipe to frost and finish.
- **USE A PASTRY BAG FOR A FANCY FINISH:** Fit a large star tip (I use an Ateco #6) into a pastry bag and fill with the frosting (see the sidebar on p. 18). Evenly pipe the frosting onto the cooled cone cakes, leaving a border of cake around each one.

FOR THE WHOOPIES

- 2 cups (9 ounces) unbleached all-purpose flour
- 2 teaspoons baking powder
- ¼ teaspoon baking soda
- ½ teaspoon table salt
- 6 tablespoons (3 ounces) unsalted butter, softened
- 1 cup (7 ounces) granulated sugar
- 4 teaspoons finely grated orange zest
- 2 large eggs, at room temperature
- 1 teaspoon pure vanilla extract
- ½ cup buttermilk, at room temperature

FOR THE FILLING

- 8 tablespoons (4 ounces) unsalted butter, at room temperature
- 2 cups (8 ounces) confectioners' sugar
- 6 tablespoons honey (preferably orange blossom)
- 2 tablespoons heavy cream
- 1 tablespoon finely grated orange zest

Pinch of table salt

Colored sprinkles, for garnish (optional)

Makes 24 filled whoopie pies

Orange Whoopie Pies with Orange–Honey Buttercream

After tasting these whoopie pies, my dear friend Laura Clark asked if she could have the recipe for a contest of sorts at Macy's, where she works. From what I gather, Laura's corporate division of Macy's sets aside a day for a "taste-off" and all the departments bring in samples of their best homemade recipes—sweet and savory—and everyone votes for a winner. It seems that Laura came up one vote shy of first place the previous year so she was angling for a win. After plating and passing these honey-scented, double orange three-biters to a room full of ooohs and ahhhs, Laura was sure she had the win "in the bag." To Laura's dismay, it was determined that it was no longer "PC" to have a winner, so no votes were tabulated and no winner announced. But as Laura and I agreed, we knew that these whoopies stole the show, and I know you'll feel the same, too.

make the whoopies

1 Position an oven rack in the center of the oven and heat the oven to 350°F. Line three cookie sheets with parchment or nonstick liners.

2 Whisk the flour, baking powder, baking soda, and salt in a medium bowl until well blended and no lumps remain. Put the butter, sugar, and orange zest in a large bowl. Beat with an electric mixer fitted with the paddle attachment on medium speed until well blended and smooth, about 3 minutes. Add the eggs, one at a time, beating until just blended between additions. Add the vanilla with the last egg. Stop to scrape down the bowl and the beater as needed. Add half of the flour mixture and mix on low speed until just blended. Add the buttermilk and mix until just blended. Add the remaining flour mixture and mix on low speed until just blended.

3 Using a 1-tablespoon mini scoop, shape the dough into balls and arrange about 1½ inches apart on the prepared cookie sheets. Bake, one sheet at a time, until a toothpick inserted in the center of one whoopie comes out clean, 9 to 11 minutes. Move the sheet to a wire rack, let the whoopies sit for 10 minutes, and then transfer them to a rack to cool completely.

make the filling

Put the butter and confectioners' sugar in a large bowl. Beat with an electric mixer fitted with the whisk attachment on medium speed until well blended and smooth, about 2 minutes. Add the honey, heavy cream, orange zest, and salt. Continue beating until smooth and fluffy, about 2 minutes.

assemble the whoopie pies

Turn half of the cooled whoopies over so they are flat side up. Spoon a slightly rounded 1 tablespoon of the filling onto the center of each whoopie. Top with the remaining whoopies, flat side down. Press gently on each top to spread the filling almost to the edge. Roll the edges of the whoopie pies in colored sprinkles, if you like. Serve immediately or chill for 30 minutes. Whoopie pies are best when served at room temperature.

finishing touches

- Before baking, sprinkle the tops of half of the whoopies with coarse sugar or finely chopped walnuts. Bake and let cool as directed and, when assembling the pies, use the sugar- or walnut-coated whoopies as the tops.

- Fit a large round or star tip (I use an Ateco #6) into a pastry bag and fill with the frosting (see the sidebar on p. 18). Evenly pipe the frosting onto half of the cooled whoopies and continue as directed in Assemble the Whoopie Pies.

twists

MAKE IT LEMON: Use 2 teaspoons finely grated lemon zest instead of the orange zest in the cakes; eliminate the orange zest in the filling.

do ahead

- The whoopies can be prepared through Step 3 in Make the Whoopies, covered, and stowed at room temperature for up to 1 day before filling.

- Filled whoopies can be stowed in the refrigerator for up to 2 days. Serve at room temperature.

Almost-Instant Yellow Cupcakes with Strawberry Cream Frosting

When I wrote *The Weekend Baker,* I included a recipe for Emergency Chocolate Cupcakes, which can be whipped up from on-hand ingredients in the time it takes for the oven to heat. Perfect for last-minute desserts yet still from-scratch delicious, these have long been a reader favorite. In this yellow cake version, I call for butter because I prefer the flavor it packs, but you could use a mild, flavorless oil, like canola or vegetable, too. Make sure your oil is fresh and doesn't smell "off" or rancid—the cupcakes' flavor would suffer.

A word about the frosting: The base is a combination of lightly sweetened heavy cream and mascarpone (the mascarpone stabilizes the heavy cream so the frosting will keep its shape and not weep like ordinary whipped cream). For a pretty pink color and fresh flavor, I've added a reduced strawberry purée. If you want to skip the step of cooking down the purée, use ³⁄₄ cup uncooked purée or, instead, use Toasted Walnut Buttercream Frosting (pp. 88–89).

make the purée
Put the strawberries in a food processor (a blender also works) and whiz until completely smooth, 1 to 2 minutes. Pour the purée into a medium saucepan and bring to a boil over medium-high heat, stirring occasionally. Reduce the heat to low and cook, stirring often, until very thick and reduced to ³⁄₄ cup, 18 to 22 minutes. Slide the pan from the heat and let cool completely.

make the cupcakes
1 Position an oven rack in the center of the oven and heat oven to 375°F. Line 12 regular-sized (2³⁄₄-inch diameter) muffin cups with paper or foil liners.

2 Put the flour, sugar, baking powder, and salt in a medium bowl and whisk until well blended.

3 Put the melted butter, water, egg, egg yolk, and vanilla in a small bowl and whisk until well blended. Pour over the dry ingredients and whisk until well blended and smooth, about 1 minute.

recipe continues

FOR THE CONDENSED STRAWBERRY PURÉE

1 pound fresh strawberries, rinsed, dried, and stemmed

FOR THE CUPCAKES

1¼ cups (5½ ounces) unbleached all-purpose flour

¾ cup granulated sugar

2 teaspoons baking powder

½ teaspoon table salt

6 tablespoons (3 ounces) unsalted butter, melted

½ cup water

1 large egg, at room temperature

1 yolk from a large egg

1 tablespoon pure vanilla extract or paste

FOR THE FROSTING

1 cup heavy cream

½ cup mascarpone

¾ cup (3 ounces) confectioners' sugar

1 teaspoon pure vanilla extract

Pinch of table salt

FOR SERVING

12 small fresh strawberries, rinsed and dried

Makes 12 cupcakes

twists

- **USE OIL INSTEAD OF BUTTER:** Use
1/3 cup neutral-flavored oil like
canola, vegetable, or corn. The
flavor won't be as deep, but the
cupcakes will still be delicious.

- **CHANGE UP THE FROSTING:**
Instead of topping the cupcakes
with strawberry cream frosting,
substitute Brown Sugar Whipped
Cream Frosting (p. 90).

- **USE A PASTRY BAG FOR A FANCY
FINISH:** Fit a large plain tip (I use
an Ateco #5) into a pastry bag
and fill with the frosting (see
the sidebar on p. 18). Evenly pipe
the frosting onto the cooled
cupcakes, leaving a border of cake
around each one.

do ahead

- The condensed strawberry
purée can be made, covered,
and refrigerated for up to 2 days
before using.

- The strawberry cream frosting
can be made, covered, and
refrigerated up to 1 day ahead.

4 Portion the batter evenly among the prepared muffin cups (3 tablespoons batter per cup will be about two-thirds of the way full). Bake until a toothpick inserted in the center comes out clean, 14 to 16 minutes. Move to a wire rack and let cool for 15 minutes. Carefully remove the cupcakes from the pan, set them on a wire rack, and let cool completely.

make the frosting

Put the heavy cream and mascarpone in a large bowl. Beat with an electric mixer fitted with the whip attachment on medium-low speed until well blended and smooth, about 1 minute. Add the confectioners' sugar, vanilla, and salt. Beat on medium-high speed until thick enough to hold firm peaks when the beater is lifted, about 2 minutes. Add 3/4 cup of the cooled, reduced strawberry purée and beat on medium until well blended.

assemble the cupcakes

Portion the frosting evenly among the cooled cupcakes (about 2 tablespoons per cupcake). Using a small metal spatula, mound and swirl the frosting on top of the cupcakes, leaving a border of cake around each one. Top each cupcake with a small strawberry. Serve immediately or chill for 30 minutes. The cupcakes are best when frosted and eaten the day they're baked. Serve slightly chilled but not cold.

Mini Spiced Sour Cream Coffee Cakes

These comforting coffee cakes are inspired by one of my favorite recipes that I used to bake with my mom when I was first starting out. Mom had torn out a recipe for Spiced Yogurt Cake from, of all places, an issue of *Vogue* (continued proof that food is fashionable, I suppose). It was a straightforward single-layer cake, and while I think the recipe included some sort of topping, Mom and I always made it straight up. The cake's flavor was perfectly balanced: just the right amount of spices paired with the tang of yogurt. It also had the added allure of an improving flavor and texture the longer it sat.

This cupcake version has all the elements of the original plus the addition of a slightly crunchy streusel topping—perfect for breakfast, brunch, or teatime.

make the streusel

In a small bowl, combine the brown sugar, flour, and cinnamon. Drizzle the melted butter on top and, using a fork or your fingers, mix the ingredients until well blended and small crumbs form when pinched together with your fingers. Pop in the refrigerator while you make the cupcake batter.

make the cupcakes

1 Arrange an oven rack in the center of the oven and heat the oven to 350°F. Line 16 regular-sized (2¾-inch-diameter) muffin cups with foil or paper liners.

2 Whisk the flour, baking soda, cinnamon, nutmeg, and salt in a medium bowl until well blended. Put the butter in a large bowl. Beat with an electric mixer fitted with the paddle attachment on medium speed until well blended, about 1 minute. Add the brown sugar and beat on medium-high speed until well blended, about 2 minutes. Add the eggs, one at a time, beating well after each addition. Add the vanilla with the last egg. Stop to scrape the bowl and beaters as needed. Add about half of the flour mixture and mix on low speed until just blended. Add the sour cream and continue mixing until just blended. Using a rubber spatula, fold in the remaining flour mixture.

3 Spoon the batter evenly among the prepared muffin cups. Tap the muffin tin on the counter a few times to settle the batter. Evenly scatter the streusel mixture over the batter and press gently into the batter (this also helps even out the batter in the liners). There will be a lot of streusel, but you'll like the cakes this way.

4 Bake until the top of the cake springs back when lightly pressed and a toothpick inserted in the center comes out clean, 18 to 20 minutes. Move the muffin tins to a wire rack and let the cakes cool. Serve warm or at room temperature.

FOR THE STREUSEL TOPPING

- ⅓ cup (2⅜ ounces) firmly packed light brown sugar
- ½ cup (2¼ ounces) unbleached all-purpose flour
- ¾ teaspoons ground cinnamon
- 2 tablespoons (1 ounce) unsalted butter, melted

FOR THE CUPCAKES

- 2 cups (9 ounces) unbleached all-purpose flour
- 1 teaspoon baking soda
- ½ teaspoon ground cinnamon
- ½ teaspoon ground nutmeg
- ½ teaspoon table salt
- 8 tablespoons (4 ounces) unsalted butter, softened
- 1⅓ cups (9⅜ ounces) firmly packed light brown sugar
- 2 large eggs, at room temperature
- 1 teaspoon pure vanilla extract
- 1 cup sour cream, at room temperature

Makes 16 cakes

do ahead

The cupcakes can be prepared through Step 4, covered, and stowed at room temperature for up to 1 day before serving.

twists

- Instead of the sour cream, substitute the same amount of plain yogurt (Greek style is best) or the same amount of buttermilk.

- Add to the streusel one of the following (or a combination of both): 2 ounces chopped bittersweet chocolate (⅓ cup) or ¼ cup (1 ounce) lightly toasted chopped pecans, walnuts, or slivered almonds.

12 flat-bottomed ice cream cones

FOR THE CAKE

1 cup (4½ ounces) unbleached
    all-purpose flour

½ teaspoon baking powder

¼ teaspoon baking soda

¼ teaspoon table salt

4 tablespoons (2 ounces) unsalted
    butter, softened

⅓ cup (3 ounces) smooth peanut
    butter

⅔ cup (4⅝ ounces) firmly packed
    light brown sugar

2 large eggs, at room temperature

1 teaspoon pure vanilla extract

⅓ cup buttermilk

FOR THE FROSTING

¼ cup (¾ ounce) unsweetened
    natural cocoa powder, sifted
    if lumpy

⅓ cup whole milk

16 tablespoons (8 ounces) unsalted
    butter, softened

1 cup (4 ounces) confectioners'
    sugar

1 teaspoon pure vanilla extract

Pinch of table salt

4 ounces bittersweet chocolate,
    melted and cooled

3 Reese's® Peanut Butter Cups®,
    cut into quarters, for garnish
    (optional)

Makes 12 cone cakes

do ahead

• The cone cakes can be prepared
  through Step 3 covered, and
  stowed at room temperature for
  up to 1 day before frosting.

• The frosted cone cakes can be
  covered and stowed at room
  temperature for up to 2 days.

Peanut Butter Cone Cakes with Bittersweet Frosting

Finding the perfect balance for a peanut butter cake can be tricky. Clearly, the cake needs to be moist and full of peanut butter flavor, but it's easy to take the texture and flavor too far. These cakes confidently walk that tightrope.

Many will say that the cake is the scene-stealer of this dessert but don't discount the chocolate frosting. The flavor is deep and chocolaty and lacks the cloying sweetness of typical confectioners' sugar-based frostings. Claire Van de Berghe, my trusted testing assistant, says it's one of the best she's ever had and for more than just these cakes.

Position an oven rack in the center of the oven and heat the oven to 350°F. Arrange 12 flat-bottomed ice cream cones in the cups of a mini (scant 2-inch diameter) muffin tin.

make the cake

1 Whisk the flour, baking powder, baking soda, and salt in a small bowl until well blended. Put the butter and peanut butter in a large bowl. Beat with an electric mixer fitted with the paddle attachment on medium speed until well blended, about 1 minute. Add the brown sugar and beat on medium-high speed until well blended, about 2 minutes.

2 Add the eggs, one at a time, beating well after each addition. Add the vanilla with the last egg. Stop to scrape down the bowl and the beater as needed. Add half of the flour mixture and mix on low speed until just blended. Add the buttermilk and mix until just blended. Add the remaining flour mixture and mix on low speed until just blended.

3 Portion the batter evenly among the prepared cones. They'll be about three-quarters of the way full. Bake until the top of the cake springs back when lightly pressed and a toothpick inserted in the center comes out clean, 22 to 25 minutes. Move the muffin tin to a wire rack and let the cone cakes cool completely.

make the frosting

1 While the cone cakes are cooling, make the frosting. Put the cocoa powder in a small saucepan and slowly whisk in the milk until smooth and blended. Cook, whisking constantly, over medium heat until just boiling and very thick. Slide the pan from the heat and set aside, whisking occasionally, to cool completely.

2 Put the butter and confectioners' sugar in a large bowl. Beat with an electric mixer fitted with the paddle attachment on medium speed until well blended and smooth, about 1 minute. Add the cooled cocoa mixture, vanilla, and salt and beat on medium-high speed until light and fluffy, about 2 minutes. Add the cooled, melted chocolate and beat on medium speed until blended.

assemble the cone cakes

Portion the frosting evenly among the cooled cone cakes (about 2 tablespoons per cake). Using a small metal spatula, mound and swirl the frosting on top of the cupcakes, leaving a border of cake around each one. Top with a piece of Reese's Peanut Butter Cup, if using. Serve immediately.

twists

- **MAKE 'EM CUPCAKES:** Instead of using ice cream cones, line 10 regular-sized (2¾-inch diameter) muffin cups with paper or foil liners and bake for 17 to 19 minutes.

- **MAKE 'EM CHOCO-CHIPPERS:** Add 4 ounces (⅔ cup) chopped bittersweet chocolate to the batter along with the final addition of flour.

- **USE A PASTRY BAG FOR A FANCY FINISH:** Finish Fit a large star tip (I use an Ateco #6) into a pastry bag and fill with the frosting (see the sidebar on p. 18) Evenly pipe the frosting onto the cooled cupcakes, leaving a border of cake around each one.

- **MAKE THE FROSTING MARSHMALLOW:** Instead of chocolate frosting, spread the marshmallow filling on pp. 103–104 as a frosting. You won't use all of it, so stow the remainder in the refrigerator and bring to room temperature before frosting your next batch of cone cakes.

- **ADD NUTS:** Instead of the Reese's Peanut Butter Cups, scatter chopped, lightly salted peanuts onto the frosting.

·4·

Bite-Sized Treats

....

ONE- AND TWO-BITE
MINI SWEETS

¾ cup (3¾ ounces) finely ground chocolate cookies (I use Nabisco® Famous® Chocolate Wafers)

2 tablespoons (1 ounce) unsalted butter, melted

FOR THE CHEESECAKE

2 packages (8 ounces each) cream cheese, softened

⅔ cup (4⅝ ounces) granulated sugar

1½ teaspoons pure vanilla extract
Pinch of table salt

2 large eggs, at room temperature

1 cup (10 ounces) Nutella

Makes 12 cheesecakes

Black-Bottomed Nutella Swirl Cheesecakes

In my opinion, any decent dessert cookbook must include at least one cheesecake recipe or it's incomplete. My challenge with this utensil-free cookbook was to find a way to experience that same rich creaminess that you get from a slice of cheesecake. The answer came to me on my birthday last year, when my husband and daughter served me super-creamy cupcakes from a local bakery. My cheesecake in a cupcake idea was born. Thanks to C and T for the inspiration!

make the black bottom

1 Line 12 regular-sized (2¾-inch diameter) muffin cups with foil liners (paper ones won't work here) and lightly grease the bottom and sides.

2 Put the cookie crumbs and butter in a small bowl and mix with a fork until the crumbs are evenly moistened.

3 Portion the crumbs evenly among the foil liners (1 firmly packed tablespoon in each). If you have a tart tamper, this is a great time to use it. If not, tear off a piece of plastic wrap, place it over the crumbs, and use your fingers to press firmly to make a compact layer. Slide the tin into the refrigerator while you make the filling. (This helps keep the crumbs on the bottom when you are swirling the batters together.)

make the cheesecake

1 Position an oven rack in the center of the oven and heat the oven to 300°F. Put the cream cheese in a large bowl and beat with an electric mixer fitted with the paddle attachment on medium high until very smooth and fluffy, about 2 minutes. Add the sugar, vanilla, and salt. Continue beating until well blended and smooth, scraping down the sides of the bowl frequently; there should be no lumps. Add the eggs, one at a time, beating on medium speed until just blended. Once the eggs have been added to the batter, it's important to mix thoroughly without overbeating or the cheesecake will puff and crack during baking.

2 Scoop out 1 cup of the vanilla batter and set aside. Add the Nutella to the remaining batter and stir until well blended. Portion the Nutella batter evenly among the prepared muffin cups (about 4 tablespoons per cup). Next, portion the vanilla batter evenly among the cups (about 1 tablespoon in each). The cups should be completely filled.

recipe continues

do ahead

The cheesecakes can be prepared and baked ahead. Once cooled, cover the muffin tins with plastic and refrigerate for up to 3 days or freeze (tin and all to keep the foil perky and pretty) for up to 1 month.

finishing touches

- Cut some of the same cookies you used for the bottom into quarters. Just before serving, top each chilled cheesecake with a dollop of whipped cream and arrange one or two cookie wedges in the cream.

- In place of cookie quarters, top each cheesecake with toasted, chopped hazelnuts.

3   Drag and fold the tip of a wooden skewer, toothpick, or paring knife through the two batters in a swirled pattern. There should still be solid streaks of each batter visible, and the cups should be filled to the brim. Tap the muffin tin on the counter to settle the batters. Bake until the centers barely jiggle when the pan is nudged, 20 to 22 minutes. Set the muffin tin on a rack and let cool completely. Cover and refrigerate until very cold, at least 6 hours.

twists

PUMPKIN SWIRL: Use the same amount of ground gingersnaps instead of the chocolate cookies for the base. Eliminate the Nutella and the yolk from the batter and add the following to the 1 cup vanilla batter in a small bowl.

$\frac{1}{3}$ cup canned solid-pack pumpkin (see Kitchen Wisdom on p. 83)

$2\frac{1}{4}$ teaspoons unbleached all-purpose flour

$\frac{1}{2}$ teaspoon ground cinnamon

$\frac{1}{4}$ teaspoon ground ginger

$\frac{1}{8}$ teaspoon ground nutmeg

The cups won't be filled as high with the pumpkin batter as with the Nutella batter, but they will still be very full and will bake in 17 to 19 minutes using the same doneness test.

> ### KITCHEN WISDOM ☺☺ crushing cookies
>
> To make crumbled cookies or cookie crumbs, pop the cookies into a food processor and pulse until you reach the desired texture. Or pop them into a heavy-duty zip-top bag, press out all the air, and seal. Using a rolling pin or a small skillet, pound on the cookies until they are the correct consistency.

Brown Sugar Crème Brûlée Tarts

I bet you never thought you'd find a crème brûlée recipe in a book of no-fork desserts. But I couldn't leave out such a glorious dessert! In lieu of a spoon, this recipe relies on the same crisp, buttery phyllo tarts I used for the S'mores Tarts (see p. 126) and Hazelnut Phyllo Tarts with Nutella Mousse (see p. 146).

Make the phyllo cups as described on p. 146.

make the custard

1 Put the yolks in a small bowl and whisk until well blended. Set aside.

2 In a medium saucepan, whisk the brown sugar, cornstarch, and salt until well blended. Slowly pour in the half-and-half or heavy cream, whisking constantly. Cook, whisking often, over medium heat until barely boiling, about 3 minutes. Slowly pour into the egg yolks, whisking constantly. Scrape the mixture back into the saucepan. Cook, whisking constantly (including the sides and bottom), over medium heat until the mixture boils, then cook for 1 minute. Slide the pan from the heat, add the butter and vanilla, and whisk until well blended.

3 Pour the hot custard into a clean medium bowl. Gently press a piece of plastic wrap directly on the custard's surface to prevent a skin from forming. Refrigerate until chilled, about 4 hours.

assemble and serve

1 Spread the brown sugar over a plate in a thin layer and set aside at room temperature until dry, 1 to 2 hours or up to 1 day ahead.

2 Evenly portion the custard among the cooled tart shells (about 1 tablespoon per shell) and sprinkle the dried brown sugar evenly over the tops. Using a kitchen torch, pass the flame over the brown sugar, being careful not to ignite the pastry, until it's melted and caramelized. Serve immediately or refrigerate for up to 1 hour before serving.

> **KITCHEN WISDOM** ✎✎ **puddings and custards**
>
> This custard is adapted from my favorite vanilla pudding recipe—I make the pudding with whole milk instead of half-and-half. I like to thicken my puddings and brûlée fillings with cornstarch because the finished flavor and texture is smoother than when using flour. Overcooking cornstarch-based types can break down the thickening effect of the cornstarch, though, so boil it only as long as directed.

FOR THE PHYLLO CUPS

See the recipe on p. 146.

FOR THE CUSTARD

- 4 large egg yolks, at room temperature
- ⅓ cup (2⅜ ounces) firmly packed light brown sugar
- 5 teaspoons cornstarch
- ⅛ teaspoon table salt
- 1¾ cups half-and-half or heavy cream
- 2 tablespoons (1 ounce) unsalted butter, cut into 4 pieces and softened
- 1¼ teaspoons pure vanilla extract

- ½ cup (3½ ounces) firmly packed light brown sugar

Makes 30 tarts

do ahead

The custard can be made, covered, and refrigerated for up to 2 days before filling and serving.

twists

• Instead of brown sugar, use the same amount of granulated sugar in the custard.

• Instead of making your own pastry shells, use the same amount of frozen, store-bought phyllo shells or frozen tart shells (I like Dufour brand), but they won't have the sugar-nut filling.

• Instead of using pure vanilla extract, use the same amount of pure vanilla paste for the same great flavor with the addition of those pretty tiny black seeds.

⅓ cup (1½ ounces) graham cracker crumbs

2 tablespoons granulated sugar

Pinch of table salt

½ package (8 ounces) phyllo dough (one roll from a twin-pack), thawed (you'll need 6 sheets + a few extras in case of breakage)

4 tablespoons (2 ounces) unsalted butter, melted

FOR THE MILK CHOCOLATE GANACHE FILLING

12 ounces milk chocolate, chopped

¾ cup heavy cream

FOR SERVING

60 mini marshmallows

Makes 30 tarts

do ahead

The phyllo shells can be baked, covered, and stowed (in their muffin cups) at room temperature for up to 2 days before filling and serving.

S'mores Tarts

Growing up on the Connecticut shoreline meant that summer nights were filled with beach cookouts, evening swims, and, as the grill fire subsided, s'mores. I think most of you who have ever tasted this iconic treat made with milk chocolate, graham crackers, and toasted marshmallow will agree that kids—both young and young at heart—dig this combo. For this book, I developed a slightly more polished version of the classic: crispy, buttery phyllo cups layered with crushed graham crackers are filled with a creamy milk chocolate ganache, topped with mini marshmallows and toasted until golden brown (or darker, if you prefer). They're even better than the original.

make the phyllo cups

1 Position an oven rack in the center of the oven and heat the oven to 350°F. Lightly grease one 30-cup or two 15-cup mini (scant 2-inch diameter) muffin tins. Put the graham cracker crumbs, sugar, and salt in a small bowl and stir until blended.

2 Unroll the phyllo and lay it flat on a clean, dry surface. Cover it completely with plastic wrap or a damp (not wet) dishtowel. Working with one sheet of phyllo at a time, and keeping the rest covered to prevent it from drying out, place a sheet with one long side in front of you on a cutting board. Brush with some of the melted butter, sprinkle with about 1½ tablespoons of the graham cracker mixture, and cover with another sheet of phyllo. Press lightly on the top sheet. Brush the sheet with some of the butter and sprinkle another 1½ tablespoons of graham cracker mixture evenly over the phyllo. Cover with a third sheet of phyllo and press gently. Brush again with some of the butter.

3 Using a sharp knife or pizza wheel (use a ruler for a straight edge), cut the layered sheets lengthwise into three equal strips about 2¾ inches wide. Cut the strips crosswise into five 2¾-inch squares.

4 Using your fingers, gently ease the phyllo squares into the prepared mini muffin cups so the bottoms fit snugly and the sides form a cup shape. The top edges will be uneven and a bit ruffly.

5 Repeat the layering process with the remaining 3 sheets of phyllo, butter, and graham cracker mixture, then transfer to the remaining muffin cups.

6 Bake until the phyllo cups are golden brown, 7 to 9 minutes. Move the muffin tins to a wire rack and let cool completely.

make the ganache

Melt the chocolate and heavy cream in the microwave or in a small bowl set over a pot of simmering water, stirring with a rubber spatula until smooth. Remove from the heat and set aside until thickened, about 2 hours. For faster chilling, set the bowl over an ice water–filled bowl and stir until the ganache is thickened but not set.

assemble and serve

Evenly portion the ganache among the cooled tart shells (about 1 tablespoon per shell) and refrigerate until chilled and firm, about 3 hours or up to 1 day before serving. Just before serving, top each tart with a couple of mini marshmallows and, using a kitchen torch, pass the flame over the marshmallows, being careful not to ignite the pastry, until they are melted and caramelized. Serve immediately or refrigerate for up to 1 hour before serving. Serve slightly chilled or at room temperature.

twists

- Instead of making your own pastry shells, use the same amount of frozen, store-bought phyllo shells or frozen tart shells (I like Dufour brand), but they won't have the sugar-graham cracker filling.
- Instead of using mini marshmallows, spoon a teaspoon or two of Marshmallow Fluff on top of the chilled chocolate ganache and toast as directed.

Cinnamon Toast Scones

The aroma of cinnamon toast is one of my favorite childhood flashbacks, so much so that I can almost smell its heady fragrance just by thinking about it. Lightly toasted Wonder® bread slathered with salted butter and thickly coated with my mom's cinnamon sugar was a favorite snack no matter what time of day.

These scones are a definite upgrade from my childhood version yet are still buttery and, yes, thickly coated with Mom's cinnamon sugar. They taste best warm from the oven, but leftovers can be gently warmed in a toaster oven set on bake. Or do as my kids do and pop them in the microwave for a second or two.

make the scones

1 Position an oven rack in the center of the oven and heat the oven to 375°F. Line a cookie sheet with parchment or a nonstick liner.

2 Cut the butter in half lengthwise, cut each half lengthwise again, and then cut each strip into 8 pieces. Pile the butter onto a plate and slide it into the freezer until ready to use. Measure the half-and-half in a 1-cup glass measure; add the egg and vanilla. Using a fork, whisk until blended and keep in the refrigerator until ready to use.

3 Whisk the flour, sugar, baking powder, and salt in a large bowl until well blended. Add the cold butter pieces and, using a pastry blender or two knives, cut the butter into the flour mixture until the butter is pea-sized, about 3 minutes. (You can also do this in a food processor using short pulses, scraping the blended mixture into a large bowl before proceeding.)

4 Pour the egg mixture over the flour and, using a rubber spatula, stir and fold until it forms a shaggy, moist dough with some floury bits remaining. Scrape the dough and any remaining floury bits onto the counter and knead a few times until the dough is evenly moist and holds together. Be careful not to overknead the dough or the scones will be dense.

5 Shape the dough into an 8x4-inch rectangle. With a large knife, cut the dough crosswise into six equal strips, then cut each strip into three pieces (they'll be about 1⅓ inches each). Arrange the strips about 2 inches apart on the prepared cookie sheet. Bake until the tops are golden brown, 19 to 21 minutes. Move the cookie sheet to a wire rack and let the scones sit until they're cool enough to handle, about 10 minutes.

finish the scones

Put the sugar and cinnamon in a small bowl (I use a 6-ounce ramekin) and stir with a spoon until well blended. Put the melted butter in a similar bowl and arrange them both near the cookie sheet. Working with one scone at a time, dip the tops in the butter and gently press the buttered top into the cinnamon sugar. Arrange, cinnamon side up, on a wire rack. The scones can be served warm or at room temperature.

---

8   tablespoons butter, chilled

½   cup half-and-half, chill

1   large egg, chilled

1   teaspoon pure vanilla extract

2   cups (9 ounces) unbleached all-purpose flour

¼   cup (1¾ ounces) granulated sugar

1   tablespoon baking powder

½   teaspoon table salt

FOR THE TOPPING

⅓   cup (2⅜ ounces) granulated sugar

1½ teaspoons ground cinnamon

4   tablespoons (2 ounces) unsalted butter, melted

Makes 18 scones

do ahead

Cover the cooled scones and stow at room temperature for up to 1 day. Reheat in the oven, toaster oven, or microwave (briefly), if desired.

twists

• In place of the cinnamon sugar, use an equal amount of Chicago Old Town Spiced Sugar (www.spicehouse.com).

• Add ½ cup cinnamon chips to the dough along with the flour.

.nces) unsalted

_ milk, chilled

⌐on pure vanilla extract

⌐ps (10⅛ ounces) unbleached
all-purpose flour

½ cup (3½ ounces) granulated
sugar

5 teaspoons instant espresso
granules or coffee powder

1 teaspoon baking powder

¼ teaspoon baking soda

¼ teaspoon table salt

Makes 10 scones

finishing touches

Make a vanilla glaze by mixing
1 cup (4 ounces) confectioners'
sugar, 1 to 2 tablespoons milk, and
¼ teaspoon pure vanilla extract
in a small bowl until well blended.
Using a small spoon, drizzle the
glaze over the cooled scones. If
you like, you can add ¼ teaspoon
ground cinnamon to the glaze.

twists

• Add ½ cup cinnamon chips or
bittersweet chocolate chips to
the butter-flour mixture and
proceed as directed.

• In place of the vanilla glaze, use
Milk Chocolate Drizzle (see p. 14).

do ahead

Cover and stow the scones at
room temperature for up to 3 days.
Reheat gently in a low oven.

Café au Lait Scones

While I'm not a coffee drinker, I am crazy for the deep, roasted flavor that coffee imparts to desserts. That said, I'm not a fan of adding ground coffee to my baked goods. Although they pack the dessert full of coffee flavor, I find the gritty texture most unpleasant. Instead, I like to use instant espresso granules, which provide all the flavor but no grit. Whizzing them with the other dry ingredients in a food processor grinds them into a fine powder, so they quickly dissolve and infuse into the baked scones.

These small coffee-flavored scones are delicious for breakfast or brunch, and they also make a delicious afternoon treat served alongside a cup of hot coffee or, as in my case, tea.

1 Position an oven rack in the center of the oven and heat the oven to 400°F. Line a cookie sheet with parchment or a nonstick liner.

2 Cut each tablespoon of butter in half lengthwise, cut each half lengthwise again, and then cut each strip into 8 pieces. Pile the butter onto a plate and slide it into the freezer until ready to use. Measure the milk in a 1-cup liquid measure; add the vanilla. Using a fork, whisk until blended and keep in the refrigerator until ready to use.

3 Put the flour, sugar, espresso granules, baking powder, baking soda, and salt in a food processor and pulse until well blended and the espresso is finely ground, about 1 minute. Add the cold butter pieces and, using short pulses, cut the butter into the flour until the mixture resembles coarse meal with small pieces of butter (not the pea-sized kind as in other scone recipes) still visible, about 1 minute. Scrape the mixture into a large bowl.

4 Pour the milk and vanilla over the flour mixture and, using a rubber spatula, stir and fold until it forms a shaggy, moist dough with some floury bits remaining. Scrape the dough and any remaining floury bits onto the counter and knead a few times, a style of kneading called *fraisage* (see Kitchen Wisdom on p. 53) until the dough is evenly moist and holds together. Be careful not to overknead the dough because that will make the scones dense.

5 Shape the dough into a 12x2-inch rectangle. With a large knife, cut the dough crosswise into triangles about 2 inches at their base. You'll have 9 triangles and 2 end pieces. Gently press these end pieces together to form one triangle for a total of 10. Arrange the triangles about 2 inches apart on the prepared cookie sheet. Bake until the tops and edges are golden brown, 17 to 19 minutes. Move the sheet to a wire rack and let the scones sit until they're cool enough to handle, about 10 minutes. Serve warm or at room temperature.

Toasted Almond Scones

Homemade scones are so easy to make and taste so much better than store-bought. But if you really need convincing, give these scones a test-drive. They are loaded with almond flavor, lightly sweetened, and have the perfect crumbly texture. You'll be convinced.

1 Position an oven rack in the center of the oven and heat the oven to 375°F. Line a cookie sheet with parchment or a nonstick liner.

2 Cut the butter in half lengthwise, cut each half lengthwise again, and then cut each strip into 6 pieces. Pile the butter onto a plate and slide it into the freezer until ready to use. Measure the heavy cream in a 1-cup liquid measure; add the egg yolks and almond and vanilla extracts. Using a fork, whisk until blended and keep in the refrigerator until ready to use.

3 Whisk the flour, brown sugar, baking powder, and salt in a large bowl until well blended. Add the cold butter pieces and, using a pastry blender or two knives, cut the butter into the flour mixture until the butter is pea-sized, about 3 minutes. (You can also do this step in a food processor using short pulses, scraping the blended mixture into a large bowl before proceeding.) Add the almonds and toss until blended.

4 Pour the egg mixture over the flour and, using a rubber spatula, stir and fold until it forms a shaggy, moist dough with some floury bits remaining. Scrape the dough and any remaining floury bits onto the counter and knead (see Kitchen Wisdom on p. 53) a few times until the dough is evenly moist and holds together. Be careful not to overknead the dough or the scones will be dense.

5 Shape the dough into a 6-inch round. Sprinkle the top evenly with the demerara sugar and, using your fingertips, gently press it into the dough. With a large knife, cut the dough into eight wedges. Arrange the wedges about 2 inches apart on the prepared cookie sheet. Bake until the tops are golden brown, 20 to 22 minutes. Move the sheet to a wire rack and let the scones sit until they're cool enough to handle, about 10 minutes.

twists
- For less-rich scones, substitute 1 large egg for the 2 egg yolks.
- Instead of the light brown sugar, use the same amount of granulated sugar.
- For a dried fruit scone, use the same amount of coarsely chopped dried fruit for the slivered almonds and use a total of 1 teaspoon pure vanilla extract instead of the vanilla/almond extract combination.

6 tablespoons (3 ounces) unsalted butter, chilled

¾ cup heavy cream, chilled

2 yolks from large eggs, chilled

1 teaspoon pure almond extract

½ teaspoon pure vanilla extract

2 cups (9 ounces) unbleached all-purpose flour

¼ cup (1¾ ounces) firmly packed light brown sugar

1 tablespoon baking powder

½ teaspoon table salt

1 cup (4 ounces) slivered almonds, toasted

FOR THE TOPPING

⅓ cup demerara or turbinado sugar (Sugar in the Raw)

Makes 8 scones

do ahead
- The butter can be cut into the dry ingredients, covered, and stowed in the refrigerator alongside the mixed wet ingredients up to 1 day ahead. When ready to serve, proceed with the recipe while the oven heats up.
- The scones can be served warm or at room temperature (I prefer them warm). If you're not serving them immediately, cover the cooled scones and stow at room temperature for up to 2 days and reheat in the oven or toaster oven.

finishing touches
Make an almond glaze by mixing 1 cup (4 ounces) confectioners' sugar and 1 tablespoon almond liqueur (or 1 tablespoon whole milk and ⅛ teaspoon pure almond extract) in a small bowl until well blended. Using a small spoon, drizzle some of the glaze over the cooled scones.

Dusty Sundae Éclairs

At a young age, my mom taught me how to bake amazing desserts like Floating Island and Virginia Sponge Cake, but my favorite was éclairs. I'd stare through the oven window and watch, in wonderment, as the soft and mushy dough would transform into puffed, airy shells. While it seemed like magic back then, there's no magic needed to make these adorable little éclairs—I promise. I'm fond of saying, "If you can boil water, then you can make this recipe." Really.

What's a Dusty Sundae, you ask? To start with, it's my all-time favorite childhood summer beach dessert, one that has endured into my adulthood. Although my friends hotly debate the iconic ingredients, *my* ultimate dusty sundae is made of vanilla ice cream and chocolate sauce (not the hot stuff) and topped with plenty of malted milk powder. It's a scoop of heaven.

make the pastry shells

1 Position an oven rack in the center of the oven and heat the oven to 400°F. Line two cookie sheets with parchment or nonstick liners.

2 Put the water, butter, sugar, and salt in a medium saucepan. Cook, stirring occasionally, over medium heat until the butter is melted, about 2 minutes. Increase the heat to high and bring to a boil. As soon as the mixture is boiling, slide the pan from the heat and immediately add the flour. Using a wooden spoon or spatula (I like to use an angled wooden spatula), stir quickly until the dough is smooth and thick. Cook over low heat, stirring constantly, until the dough is shiny, about 1 minute (see the photo at right).

3 Slide the pan from the heat and add the eggs, one at a time, beating with a wooden spoon until the dough and egg are well blended and smooth before adding the next egg. After adding the eggs, the dough will be soft and should fall from the spoon by the count of three. (You can also do this step using a stand mixer fitted with the paddle attachment.)

4 Fit a ½-inch pastry tip (I use an Ateco #6) into a pastry bag and fill with the dough (see the sidebar on p. 18). Evenly pipe the dough into 2-inch-long strips spaced about 2 inches apart onto the prepared cookie sheets. Bake, one sheet at a time, until the pastry is an even, deep golden brown, 24 to 26 minutes. Transfer the sheet to a cooling rack. Using the tip of a chopstick or wide skewer, pierce one end of each shell to let the steam escape. Let cool completely. Use immediately or cover and store at room temperature for up to 1 day or freeze for up to 1 month.

recipe continues

FOR THE PASTRY SHELLS

- ¾ cup water
- 6 tablespoons (3 ounces) unsalted butter, cut into 8 pieces
- 2 tablespoons granulated sugar
- ¼ teaspoon table salt
- ¾ cup (3⅓ ounces) unbleached all-purpose flour
- 3 large eggs, at room temperature

FOR THE MALTED MILK CREAM FILLING

- 1¼ cups whole milk
- 3 yolks from large eggs
- ⅓ cup (2⅜ ounces) granulated sugar
- 6 tablespoons malted milk powder + more for sprinkling
- 5 teaspoons unbleached all-purpose flour
- Pinch of table salt
- 1 teaspoon pure vanilla extract

FOR THE CHOCOLATE GLAZE

- 4 ounces bittersweet chocolate, finely chopped
- ½ cup heavy cream

Makes forty 2-inch éclairs

Cream puff dough should be smooth, thick, and shiny.

do ahead

- The éclair shells can be prepared through Step 4, covered, and stowed at room temperature for up to 1 day or frozen for up to 1 month.
- The filled and glazed éclairs can be stowed in the refrigerator for up to 1 day.

twists

MAKE A PEANUT BUTTER FILLING: Follow the directions for making the malted milk cream filling, but substitute the same amount of brown sugar for the granulated sugar and add ¼ teaspoon table salt. Eliminate the malted milk powder and whisk ½ cup (4½ ounces) creamy peanut butter into the cream along with the vanilla. Instead of sprinkling the tops of the glazed éclairs with malted milk powder, sprinkle with chopped, lightly salted peanuts.

make the filling

In a medium saucepan, bring the milk to a simmer. Meanwhile, in a medium bowl, whisk the egg yolks, sugar, malted milk powder, flour, and salt until well blended and pale. Slowly add the hot milk, whisking constantly. Pour the mixture back into the saucepan. Cook over medium-low heat, whisking constantly, until the cream comes to a boil. Cook, whisking constantly, for 1 minute. Slide the pan from the heat, whisk in the vanilla, and scrape the cream into a medium bowl. Gently press a piece of plastic wrap directly on the cream's surface to prevent a skin from forming. Refrigerate until cold, about 4 hours, or up 2 days before proceeding with the recipe.

make the glaze

Put the chocolate and heavy cream in a small heatproof bowl and cook, whisking occasionally, in a microwave or over a double boiler until the chocolate is melted and the mixture is smooth. Set aside.

assemble the éclairs

1 Fit a ¼-inch round pastry tip (I use an Ateco #3) into a pastry bag and fill with the cream (see the sidebar on p. 18). Working with one éclair at a time, gently push the tip into the vent hole on one end of the éclair and pipe the filling into each pastry.

2 Working with one éclair at a time, dip the top half of the pastry into the warm chocolate and tap it gently on the side of the bowl to eliminate any excess chocolate. Arrange the éclairs chocolate side up on a cookie sheet or flat plate. Refrigerate until the glaze is set, about 30 minutes or up to 2 days. Just before serving, sprinkle the tops with a little malted milk powder. Serve chilled.

Mini Mocha Roll Cakes

My mom wasn't a big fan of packaged chocolate baked treats—those chocolate cakes filled or rolled with vanilla cream and covered in chocolate. They were a kid's culinary bliss. I was particularly fond of the rolled kind because those little mini jellyrolls had the best cake to filling to chocolate ratio.

These made-from-scratch mini rolls are my adult ode to those of my past. Unlike their forefathers, I decided not to cover them with chocolate because the cake and filling are delicious without the added step. I love these mini cakes even more than my memories of the store-bought kind. Kids of all ages will agree.

make the cake

1 Position an oven rack in the center of the oven and heat the oven to 350°F. Lightly grease the sides and bottom of a 16¾x11¾-inch half-sheet pan and line the bottom with parchment. Lightly grease and flour the parchment and the sides of the pan.

2 Whisk the flour, cocoa powder, baking powder, and salt in a small bowl until blended. Set aside.

3 Crack the eggs into a large bowl. Beat with an electric mixer fitted with the whisk attachment on medium-high speed until pale in color, about 2 minutes. Add the confectioners' sugar and vanilla and beat on medium-high speed until thick enough that a ribbon forms when the beater is lifted, about 3 minutes.

4 Sprinkle the flour mixture over the eggs and, using a large rubber spatula, fold until just blended. Scrape the batter into the prepared pan and spread it evenly with an offset spatula. Bake until the cake begins to pull away from the sides of the pan, 6 to 8 minutes.

5 While the cake is baking, have ready four long sheets of paper towels (I use two sheets still connected for each long sheet), a large wire rack, a small wire rack, and a sifter or sieve filled with the confectioners' sugar for dusting.

6 Remove the cake from the oven and set on the smaller rack. Immediately and carefully, run a knife around the edges to loosen them from the pan using a chopping motion (not dragging the knife). Generously and evenly dust the entire top of the cake with the confectioners' sugar. Arrange two long sheets of paper towel over the cake, overlapping them about 1½ inches lengthwise down the center and leaving about 1 to 2 inches extra over the long sides. Place the large cooling rack on top of the paper towels and, using pot holders, invert the pan onto the rack. Lift the pan from the cake and carefully peel away the parchment. Cover the cake with the remaining two sheets of paper towels and set aside to cool.

recipe continues

FOR THE CHOCOLATE CAKE

- 2 tablespoons unbleached all-purpose flour
- 2 tablespoons unsweetened natural cocoa powder, sifted if lumpy
- ⅛ teaspoon baking powder
- Pinch of table salt
- 3 large eggs, at room temperature
- ¾ cup (3 ounces) confectioners' sugar
- ½ teaspoon pure vanilla extract

Confectioners' sugar, for dusting (about ¾ cup or 3 ounces)

FOR THE FILLING

- 6 tablespoons (3 ounces) unsalted butter, cut into 4 pieces
- ¾ teaspoon instant espresso granules or coffee powder
- 2 cups (8 ounces) confectioners' sugar
- 3 tablespoons heavy cream or coffee-flavored liqueur
- 1 teaspoon pure vanilla extract
- Pinch of table salt

Makes 14 mini roll cakes

do ahead
The finished mini rolls can be prepared completely and stored at room temperature for up to 3 days.

finishing touches
Cut the rolls on a sharp angle, as you would for biscotti. Your yield will be smaller but they sure are pretty this way.

twists
- **MAKE THE CAKE CINNAMON FLAVORED:** Add ¾ teaspoon ground cinnamon to the flour mixture along with the cocoa.
- **MAKE THE CAKE ORANGE FLAVORED:** Add 2 teaspoons finely grated orange zest to the cake batter along with the vanilla extract.

Pour the filling over the cake and spread to the edges.

Cut the cake in half.

Roll up the cake jellyroll style.

make the filling and assemble the mini rolls

1 Put the butter in a medium saucepan and cook over low heat until melted, about 2 minutes. Slide the pan from the heat, add the instant espresso granules and whisk until dissolved. Add the confectioners' sugar, heavy cream or coffee liqueur, vanilla, and salt and whisk until well blended and smooth, about 1 minute. Set aside, whisking occasionally, until barely warm to the touch, about 25 minutes.

2 Line a cookie sheet with parchment or a nonstick liner. Remove the paper towels from the top of the cake.

3 Using a rubber spatula, pour the barely warm filling by spoonfuls evenly over the cake and carefully spread over the cake all the way to the edges. Using a serrated knife, cut the cake crosswise into two equal pieces. Working with one half of the cake at a time and beginning at one short end, roll up the cake and filling in a tight jellyroll style. If the roll seems very soft, let it sit for 10 to 15 minutes before moving. Using a long offset spatula, move the roll and arrange it seam side down on one side of the prepared cookie sheet, being careful to keep the log rounded. Repeat with the remaining cake. Refrigerate the logs until the filling is set, about 1 hour.

4 Using a serrated knife, trim each end to neaten and cut each roll into 7 pieces. Serve immediately or cover and stow at room temperature for up to 3 days. Just before serving, lightly dust the tops with more confectioners' sugar, if you like.

> **KITCHEN WISDOM** ◎◎ **rolling cake**
>
> Unlike most rolled cakes, this cake doesn't get rolled while it's hot and then set aside to cool. This cake is moist enough to roll after it has cooled and is spread with the filling. I find this method much less stressful and it makes these Ho Ho®-inspired cakes easy to make.

FOR THE EGG WASH

FOR THE EGG WASH

1 large egg

1 tablespoon water

FOR THE PASTRY SHELLS

½ cup water

3 tablespoons (1½ ounces) unsalted butter, cut into 3 pieces

1 tablespoon granulated sugar

¼ teaspoon table salt

½ cup (2¼ ounces) unbleached all-purpose flour

2 large eggs, at room temperature

⅓ cup chopped walnuts

FOR THE FILLING

½ cup finely chopped mixed dried fruit (I use a combo of apricots, cherries, and apples)

½ cup water

4 ounces cream cheese, at room temperature

½ cup whole-milk ricotta

2 tablespoons firmly packed light brown sugar

Pinch of table salt

½ teaspoon pure vanilla extract

Makes 18 gougères

do ahead

• The pastry shells can be prepared, covered, and stowed at room temperature up to 1 day or frozen for up to 1 month.

• The cream filling can be refrigerated for up to 1 day before using.

Dried Fruit Gougères

One of my favorite go-to appetizers are cheese-nut gougères, a savory version of cream puffs made with a similar egg dough that's cooked on top of the stove. For my dessert version, I've topped the slightly sweetened puffs with toasty walnuts and filled them with an Italian-inspired creamy ricotta and dried fruit filling.

Since these don't take up much room in my freezer, I like to keep a batch of the unfilled shells tucked away so I'm always ready with a dessert.

Arrange an oven rack in the center of the oven and heat the oven to 425°F. Line a cookie sheet with parchment or a nonstick liner.

make the egg wash

Put the egg and water in a small bowl or ramekin and, using a fork, mix until well blended.

make the pastry shells

1 Put the water, butter, sugar, and salt in a medium saucepan. Cook, stirring occasionally, over medium heat until the butter is melted, about 2 minutes. Increase the heat to high and bring to a boil. As soon as the mixture is boiling, slide the pan from the heat and immediately add all the flour. Using a wooden spoon or spatula (I like to use an angled wooden spatula), stir quickly until the dough is smooth and thick. Cook over low heat, stirring constantly, until the dough is shiny, about 1 minute.

2 Slide the pan from the heat and add the eggs, one at a time, beating until the dough and egg are well blended and smooth before adding the next egg. After adding the eggs, the dough will be soft and should fall from the spoon by the count of three. (You can also do this step using a stand mixer fitted with the paddle attachment.)

3 Using a 1-tablespoon mini scoop, shape the dough into balls and arrange about 1½ inches apart on the prepared cookie sheet. Using a small pastry brush, brush the dough with egg wash and sprinkle the tops with walnuts. Bake until the pastry is puffed and deep golden brown, 24 to 26 minutes. Move the sheet to a wire rack. Using the tip of a chopstick or wide skewer, pierce each shell to let the steam escape. Let cool completely.

make the filling

1 Put the dried fruit and water in a small saucepan. Bring to a boil over medium heat. Reduce the heat to low and simmer, stirring occasionally, until the liquid is evaporated, 2 to 3 minutes. Set aside to cool completely.

2 Put the cream cheese, ricotta, brown sugar, and salt in a medium bowl. Beat with a hand-held electric mixer on medium speed until well blended and smooth, about 3 minutes. Add the dried fruit and vanilla and continue beating until well blended, about 1 minute.

to assemble

Fit a ¼-inch round pastry tip (I use an Ateco #3) into a pastry bag and fill with the cream (see the sidebar on p. 18). Using the vent hole on one side, gently push the tip into the shell and pipe the filling into each pastry. Serve immediately or refrigerate for up to 2 hours before serving.

KITCHEN WISDOM ◉◉ dried fruit

Use only plump dried fruit in any recipe. Dried fruit that's past its prime will look dry and especially pruney, and the sugars will have crystallized, giving the fruit an unpleasant, granular texture.

---

twists

- Instead of the walnuts, use any type of nut you like.
- Substitute the same amount of any combination of dried fruit or use just one kind.
- Make the filling orange by substituting the same amount of orange juice and 1 teaspoon finely grated orange zest for the water.

4 ounces cream cheese, at room temperature

¼ cup whole-milk ricotta

¼ cup (1 ounce) confectioners' sugar

2 teaspoons finely grated orange zest

1 teaspoon orange-flavored liqueur or freshly squeezed orange juice

Pinch of table salt

1 quart large fresh strawberries, rinsed and dried

Makes 16 to 20 filled strawberries (depending on their size)

finishing touches

Just before serving, garnish the top of each berry with a small sprig of basil or mint.

twists

- **MAKE THE FILLING LEMON-FLAVORED:** Substitute 1½ teaspoons grated lemon zest for the orange zest and use lemon-flavored liqueur or freshly squeezed lemon juice instead of the orange liqueur.

- **USE APRICOTS INSTEAD OF STRAWBERRIES:** Cut small ripe apricots in half lengthwise and scoop out the pit and some of the flesh from the center. Slice off a bit of the back side so it doesn't wobble. Pipe the filling into the center and proceed as directed for the strawberries.

- **CHANGE UP THE GARNISH:** Instead of garnishing with basil or mint, sprinkle the filled strawberries with toasted, finely chopped pistachios, toasted coconut, or colored sprinkles, or drizzle with a little melted bittersweet chocolate.

Orange and Ricotta Cheesecake-Stuffed Strawberries

These stuffed strawberries are to the dessert table what deviled eggs are to an appetizer spread. They're small enough to be a two-biter, and the filling can be switched up depending on what flavor you're in the mood for or what ingredients you have on hand.

make the filling

Put the cream cheese and ricotta in a medium bowl. Beat with a hand-held electric mixer on medium speed until well blended and smooth, about 3 minutes. Add the confectioners' sugar, orange zest, orange liqueur or juice, and salt and continue beating until well blended, about 1 minute. Refrigerate until chilled, about 2 hours, or up to 1 day before filling the strawberries.

assemble the strawberries

Using a small knife, cut off the tops of the strawberries and cut off a little bit of the bottom tips so the filled berries will sit upright. Using a paring knife or a very small melon baller, scoop out some of the center of the strawberries, leaving the bottom and sides intact. Fit a star tip (I use an Ateco #4) into a pastry bag and fill it with the chilled ricotta filling (see the sidebar on p. 18). Pipe the filling evenly into the center of the each strawberry, making sure the filling comes slightly over the berry's flat edge to create a swirled peak. Arrange the berries on a serving platter and refrigerate for up to 1 day. They are best when served slightly chilled.

14 frozen pastry tart shells (Dufour is my brand of choice), baked according to package directions

FOR THE CHEESECAKE

4 ounces cream cheese, softened

½ cup dulce de leche, at room temperature

Pinch of table salt

1 yolk from a large egg, at room temperature

Makes 14 mini cheesecake tarts

finishing touches

Top with a drizzle of dulce de leche, a few toasted, chopped walnuts, and a sprinkle of fleur de sel.

twists

ADD WHITE CHOCOLATE–TOASTED ALMOND BRITTLE TOPPING:
In a small heatproof bowl, melt 2 ounces chopped white chocolate in the microwave or over simmering water. Add ½ cup (2 ounces) toasted, slivered almonds and stir until the nuts are evenly coated. Scrape onto a parchment- or nonstick-lined cookie sheet and spread into a thin layer. Slide the sheet into the refrigerator and chill until the brittle is firm. Chop or break the brittle into small pieces and sprinkle a few pieces over each tart before serving. The brittle can be made and refrigerated for up to 1 week before using.

Dulce de Leche Cheesecakes

My daughter, Tierney, loves cheesecake, especially when it's flavored with smooth, creamy caramel-flavored dulce de leche. She was home from college when I was developing this recipe and deemed it "like a slice of a whole, amazingly good cheesecake." After a day or two, when the cheesecakes were nothing but a memory, Tierney offered that she thought I should retest the recipe just so she could be sure there was the right amount of dulce de leche in it. Nice try, T!

1 Position an oven rack in the center of the oven and heat the oven to 300°F. Arrange the baked and cooled tart shells in their foil cups on a cookie sheet.

2 Put the cream cheese in a large bowl and beat with an electric mixer fitted with the paddle attachment on medium-high speed until very smooth and fluffy, about 2 minutes. Add the dulce de leche and salt. Continue beating until well blended and smooth, scraping down the sides of the bowl frequently; there should be no lumps. Add the yolk and beat on medium speed until just blended. Once the yolk has been added to the batter, it's important to mix thoroughly without overbeating or the cheesecake will puff and crack during baking.

3 Evenly portion the mixture among the cooled tart shells (about 1 tablespoon per shell). Gently tap and shake the shells on the counter to settle the batter. Bake until the centers barely jiggle when the pan is nudged, 15 to 17 minutes. Move the sheet to a wire rack and let the tarts cool completely. Cover and refrigerate until chilled, about 2 hours or up to 2 days before serving. Serve slightly chilled.

Chocolate-Glazed Peanut Butter Fingers

Who says peanut butter and chocolate is just for kids? These peanut butter "fingers" are my adult version of a Reese's Peanut Butter Cup, and they're sophisticated enough to serve at a dinner party. A shortbread crust is the base for a creamy peanut butter–custard filling, and the bittersweet chocolate glaze adds an elegant and delicious final touch. According to my daughter, Tierney, "It's like a bite-sized peanut butter cream pie!"

make the crust

1 Position an oven rack in the center of the oven and heat the oven to 350°F. Line a 9x13-inch baking pan (I like the straight-sided kind) with foil, leaving about a 1-inch overhang on two sides (see p. 5). Lightly coat the bottom and sides with cooking spray.

2 Put the flour, confectioners' sugar, and salt in a food processor. Pulse until combined, about 15 seconds. Scatter the cold butter pieces over the flour mixture and pulse until the dough begins to form small, moist clumps, about 1 minute.

3 Dump the dough into the prepared pan. Using lightly floured fingertips, press the dough into the pan to form an even layer. Bake until the top looks dry and the edges are a pale golden brown, 18 to 20 minutes. Don't overbake or the crust will be hard and crispy. Move the pan to a wire rack and let cool completely.

make the peanut butter filling

1 Put the water in a small ramekin and sprinkle the gelatin over the top. Set aside to soften.

2 Pour the milk into a small saucepan and bring to a simmer over medium heat. In a small bowl, whisk the egg yolks, brown sugar, and salt until well blended. Slowly add the hot milk, whisking constantly. Pour the mixture back into the saucepan. Cook over medium heat, stirring constantly with a heatproof spoon, until the custard registers 170°F on an instant-read or candy thermometer and is thick enough to coat the back of the spoon (see the top photo on p. 144), 2 to 4 minutes. Slide the pan from the heat and add the gelatin; stir until dissolved. Add the peanut butter and vanilla and whisk until well blended. Set aside, stirring occasionally, until cooled to room temperature. For faster chilling, scrape the custard into a clean bowl, set the bowl over another larger bowl of ice, and stir until cooled.

recipe continues

FOR THE CRUST

- 1½ cups (6¾ ounces) unbleached all-purpose flour
- 3 ounces (¾ cup) confectioners' sugar
- ¼ teaspoon table salt
- 12 tablespoons (6 ounces) unsalted butter, cut into 10 pieces and chilled

FOR THE PEANUT BUTTER FILLING

- 3 tablespoons water
- 2 teaspoons unflavored gelatin
- 2⅓ cups whole milk
- 4 yolks from large eggs
- ½ cup (3½ ounces) firmly packed light brown sugar
- ½ teaspoon table salt
- ¾ cup (6¾ ounces) crunchy peanut butter
- 1 teaspoon pure vanilla extract

FOR THE CHOCOLATE GLAZE

- 5 ounces semisweet chocolate, chopped
- 5 tablespoons (2½ ounces) unsalted butter, cut into 3 pieces
- 1 tablespoon Lyle's Golden Syrup or light corn syrup

Makes twenty-eight 3-inch pieces

do ahead

The glazed treats can be refrigerated in the pan for up to 3 days before being cut and served.

twists

- Use an equal amount of creamy peanut butter instead of chunky.
- Sprinkle the top of the still-warm chocolate glaze with lightly salted, chopped peanuts.

The custard should be thick enough to coat the back of a spatula.

Add the gelatin to the pot while it's off the heat.

3 Pour the peanut butter cream over the baked crust and spread evenly. Gently press a piece of plastic wrap directly on the cream's surface to prevent a skin from forming. Refrigerate until cold, about 4 hours, or up to 1 day before proceeding with the recipe.

make the glaze, cut, and serve

1 Melt the chocolate, butter, and cane syrup in the microwave or in a small bowl set over a pot of simmering water, stirring with a rubber spatula until smooth. Remove from the heat and set aside.

2 Scrape the glaze onto the top of the chilled peanut butter filling and, using an offset spatula, spread evenly. Slide the baking pan into the refrigerator until the glaze is set, about 20 minutes.

3 Use the foil "handles" to carefully lift the entire bar from the pan onto a cutting board. Peel away the foil and toss it out. Using a large knife, cut crosswise into four equal strips, and then cut each strip into seven pieces. Serve slightly chilled.

¼ cup (1¼ ounces) coarsely chopped hazelnuts, toasted

2 tablespoons granulated sugar

¼ teaspoon ground cinnamon

Pinch of table salt

½ package (8 ounces) phyllo dough (one roll from a twin-pack), thawed (you'll need 6 sheets + a few extras in case of breakage)

4 tablespoons (2 ounces) unsalted butter, melted

FOR THE NUTELLA MOUSSE

1 cup heavy cream, chilled

Pinch of table salt

¾ cup (7½ ounces) Nutella

FOR SERVING

¼ cup (1¼ ounces) chopped hazelnuts, toasted

Makes 30 tarts

do ahead

- The phyllo shells can be baked, covered, and stowed at room temperature up to 2 days before filling and serving.

- The mousse can be made up to 3 days before serving.

Hazelnut Phyllo Tarts with Nutella Mousse

Like the other bite-sized tarts (see p. 125 and p. 126) and the filled gougères (see p. 138), I think of these small treats as the hors d'oeuvres of the dessert world. Arrange one type or a combination of a few on a pretty tray or plate and pass with cocktail napkins.

make the phyllo cups

1 Position an oven rack in the center of the oven and heat the oven to 350°F. Lightly grease one 30-cup or two 15-cup mini (scant 2-inch diameter) muffin tins.

2 Put the hazelnuts, sugar, cinnamon, and salt in a food processor and pulse until the nuts are finely chopped. Alternatively, finely chop the nuts by hand, put them in a small ramekin with the sugar and cinnamon, and stir until blended.

3 Unroll the phyllo and lay it flat on a clean, dry surface. Cover completely with plastic wrap or a damp (not wet) dishtowel. Working with one sheet of phyllo at a time, and keeping the rest covered to prevent it from drying out, place a sheet with one long side in front of you on a cutting board. Brush with the melted butter, sprinkle with about 1½ tablespoons of the cinnamon-hazelnut mixture, and cover with another sheet of phyllo. Press lightly on the top sheet. Brush the sheet with butter and sprinkle another 1½ tablespoons of cinnamon-hazelnut mixture evenly over the phyllo. Cover with a third sheet of phyllo and press gently. Brush with butter.

4 Using a sharp knife or pizza wheel (use a ruler for a straight edge), cut the layered sheets lengthwise into three equal strips about 2¾ inches wide. Cut each strip crosswise into five 2¾-inch squares.

5 Using your fingers, gently ease the phyllo squares into the prepared mini muffin cups so the bottoms fit snugly and the sides form a cup shape. The top edges will be uneven and a bit ruffly.

6 Repeat the layering process with the remaining 3 sheets of phyllo, butter, and cinnamon-hazelnut mixture and then transfer to the remaining muffin cups.

7 Bake until the phyllo cups are golden brown, 7 to 9 minutes. Move the muffin tins to a wire rack and let cool completely.

make the mousse

Put the heavy cream and salt in a medium bowl. Beat with an electric mixer fitted with the whip attachment on medium-high speed until thickened and the cream forms medium peaks when the beaters are lifted (when the machine is turned off). Add the Nutella and beat on medium-high speed until thick enough to hold firm peaks when the beater is lifted, about 1 minute. Cover and refrigerate the mousse until it's thick enough to pipe, about 2 hours.

assemble and serve

Evenly portion the mousse among the cooled tart shells (about 1 tablespoon per shell) and sprinkle the nuts evenly over the top. Serve immediately or refrigerate for up to 3 hours before serving.

twists

- **USE A PASTRY BAG FOR A FANCY FINISH:** Fit a large (about 1/2-inch) star tip (I use an Ateco #6) into a pastry bag and fill with the chilled mousse (see the sidebar on p. 18). Evenly pipe the mousse into the cooled tart shells to form a peak and sprinkle with nuts.

- **CHANGE UP THE TOPPING:** Instead of using the hazelnut topping, use the same amount of chopped chocolate-covered toffee bits.

- **INSTEAD OF MAKING YOUR OWN PASTRY SHELLS:** Use the same amount of frozen, store-bought phyllo shells or frozen tart shells (I like Dufour brand), but they won't have the cinnamon-nut filling.

FOR THE PAVLOVAS

1 cup (7 ounces) superfine sugar (see Kitchen Wisdom on p. 150)

5 teaspoons cornstarch

Pinch of table salt

½ cup egg whites (from 4 large eggs or 4¼ ounces), at room temperature

¼ teaspoon cream of tartar

2 tablespoons finely chopped crystallized ginger

1 teaspoon vinegar (distilled white, white wine, or white balsamic)

¾ teaspoon pure vanilla extract

FOR THE GINGER WHIPPED CREAM

1⅓ cups heavy cream, chilled

⅔ cup (2⅝ ounces) confectioners' sugar (sifted if lumpy)

¾ teaspoon finely grated fresh ginger

½ teaspoon pure vanilla extract

2 cups assorted, cut-up fresh fruit, such as kiwi, raspberries, pomegranate arils

Makes about 5 dozen pavlovas

Use the back of a spoon to make a small indentation in the meringue.

Double Ginger Pavlovas

With their tutu-like appearance, "pavs" are said to have been invented by either an Australian or New Zealand chef in honor of Russian ballerina Anna Pavlova. Regardless of their heritage, I love the soft, billowy texture of these meringues—so much so that I think I have included variations of this recipe in every one of my books. For this version, I've packed the mini meringues and whipped filling with ginger (crystallized and fresh). In keeping with this dessert's "Down Under" roots, I top these bites with a slice or two of kiwi and a few raspberries, but any fresh, seasonal fruit will taste delicious.

make the pavlovas

1 Position oven racks in the top and bottom thirds of the oven and heat the oven to 300°F. Line two cookie sheets with parchment (nonstick liners don't work with this recipe). For the best meringue volume, be sure to start with super clean equipment (see the sidebar on p. 41).

2 Put the superfine sugar, cornstarch, and salt in a small bowl and whisk until well blended and there are no lumps. Set aside.

3 Put the egg whites and cream of tartar in the clean bowl. Beat with an electric mixer fitted with the whisk attachment on medium speed until the whites are frothy, about 30 to 45 seconds. Increase the speed to medium high and beat until the whites form firm peaks, 1½ to 2 minutes. Continue beating while gradually adding the sugar mixture by tablespoonfuls. This will take about 3 minutes. When all the sugar mixture is added, stop the mixer, scrape down the sides, and add the crystallized ginger, vinegar, and vanilla. Beat on high speed until blended, about 30 seconds.

4 Using a 2-tablespoon mini scoop, arrange meringue mounds about 1 inch apart on the prepared cookie sheets. Using the back of a ½-teaspoon metal measure lightly coated with water, make a small indentation in the center and about halfway down each meringue. Re-wet the spoon every few uses. Don't worry if the meringues aren't all perfect.

5 Reduce the oven temperature to 200°F. Bake until the outside feels firm and the meringue moves only slightly when nudged with a fingertip (the centers will still

recipe continues

do ahead

- The baked and cooled meringues can be stowed in an airtight container at room temperature for up to 1 day.
- The filled pavlovas can be assembled and stowed in the refrigerator for up to 2 hours before serving.

twists

- **MAKE THE FILLING LEMON:** Spoon homemade or store-bought lemon curd into the meringue wells and top with fruit.
- **GIVE IT A FLAVOR:** Omit the crystallized ginger from the meringue and add ¼ teaspoon pure peppermint oil along with the vanilla. Instead of using the fresh ginger in the whipped cream, add 4 tablespoons unsweetened cocoa powder (Dutch-processed style is preferable for this recipe, but not mandatory). Instead of topping with fruit, sprinkle the piped cocoa cream with finely chopped peppermint candies.

be soft), about 1 hour to 1 hour and 15 minutes. (The temp is so low there's no need to switch placement of the cookie sheets during baking.) Turn off the oven and let the meringues cool in the oven for 1 hour, then move the sheets to wire racks and let cool completely. Carefully lift the meringues from the paper and stow in an airtight container until ready to assemble and serve.

make the cream and assemble

1 Put the heavy cream and confectioners' sugar in a large bowl. Beat with an electric mixer fitted with the whisk attachment on medium-high speed until it's thick enough to hold firm peaks when the beater is lifted, about 2 minutes. Add the grated ginger and vanilla and beat on medium until well blended.

2 Spoon or pipe about 1 tablespoon of the whipped cream into the center of each meringue and top with the fruit.

KITCHEN WISDOM ☺☺ **superfine sugar**

If you can't find superfine sugar at your grocery store, make your own by whizzing the same amount of granulated sugar in a food processor until the granules are pulverized. These finely ground sugar crystals dissolve quickly in whipped whites to make silky, sweet meringues.

Orange-Scented Chocolate–Velvet Tarts

A few weeks back, I served these to a group of pals over for one of our casual "potluck" dinners, and one friend said that the filling tasted like "chocolate velvet." Now, I'm not sure what exactly velvet tastes like, let alone chocolate velvet, but I think you can guess that he more than loved the silky, smooth, deep chocolate filling. These tarts look so sophisticated and glamorous with their chocolate filling, whipped cream, and berry topping that you'd never believe how fast and easy they are to make.

bake the tart shells

Position an oven rack in the center of the oven and heat the oven to 300°F. Arrange the baked and cooled tart shells in their foil cups on a cookie sheet.

make the filling

1 Put the chocolate and butter in a medium saucepan and set over medium heat, stirring occasionally, until the butter is melted (you can also do this in the microwave). Slide the pan from the heat and add the sugar and cocoa powder. Whisk until no lumps remain. Set aside to let cool, about 5 minutes. Once the mixture has cooled, add the egg, orange liqueur, vanilla, and salt and whisk until blended.

2 Evenly portion the mixture among the cooled tart shells (about 1 tablespoon per shell). Bake until the tops look set but still shiny, 9 to 11 minutes. Move the sheet to a wire rack and let the tarts cool completely. Cover and refrigerate until chilled, about 2 hours or up to 1 day before serving.

make the mascarpone cream

Put the mascarpone, heavy cream, vanilla, and salt in a medium bowl. Beat with an electric mixer fitted with the whip attachment on medium-high speed until thickened and stiff peaks form when the beaters are lifted.

assemble and serve

Spoon or pipe (see the sidebar on p. 18 for piping directions) the whipped mascarpone onto the tarts and top with a raspberry. Serve immediately or refrigerate for up to 2 hours before serving.

FOR THE TART SHELLS

24 frozen pastry mini tart shells (Dufour is my brand of choice), baked according to package directions

FOR THE ORANGE-CHOCOLATE FILLING

6 ounces bittersweet chocolate, chopped

6 tablespoons (3 ounces) unsalted butter, cut into 4 pieces

2 tablespoons granulated sugar

2 tablespoons unsweetened natural cocoa powder, sifted if lumpy

1 large egg, at room temperature

1 tablespoon orange-flavored liqueur

1/2 teaspoon pure vanilla extract

Pinch of table salt

FOR THE WHIPPED MASCARPONE CREAM

8 ounces mascarpone

1/2 cup heavy cream

1 teaspoon pure vanilla extract

Pinch of table salt

24 fresh raspberries

Makes 24 tarts

do ahead

• The filled tarts can be baked, covered, and stowed in the refrigerator for up to 1 day before garnishing and serving.

• The mascarpone cream can be made and stowed in the fridge for up to 8 hours before serving.

twists

• Instead of using frozen pastry shells, use 24 of the Hazelnut Phyllo cups (see p. 146), baked and cooled.

• Instead of orange liqueur, use the same amount of freshly squeezed orange juice, or raspberry liqueur, or raspberry vodka.

·5·
Frozen Treats

....

SPARKLING POPS & ICE CREAMS
FOR KIDS OF ALL AGES

FOR THE BROWN BUTTER COOKIE LAYERS

8 tablespoons (4 ounces) unsalted butter, cut into 6 pieces

1¼ cups (5½ ounces) unbleached all-purpose flour

¼ teaspoon baking soda

Pinch of table salt

½ cup (3½ ounces) firmly packed light brown sugar

2 tablespoons Lyle's Golden Syrup

2 yolks from large eggs, at room temperature

½ teaspoon pure vanilla extract

FOR THE ICE CREAM

1 container (14 ounces) dulce de leche ice cream

1 container (14 ounces) banana ice cream

Makes 12 sandwiches

finishing touches

DIP IN CHOCOLATE AND DECORATE:
Line a flat plate or tray with waxed paper or foil and arrange in the freezer. Put 9 ounces chopped bittersweet chocolate and 3 tablespoons vegetable or canola oil in deep, small heatproof bowl set over saucepan of barely simmering water until melted and smooth; let cool to lukewarm. (This can also be done in the microwave.) Arrange 1½ cups of decorations (choose one or more: toasted chopped nuts, colored sprinkles, chocolate-covered toffee bits, or cacao nibs) on shallow plates. Working with one frozen ice cream sandwich at a time, dip one end in the chocolate, allowing the excess to drip back into bowl. Press the sandwich gently into decorations. Place on the sheet in the freezer and repeat with remaining sandwiches. Freeze until the chocolate sets, about 1 hour.

Brown Butter Ice Cream Sandwiches

The tender brown butter cookies for these sandwiches are delicious on their own, but pairing them with rich, creamy ice cream brings the flavor up to a whole new level. While your kids will also love these, I'd suggest reserving them for the adult table.

make the cookie layers

1 Position an oven rack in the center of the oven and heat the oven to 325°F. Line the bottom and sides of a 9x13-inch baking pan (preferably with straight sides), with foil, leaving about a 1-inch overhang on the short sides (see p. 5). Lightly grease the bottom and sides of the foil.

2 Put the butter in a small heavy saucepan. Cook, stirring, over medium heat until it's nutty brown and the milk solids are dark brown, 6 to 7 minutes. Carefully pour the browned butter into a small bowl and let cool slightly.

3 Put the flour, baking soda, and salt in a small bowl and whisk until blended.

4 Pour the warm browned butter into a medium bowl, leaving behind the dark butter solids. Add the brown sugar and syrup and whisk until the sugar is moist and no lumps remain (the mixture will not come together at this point). Add the yolks and vanilla and whisk until well blended and smooth. Add the flour mixture and, using a rubber spatula, stir and smear the mixture until it's blended and smooth. Drop the thick batter by spoonfuls into the prepared pan. Using your fingertips, press and spread the batter to evenly cover the bottom of the pan.

5 Bake until the top is golden brown and the sides just begin to pull away from the pan, 15 to 17 minutes (don't overbake or the cookie layer will be too crisp). Transfer the pan to a wire rack and let cool completely.

assemble the sandwiches

1 When the cookie layer is completely cool, use the foil "handles" to lift it from the pan. Carefully invert onto a cutting board and peel away the foil. Turn the layer over and cut crosswise into 2 equal pieces.

2 Position two long pieces of plastic wrap in a cross shape over half of the 9x13-inch pan (this is the short side and halfway down the two long sides). Press the plastic into the pan to cover the bottom and sides, leaving the remaining length flat. Place one cookie layer, top side down, snugly into one end of the pan.

3   Remove the ice creams from the freezer and set on the counter. When they are slightly softened (a finger pressed into the ice cream should go in easily and leave a firm indent), use a spade or metal spoon to spoon alternating scoopfuls into a medium bowl. Using a chopping and stirring motion, work the ice creams until swirled but not melted, about 1 minute. (If at any time the ice creams starts to melt, pop the bowl into the freezer before proceeding.) Working quickly, drop the mixed ice cream in large scoopfuls over the cookie layer in the pan and spread evenly.

4   Position the remaining cookie layer, top side up, over the ice cream and press gently. Wrap the ends of the plastic wrap over the filled layers. Freeze until the ice cream is hard, about 4 hours.

5   Using an offset spatula, lift the package from the pan, unwrap it, and set it on a cutting board. Using a serrated knife and a sawing motion, cut crosswise through the top cookie layer before pressing down through the ice cream and bottom cookie layer. Using the same cutting technique, cut each piece into three squares and cut each into triangles or smaller rectangles. Serve immediately or wrap individually and return to the freezer until ready to serve or for up to 1 month.

> **KITCHEN WISDOM ◎◎ warming up ice cream**
>
> Ice cream warming time can vary from 5 to 15 minutes. It depends on many things: where you live, what season it is, how warm or chilly you keep your home, your freezer temperature—it should be set at o°F—and even what type of ice cream you buy.

twists
- Use about 3 cups of any flavor of ice cream or sorbet.
- Press colored sprinkles into the sides of the ice cream sandwiches.

do ahead
- The cookie layer can be made up to 1 day ahead or frozen for up to 1 month before proceeding with the recipe.
- The ice cream-filled cookie layers can be removed from the pan, wrapped tightly, and frozen for up to 1 month before finishing the recipe.

Position the top cookie layer over the ice cream.

Frozen Chocolate–Papaya Wedges

I like freezing fresh fruit, and it doesn't take much time or effort to turn a plain piece of fruit into a sumptuous treat. Tropical fruit like papayas and mangos are the perfect texture for freezing. They are somewhat soft-textured, full of flavor, and nice and juicy. For these handy treats, I dip papaya wedges in chocolate and sprinkle them with a little salt. I urge you to give this combo a try—the sweet-salty balance is just perfect, and it really heightens the papaya's natural flavor. But if that sounds too far afield for your taste buds, feel free to use one of the other options I suggest in the Twists at right.

1 Line a flat plate or small tray with waxed paper or foil and make room in the freezer.

2 Peel the papaya, cut it in half, and scoop out the seeds. Cut into ½-inch-thick wedges or 1-inch pieces.

3 Put the chocolate, butter, and orange zest in deep, small heatproof bowl set over a saucepan of barely simmering water until melted. (This can also be done in the microwave.) Whisk until the mixture is smooth and blended.

4 Working with one papaya wedge or piece at a time, lower it into the warm chocolate-butter mixture until halfway covered. Lift up, tap gently on the bowl to remove excess chocolate, and arrange on the prepared plate or tray. Dip the remaining pieces, one at a time, and arrange them about 1 inch apart on the plate. Sprinkle a little fleur de sel over the chocolate.

5 Arrange the plate in the freezer and chill until frozen, about 1 hour. Pop the pieces into a heavy-duty freezer bag or container and keep frozen until ready to serve or for up to 1 month.

1 ripe papaya

8 ounces bittersweet chocolate, finely chopped

5 tablespoons (2½ ounces) unsalted butter, cut into 2 pieces

2 tablespoons finely grated orange zest

½ teaspoon crushed fleur de sel

Makes 24 wedges

twists

- Instead of papaya, substitute 1 ripe mango or 3 ripe bananas.

- Instead of the fleur de sel, substitute ⅓ cup (1⅝ ounces) chopped toasted macadamia nuts (or another type of nut) or ½ cup (1¼ ounces) shredded sweetened coconut, toasted, or ¼ cup colored sprinkles.

½ cup (3½ ounces) granulated sugar

⅓ cup (1 ounce) unsweetened natural cocoa powder, sifted if lumpy

1 teaspoon instant espresso granules

Pinch of table salt

1½ cups skim milk, divided

½ teaspoon pure vanilla extract

2 tablespoons Kahlúa or other coffee-flavored liqueur

Makes four 4-ounce pops

twists

- Instead of the skim milk, substitute half-and-half or heavy cream.
- Instead of the Kahlúa, substitute 2 tablespoons brewed coffee.

do ahead

The milk mixture can be made ahead and stored in the refrigerator for up to 3 days before continuing with the recipe.

Skinnier Mocha Pops

My husband, Chris, will tell you that he doesn't have a sweet tooth, but don't believe him. After dinner, instead of asking, "Do we have anything sweet that I could nibble on?" he will instead ask if we have "something cold." I think he believes that "something cold" is the same as chewing on, say, ice cubes. No calories equal no guilt, right? Well, when it comes to these chocolate pops made with skim milk, Chris will be almost without guilt, and they taste way better than ice cubes.

1 Have ready four 4-ounce ice pop molds and make room in the freezer, making sure the molds are level and secure.

2 Put the sugar, cocoa powder, espresso, and salt and in a small saucepan. Slowly add about ½ cup of the milk and whisk until blended and the mixture is smooth. Cook, whisking constantly, over medium heat until the sugar is dissolved and the mixture is simmering, about 3 minutes. Slide the pan from the heat, then stir in the remaining milk, the vanilla, and Kahlúa. Cover and set aside to cool completely. To cool faster, set the pan over an ice bath and stir occasionally until chilled.

3 Using a large tablespoon, skim off any foam from the top. Pour an equal amount of the milk mixture into the molds. Cover each mold with a lid that has a stem or with foil and push a wooden ice pop stick through the foil and into the middle of each pop. Freeze until firm, about 4 hours or up to 1 week.

4 To serve, remove the lids (or foil) and slip the ice pops from the molds.

Boozy Frozen Watermelon Spears

3 tablespoons water

3 tablespoons granulated sugar

¼ cup light rum

2 teaspoons freshly squeezed lemon juice

Pinch of table salt

¼ small seedless watermelon

Makes 14 spears

Freezing fresh fruit unadorned isn't a new concept. In fact, it's something I do often in the wintertime with seedless grapes. Just pop 'em into the freezer, wait a few hours, and you have an instant, icy snack that's ready to grab and go. For this watermelon treatment, I wanted something more complex and adult so I turned to my son, Alex, my resident mixologist, for help.

I knew I wanted these spears to have a boozy hit without overpowering the fruit's flavor. After bouncing around some ideas, Alex and I took a field trip to the liquor store (which is something you can do only with a "child" of legal age). Much to the amusement of the store's staff, we scooped up a slew of those little sample bottles in a variety of flavors and headed home to test them all out. Luckily, I had anticipated a bountiful testing day and had bought a large watermelon.

Save the leftover syrup for a round of cocktails (it has a yummy watermelon taste) or freeze as ice cubes to use in a cocktail or for your next batch of spears.

The main recipe and Twists include our four favorite liquor flavors, but feel free to add your own favorite liquor or liqueur. (Can you say "limoncello"?)

twists

- **MAKE 'EM CHUNKS:** Cut the watermelon into small chunks, soak them in the syrup, turning frequently, and proceed as directed.

- **MAKE 'EM FESTIVE:** Cut the watermelon into ½-inch-thick slices and use small cookie cutters to make fun shapes; tie to holidays, like stars for July 4th or shamrocks for St. Patrick's Day.

- Instead of using light rum, use the same amount of watermelon-flavored vodka, raspberry-flavored vodka, or lemon-flavored light rum.

1 Have ready a 9x13-inch baking dish and 14 thin wooden or plastic skewers or toothpicks.

2 Put the water and sugar in a small saucepan. Bring to a boil over medium-high heat. Reduce the heat and simmer, stirring occasionally, until the sugar is dissolved, about 2 minutes. Slide the pan from the heat and add the rum, lemon juice, and salt. Stir until blended and set aside until warm but no longer hot. To cool faster, pour into a small bowl and set over a larger bowl filled with ice and some water and stir until warm but not hot.

3 Cut the watermelon into ½-inch-thick slices and trim off and discard the rind. Starting at one end, push a wooden skewer or toothpick into the middle of each slice about halfway through to the other end. Arrange the skewers, flat side down, in a single layer in the prepared baking dish. Pour the warm syrup over the watermelon and set aside for at least 1 hour or up to 3 hours, turning the skewers frequently. (If your kitchen is warm, keep the dish in the refrigerator.)

4 Line a small jelly roll pan with parchment or waxed paper and set it in the freezer, making sure it's level and secure. Move the skewers, one at a time, from the syrup onto the jelly roll pan. It's fine if some of the syrup moves with them. Freeze until very firm, about 4 hours or up to 5 days.

5 To serve, lift the spears from the pan and serve immediately.

do ahead

The syrup can made and stored in the refrigerator for up to 3 days before continuing with the recipe.

finishing touches

For a fun party presentation, arrange a half of a small watermelon or pineapple on a serving plate and stick the sharp end of the skewers into it.

2¼ cups half-and-half, divided

5   yolks from large eggs

**⅔   cup (4⅝ ounces) granulated
       sugar**

**   Pinch of table salt**

1½ teaspoons pure vanilla extract

⅔   cup sour cream

Makes 3½ cups

do ahead

The custard can be made and stored
in the refrigerator for up to 1 day
before continuing with the recipe.

twists

- **MAKE IT REGULAR NOT "TANGY":**
  Instead of using the sour
  cream, add an additional ½ cup
  half-and-half along with the
  remaining 1 cup half-and-half and
  the vanilla to the cooked custard
  in Step 3.

- **ADD IN SOMETHING SPECIAL:** Use
  one of the Add-ins in Classic
  Chocolate Ice Cream (see p. 168).

- **USE A VANILLA BEAN:** Instead of
  using vanilla extract, split 1 large
  vanilla bean in half lengthwise
  (see p. 21) and add it to the pan
  with the 1¼ cups half-and-half.
  Bring the half-and-half to a
  simmer, slide the pan from the
  heat, cover, and set aside for
  20 minutes or for up to 1 hour to
  let the vanilla flavor infuse the
  half-and-and half. Proceed with
  the recipe and once the custard is
  cooled, fish out the vanilla pieces
  and using the tip of a small knife,
  scrape any remaining seeds back
  into the custard.

- For more variations, see
  www.abbydodge.com.

Tangy Vanilla Ice Cream

Adding sour cream to ice cream might seem unusual, but this subtle tang adds a
level of sophistication to this classic recipe. Be sure to stir in the sour cream only
after the custard has chilled: It will curdle if added to the hot stuff.

1 Have ready an ice cream maker.

2 Put 1¼ cups of the half-and-half in a medium saucepan. Cook, stirring, over
medium-low heat until simmering. Slide the pan from the heat.

3 Meanwhile, put the yolks, sugar, and salt in a medium bowl and whisk until well
blended. Once the half-and-half has simmered, slowly add it to the yolk mixture,
whisking constantly, until blended. Scrape the mixture back into the saucepan and
cook over low heat, stirring constantly (including the sides and bottom), until the
custard is thick enough to coat the back of a spoon and holds a line drawn through
it with your finger or until the temperature registers between 175° and 180°F on an
instant-read or candy thermometer, 4 to 6 minutes. Pour into a clean bowl and stir
in the remaining 1 cup half-and-half and the vanilla. Set aside to cool completely and
refrigerate until chilled. For faster chilling, scrape the custard into a clean bowl, set the
bowl over another larger bowl of ice, and stir until cooled.

4 Arrange a 4½x8¼-inch loaf pan in the freezer, making sure it's level and secure. Add
the sour cream to the chilled custard and whisk until blended. Pour the mixture into
the ice cream maker and process according to the manufacturer's instructions. Serve
immediately (it will be soft) or scrape into the chilled dish, cover, and freeze until firm
or for up to 1 week.

5 Serve in Waffle Cones (see p. 166), between large soft Oatmeal Cookies (see p. 42), or
shape into bites (see p. 178).

Grown-Up Ginger Margarita Pops

I've always liked margaritas, but I never loved them until I tasted one in Cabo San Lucas, Mexico. The balance of sweet and tart was perfect, and the fresh ginger added warm and spicy elements to the traditional flavor. This is my frozen interpretation of this Mexican classic.

A note about the salt in the recipe. I like my margaritas on the salty side but not everyone feels the same so I've given a big range for the amount of salt. Before pouring the liquid into the molds, give the syrup a taste and add more salt, if you like.

1 Have ready seven 3-ounce ice pop molds and make room in the freezer, making sure the molds are level and secure.

2 Put ½ cup water, the sugar, lime juice, ginger slices, lime zest strips, and salt (start with a pinch) in a small saucepan. Bring to a boil over medium-high heat. Reduce the heat and simmer, stirring occasionally, until the sugar is dissolved, about 2 minutes. Slide the pan from the heat, cover, and set aside until completely cool. This resting time also allows the lime and ginger to infuse the syrup.

3 Set a fine-mesh sieve over a large bowl or 4-cup measure. Pour the cooled ginger syrup into the sieve and, using a rubber spatula, press firmly on the ginger and zest to extract all the juice.

4 Add the remaining ⅔ cup water, the tequila, and Cointreau and stir until well blended. Taste and add more salt, if you like. Pour an equal amount of liquid into the molds. Cover each mold with a lid that has a stem or with foil and push a wooden ice pop stick through the foil and into the middle of each pop. Freeze until firm, about 4 hours or up to 1 week.

5 To serve, remove the lids (or foil) and slip the pops from the molds.

KITCHEN WISDOM ◎◎ fresh ginger

When shopping for fresh ginger (also known as ginger root), select pieces that are hard and not shriveled or dry looking. Before grating, slicing, or chopping, remove the thin gray-brown peel by running the edge of a spoon in short, firm strokes over the ginger until the peel is scraped off. For finely grated ginger, I like to use a Microplane grater, but a small porcelain ginger grater works well, too.

- ½ cup + ⅔ cup water, divided
- ⅔ cup granulated sugar
- ⅓ cup + 1 tablespoon freshly squeezed lime juice
- 1 1½-inch piece of fresh ginger, peeled and very thinly sliced
- 2 strips of lime zest
   Pinch to ¼ teaspoon table salt
- 2 tablespoons tequila
- 4 teaspoons Cointreau®

Makes seven 3-ounce pops

twists

- **ADD FRESH GINGER:** Scatter fresh ginger slices throughout the pops. Leave the tops off and when the liquid is slushy, use a long wooden skewer to rearrange the slices.

- **ADD FRESH BERRIES:** Drop a few fresh raspberries or blackberries into the molds before pouring in the syrup. You'll need an extra pop mold or two depending on how many berries you are adding. Take a look at the note above about rearranging the fruit once the liquid is slushy.

do ahead

The ginger syrup can be made and stored in the refrigerator up to 3 days before continuing with the recipe.

⅔ cup (3⅓ ounces) unbleached all-purpose flour

½ teaspoon baking powder

¼ teaspoon table salt

12 tablespoons (6 ounces) unsalted butter, cut into 4 pieces

⅔ cup (2 ounces) unsweetened natural cocoa powder, sifted if lumpy

1½ cups (10½ ounces) granulated sugar

2 large eggs, at room temperature

1 teaspoon pure vanilla extract

FOR THE SORBET LAYER

2 containers (14 ounces each) raspberry sorbet

½ pint fresh raspberries, rinsed and well dried

1 tablespoon granulated sugar

¾ teaspoon finely grated lime zest

Pinch of table salt

Makes 12 to 16 sandwiches

do ahead

The brownie layers can be made up to 2 days before assembling.

finishing touches

• **GARNISH THE SANDWICHES:** Put your chosen garnish (see list below) in a small shallow bowl. Working with one sandwich at a time and keeping the others frozen, press some of the garnish onto some or all of the sides of the sandwich and return to the freezer.

Some garnish ideas finely crushed peppermint candies, finely chopped or grated bittersweet chocolate, minced crystallized ginger, finely chopped toasted pecans, crushed toffee chips, toasted sweetened coconut flakes, and crushed amaretti cookies.

Double Raspberry Brownie Ice Cream Sandwiches

I think the name of these frozen treats should be Ice Cream Wedges, but too many smart people told me that sounded like shoes. So we'll stick to calling them sandwiches but, as you can see, there is nothing shoe-like about them. The wedge shape comes from making the sandwich layers in a 9-inch springform pan, which makes assembly remarkably easy. Plus the shape is just downright fun.

make the brownie layer

1 Position an oven rack in the center of the oven and heat the oven to 325°F. Line the bottom of two 9-inch springform pans with foil (or use a 9-inch round cake pan for one of the springform pans). Fit the bottoms into the rings and secure each clasp. Lightly grease the foil.

2 Whisk the flour, baking powder, and salt in a small bowl until well blended. Put the butter in a medium saucepan and set over medium-low heat, stirring occasionally, until the butter is melted, about 2 minutes. Slide the pan from the heat, add the cocoa powder, and whisk until the mixture is smooth. Add the sugar and whisk until blended. Using your fingertip, check the temperature of the batter—it should be warm but not hot. If it's hot, set the pan aside for a minute or two before continuing with the recipe.

3 Add the eggs and vanilla and whisk until well blended. Add the flour mixture and stir with a rubber spatula until just blended. Divide the batter evenly into the prepared pans (1¼ cups or 12⅓ ounces in each pan) and spread evenly. Bake until a toothpick inserted in the center comes out with small bits of brownie sticking to it, 16 to 18 minutes. Move the pans to a wire rack and let cool completely. To unmold, unclasp the outer rings and remove. Carefully lift the brownie layers from the foil. Place a fresh piece of foil over one of the pan bottoms and replace one brownie layer and the outer ring and secure the clasp. Set the remaining brownie layer, top side up, on a wire rack.

recipe continues

twists

- **USE A CAKE PAN:** I've called for using two 9-inch springform pans because it's the easiest way to bake and assemble these brownies. But if you don't have two of them and you don't want to buy more than one, you can substitute a 9-inch cake pan lined with parchment for one of the springforms and proceed as directed. Assemble in the springform, not the cake pan.

- **USE OTHER FLAVORS:** Feel free to use any flavor store-bought ice cream or about 3 cups homemade ice cream or sorbet.

make the sorbet

Remove the containers of sorbet from the freezer and set on the counter. Put the raspberries, sugar, lime zest, and salt in a small bowl and toss to coat the berries. When the sorbet is slightly softened, use a spade or metal spoon to spoon it into a medium bowl. Using a chopping and stirring motion, work the sorbet until pliable but not melted, about 1 minute. And the raspberry mixture and stir until the raspberries are partially crushed and evenly mixed into the sorbet. (If at any time the sorbet starts to melt, pop it, bowl and all, into the freezer before proceeding.) Working quickly, drop the sorbet in large scoopfuls over the brownie layer in the pan and spread evenly. Top with the second brownie layer, pressing lightly to make an even layer. Cover and freeze until very firm, about 6 hours or for up to 3 days.

to serve

1 Remove the pan from the freezer and set on the counter. Dip a small knife or metal spatula into hot tap water, wipe dry, and slide between the pan and the ice cream. Unclasp the outer ring and remove. Using the foil, lift the layers from the bottom, peel away the foil and set the layered brownie on a cutting board. Using a small metal spatula, smooth the sorbet around the edges, if necessary.

2 Dip a large knife into hot water and wipe it dry, then cut the layered brownie into 12 or 16 wedges, dipping the knife into water and wiping it between cuts. Serve immediately or wrap individually in waxed paper and return to the freezer until ready to serve or for up to 1 month.

EZ Strawberry Ice Cream Cones

This is one of my most versatile recipes as well as one of my most refreshing. You can use any type of frozen fruit and any type of dairy or nondairy liquid (soy milk, half-and-half, coconut milk, yogurt, or fruit juice) to make this speedy, fresh, and fruity ice cream year-round. You can double this recipe, but, unless you have a very large processor, I'd suggest you make it in two separate batches.

Throughout the spring and summer months, I like to freeze fruit at its ripest to save a blast of summer sunshine for the cold winter months. Pick-your-own berries like raspberries, blueberries, and strawberries are all easy to find here in the Northeast, but you should harvest whatever fruit is local in your neck of the woods. (See the sidebar on p. 166 for easy instructions for freezing berries.)

1 Arrange a 4½x8¼-inch loaf pan in the freezer (I like this shape because it makes scooping easy, but any deep plastic or glass dish will work).

2 Put the frozen strawberries in a food processor. Pulse a few times until they're broken up. The frozen berries will bounce around in the beginning and then settle down a bit after about 1 minute of pulsing. Add the half-and-half, sugar, orange liqueur or vanilla extract, and salt and then whiz until smooth, 2 to 3 minutes. Taste and add another 1 tablespoon sugar, if needed, and then process until blended.

3 Scrape into the chilled dish, cover, and freeze until firm enough to scoop, about 1 hour or up to 2 days. When freezing for longer than just an hour or two, let the ice cream sit at room temperature until the consistency is scoopable, 15 to 30 minutes.

4 Serve in cones with toppings, if you like.

recipe continues

1 package (12 ounces) or 3 cups frozen unsweetened strawberries

½ cup half-and-half

4 to 5 tablespoons granulated sugar

1 tablespoon orange liqueur or ¼ teaspoon pure vanilla extract

Pinch of table salt

Waffle cones (homemade or store-bought; see p. 166)

Chocolate shavings (see below), chocolate sprinkles, or toasted sweetened coconut (optional)

Makes about 2 cups ice cream, or 6 cones

finishing touches

CHOCOLATE SHAVINGS: Wrap a large piece or block of bitter- or semisweet chocolate with plastic wrap. Holding the block in one hand, rub your palm quickly over one edge of the block to warm but not melt the chocolate. Unwrap the rubbed portion of the chocolate and, using a vegetable peeler and short, quick strokes, peel away strips of the chocolate, letting them drop onto a parchment- or foil-lined cookie sheet. If you need more chocolate shavings, rewrap the block, rub, and then make more strips with the peeler.

twists

• CHOOSE ANOTHER FRUIT: Substitute an equal amount of any frozen fruit for the strawberries.

• MAKE IT YOGURT: Substitute unsweetened, plain yogurt (I like Greek style) for the same amount of half-and-half.

• MAKE IT ORANGE: Substitute freshly squeezed orange juice for the same amount of half-and-half.

1 large egg, at room temperature

1 large yolk, at room temperature

1/3 cup (2 3/8 ounces) granulated sugar

1/2 teaspoon pure vanilla extract

1/4 teaspoon table salt

1/8 teaspoon pure almond extract (optional)

1/2 cup (2 1/4 ounces) unbleached all-purpose flour

3 tablespoons (1 1/2 ounces) unsalted butter, melted

1/4 cup whole milk

Makes about 8 large cones

do ahead

The cones will keep in an airtight container for up to 5 days.

homemade waffle cones

1 Put the egg, egg yolk, sugar, vanilla, salt, and almond extract (if using) in a medium bowl and whisk until well blended and pale in color, about 1 minute. Add the flour and whisk just until blended. Add the melted butter and milk and whisk until blended and smooth.

2 Heat an electric ice cream cone maker according to the manufacturer's instructions.

3 Pour 3 tablespoons batter onto the center of the hot cone maker and, using a small offset spatula, spread evenly. Cook according to the manufacturer's instructions or until evenly golden brown.

4 Using an offset spatula, lift the cookie from the cone maker and set on a work surface. Working quickly, roll the hot cookie around the cone roller and set, seam side down until it holds its shape, about 30 seconds. Using the roller, move the cone to a wire rack, seam side down, and gently slide the cone off the roller and onto the rack; let cool completely. Repeat with the remaining batter.

> **KITCHEN WISDOM** ⊙⊙ **freeze your own berries**
>
> Follow this method for freezing any kind of berries. Rinse and thoroughly dry the berries (if freezing strawberries, hull them and cut in half). Line a cookie sheet with parchment or foil and spread the fruit into a single layer. Slide the sheet into the freezer until the berries are rock-hard, about 2 hours. Break them apart, if needed, and toss into zip-top freezer bags for up to 6 months.
>
> To hull strawberries, use a small knife to cut away the stem and white core of the rinsed and dried berries. Proceed according to the recipe's directions.

2¾ cups half-and-half, divided

6 ounces bittersweet chocolate, chopped

4 yolks from large eggs

½ cup (3½ ounces) granulated sugar

Pinch of table salt

1 teaspoon pure vanilla extract

Makes 3½ cups

twists

- **MAKE IT MOCHA:** Add 2 teaspoons instant espresso granules to the half-and-half and chocolate mixture. It will dissolve as the chocolate melts.

- **ADD IN SOMETHING SPECIAL:** When the ice cream is finished churning, add one or more of the following and continue to churn until blended: ⅔ cup chocolate-covered toffee bits; ⅔ cup finely grated bittersweet, semisweet, or white chocolate (using the small holes on a box grater and a block of chocolate); or ⅔ cup toasted chopped nuts (pick your favorite).

do ahead

The custard can made and stored in the refrigerator up to 1 day before continuing with the recipe.

Classic Chocolate Ice Cream

Testing recipes for a book of this size is a daunting but important process. For this recipe, I turned to one of the biggest chocolate ice cream lovers I know: my 11-year-old goddaughter Tory. Even at this young age, she really knows her chocolate ice creams, and I'm happy to tell you that this chocolate ice cream is Tory approved!

1 Have ready an ice cream maker.

2 Put 1¾ cups of the half-and-half and the chocolate in a medium saucepan. Cook, stirring, over medium-low heat until the chocolate is melted and the mixture is smooth. Slide the pan from the heat.

3 Meanwhile, put the yolks, sugar, and salt in a medium bowl and whisk until well blended. Once the half-and-half mixture is smooth, slowly add to yolk mixture, whisking constantly, until blended. Scrape the mixture back into the saucepan and cook over low heat, stirring constantly (including the sides and bottom), until the custard is thick enough to coat the back of a spoon and holds a line drawn through it with your finger or until the temperature registers between 175° and 180°F on an instant-read or candy thermometer, 4 to 6 minutes. Pour into a clean bowl and stir in the remaining 1 cup half-and-half and the vanilla. Set aside to cool completely, cover, and refrigerate until chilled. For faster chilling, scrape the custard into a clean bowl, set the bowl over another larger bowl of ice, and stir until cooled.

4 Arrange a 4½x8¼-inch loaf pan in the freezer, making sure it's level and secure. Pour the chilled mixture into the ice cream maker and process according to the manufacturer's instructions. Serve immediately (it will be soft) or scrape into the chilled pan, cover, and freeze until firm or for up to 1 week.

5 Serve in Waffle Cones (see p. 166), between large soft Oatmeal Cookies (see p. 42), or shape into bites (see p. 178).

> **KITCHEN WISDOM ⊙⊙ cooking custard**
>
> - Use an angled wooden spatula for stirring a custard while it cooks; a heatproof plastic spatula works well, too.
> - Stir in a figure-eight motion, making sure to scrape the entire bottom of the pan, including the corners.
> - In the early stages, the custard will have a foamy layer on the top. This will disappear as you get closer to the perfect doneness.
> - If the custard has specks of cooked yolk, pour through a fine-mesh sieve.

Classic Summer Raspberry Sorbet

I never know when the urge-to-churn will hit me, so I keep my ice cream maker's freezing canister tucked into my freezer all year. This way, it's ready to produce an amazing fresh fruit sorbet when I come across great-looking berries or fruit at the grocery store or, in the summer, at the farmers' market. Feel free to experiment not only with different fruits but also with the amount of lemon juice and salt, as some fruits might need a bit more to brighten their flavors.

1 Have ready an ice cream maker.

2 Put the water, sugar, lemon juice, zest, and salt into a medium saucepan. Cook, stirring, over medium heat until the sugar is dissolved and the mixture is barely simmering, about 3 minutes. Slide the pan from the heat and set aside.

3 Pile the berries into a food processor and whiz until smooth, about 1 minute (you'll have 2 cups). Add the fruit purée to the sugar syrup and stir until blended. Set aside to cool completely and refrigerate until chilled. For faster chilling, scrape the syrup into a clean bowl, set the bowl over another larger bowl of ice, and stir until cooled.

4 Arrange a $4\frac{1}{2}$x$8\frac{1}{4}$-inch loaf pan in the freezer, making sure it's level and secure. Pour the chilled mixture into the ice cream maker and process according to the manufacturer's instructions. Serve immediately (it will be soft) or scrape into the chilled dish, cover, and freeze until firm or for up to 1 week.

5 Serve in Waffle Cones (see p. 166), between large soft chocolate or vanilla cookies or shape into bites (see p. 178).

KITCHEN WISDOM ◎◎ handling berries

Pick through the berries, discarding any leaves and stems, as well as bruised or moldy berries. Put the berries in a colander and rinse with cold water. Line a baking sheet with several layers of paper towel or a clean kitchen towel and arrange the berries in an even layer. Cover with more towels and pat dry.

- 1 cup water
- ¾ cup (5¼ ounces) granulated sugar
- 1 tablespoon freshly squeezed lemon juice
- 1 teaspoon finely grated lemon zest
-    Pinch of table salt
- 1 quart fresh raspberries

Makes 3½ cups

twists

- **MAKE A GRANITA:** In place of using an ice cream maker, arrange a 9x13-inch baking pan or 9½-cup rectangular plastic container (Ziploc®) in the freezer, making sure it's level and secure. (Other sizes and shapes work, too, but you'll need to adjust your stirring and scraping times accordingly.) Follow Steps 2 and 3 for making the mixture. Pour the chilled mixture into the baking dish and freeze for about 2 hours until frozen around the edges. Every 30 minutes thereafter, stir and scrape the mixture with a table fork. Freeze and scrape until the ice crystals are loose and frozen.

- **MAKE IT CREAMY:** Instead of the water, use the same amount of half-and-half or heavy cream

- **CHOOSE ANOTHER BERRY:** Instead of the raspberries, use 2 cups purée of another fruit or a mix of the following: blueberries, hulled strawberries, kiwi, papaya, passion fruit.

do ahead

- The syrup can be made and stored in the refrigerator for up to 2 days before continuing with the recipe.

- The sorbet can be prepared and frozen for up to 1 week.

Very Berry Cranberry Pops

I love cranberry juice. Even as a kid, I was always clamoring for it to use as the "tea" for my miniature tea parties. Was it the ruby red color (stain attack waiting to happen)? That it was called "cocktail" and made me feel grown up to drink it? It was probably a bit of both, but the bottom line was that I loved the flavor—crisp, slightly sweet, and impossibly refreshing.

In these pops, whole berries add a burst of complementary flavor as well as a frozen crunch, and there's a hint of fresh rosemary (you don't have to use it, but it sure is good) in the syrup, which adds a touch of intrigue.

1 Have ready six 4-ounce ice pop molds and make room in the freezer, making sure the molds are level and secure.

2 Put 1 cup of the cranberry juice, the sugar, lemon juice, rosemary, and salt in a small saucepan. Bring to a boil over medium-high heat. Reduce the heat and simmer, stirring occasionally, until the sugar is dissolved, about 2 minutes. Slide the pan from the heat, cover, and set aside until completely cool. This resting time also allows the rosemary flavor to infuse the syrup.

3 Set a fine-mesh sieve over a large bowl or 4-cup measure. Poor the cooled syrup into the sieve and, using a rubber spatula, press firmly on the rosemary to extract all the juice.

4 Add the remaining 1 cup cranberry juice and stir until well blended. Divide the berries evenly in the molds. They are big enough to hold their place in most molds and not fall to the bottom. Pour an equal amount of liquid into the molds. If the berries end up sinking to the bottom or floating to the top, leave the tops off and, when the liquid is slushy, use a long wooden skewer to rearrange them. Cover each mold with a lid that has a stem or with foil and push a wooden ice pop stick through the foil and into the middle of each pop. Freeze until firm, about 4 hours or up to 1 week.

5 To serve, remove the lids or foil and slip the ice pops from the molds.

2 cups white cranberry juice cocktail, divided

6 tablespoons granulated sugar

1 teaspoon freshly squeezed lemon juice

1 small sprig of fresh rosemary
   Pinch of table salt

½ pint fresh raspberries or blackberries, or a mix

Makes six 4-ounce pops

finishing touches
Arrange a small rosemary sprig or a few leaves in each mold when the liquid becomes slushy.

twists
Instead of the raspberries and blackberries, substitute the same amount of blueberries and sliced strawberries, arranging them in the molds when liquid is slushy.

do ahead
• The syrup can made and stored in the refrigerator for up to 3 days before continuing with the recipe.

• The pops can be prepared and frozen for up to 1 week—but they won't last that long!

KITCHEN WISDOM ໑໑
pop molds
Pop molds come in all sizes and shapes. While I encourage you to try different ones, remember that your yield will change as the molds change.

- ¾ cup freshly squeezed blood orange juice
- 4 tablespoons granulated sugar, divided
- 1 tablespoon tequila (optional)
- ⅔ cup freshly squeezed tangerine juice
- 3 tablespoons heavy cream

Makes four 4-ounce pops

twists

- Instead of the blood orange and tangerine juices, substitute the same amount of fresh orange juice for both layers.
- Instead of the tequila, substitute an equal amount of vodka.

do ahead

The syrups can made and stored in the refrigerator for up to 3 days before continuing with the recipe.

Blood Orange and Creamy Tangerine Pops

These pops remind me of my favorite college cocktail (for those of you who are raising an eyebrow here, the legal drinking age back then was 18), a Tequila Sunrise. This creamy pop version is just as pretty and refreshing as the original drink—with or without the "hootch."

1 Have ready four 4-ounce ice pop molds and make room in the freezer, making sure the molds are level and secure.

2 Put the blood orange juice and 2 tablespoons of the sugar in a small saucepan. Bring to a boil over medium-high heat. Reduce the heat and simmer, stirring occasionally, until the sugar is dissolved, about 1 minute. Slide the pan from the heat and stir in the tequila, if using. Set aside to cool completely and then pour into a 1-cup measure and chill until ready to use.

3 Put the tangerine juice, heavy cream, and the remaining 2 tablespoons sugar in a small saucepan. Bring to a boil over medium-high heat. Reduce the heat and simmer, stirring occasionally, until the sugar is dissolved, about 1 minute. Slide the pan from the heat and set aside to cool completely; for faster chilling, pour the liquid into a 1-cup glass measure and set over a bowl of ice.

4 Pour an equal amount of the tangerine juice mixture into the molds. Cover each mold with a lid that has a stem or with foil and push a wooden ice pop stick through the foil and into the middle of each pop. Freeze until almost firm, about 2 hours.

5 Carefully lift off the lids (or foil), keeping the sticks in place. Pour an equal amount of the blood orange juice mixture into the molds on top of the first layer. Don't worry if some of it leaks into the first layer; it will just add to the visual drama. Re-cover and freeze until firm, about 2 hours, or for up to 1 week.

6 To serve, remove the lids or foil and slip the ice pops from the molds.

- 1 cup water
- ⅓ cup (2⅜ ounces) granulated sugar
- ⅓ cup packed fresh lemon basil leaves, or regular basil
- 1 tablespoon finely grated lemon zest
- ⅛ teaspoon table salt
- ⅓ cup freshly squeezed lemon juice
- 2 tablespoons vodka (I like Absolut®)

Makes four 3-ounce pops

twists

- **MAKE MINTY MOJITO POPS:** Instead of the basil, use 8 hearty sprigs of fresh mint, broken up (you'll have about ⅔ cup packed mint leaves and stalks). Instead of the lemon zest and juice, use an equal amount of lime zest and juice. Instead of the vodka, use 2 tablespoons light rum.

- **ADD A MEYER LEMON SLICE OR TWO:** When the liquid is slushy, remove the lids or foil and use a wooden skewer to slide one or two very thin slices of Meyer lemon down each side of the molds. Replace the lids or foil.

do ahead

The syrup can made and stored in the refrigerator for up to 3 days before continuing with the recipe.

Grown-Up Lemon Basil Drop Pops

I bet you didn't know that Bill Belichick, head coach of the New England Patriots, enjoys a Lemon Drop cocktail now and then. It's a strange tidbit for me to know, especially since I'm a New Yorker and a die-hard Jets fan (and Giants, too, but don't tell my husband). The info came through my son, Alex, who waited on the esteemed coach while working in a Nantucket restaurant. All I can say is that while our football loyalties lie in different camps, Bill and I do agree on enjoying a nice Lemon Drop cocktail on a summer evening.

My frozen and much less boozy version of Bill's favorite drink is sweet-tart perfection with spicy undertones from the basil—a perfect summertime pop.

1 Have ready four 4-ounce ice pop molds and make room in the freezer, making sure the molds are level and secure.

2 Put the water, sugar, basil, lemon zest, and salt in a small saucepan. Bring to a boil over medium-high heat. Reduce the heat and simmer, stirring occasionally, until the sugar is dissolved, about 3 minutes. Slide the pan from the heat, cover, and set aside to cool completely. This gives the basil and lemon time to infuse the sugar syrup.

3 Add the lemon juice and vodka to the cooled syrup. Set a fine-mesh sieve over a 4-cup measure. Pour the syrup into the sieve and, using a rubber spatula, press firmly on the basil and zest to extract every drop of liquid and flavor.

4 Pour an equal amount of the syrup into the molds. Cover each mold with a lid that has a stem or with foil and push a wooden ice pop stick through the foil and into the middle of each pop. Freeze until firm, about 4 hours or up to 1 week.

5 To serve, remove the lids (or foil) and slip the ice pops from the molds.

Fruity Green Tea–Honey Pops

My daughter, T (short for Tierney), is the green tea drinker in my family. She likes her tea best when it's iced and lightly sweetened with honey. This past summer, as she was pouring herself a glass, she added a wedge of orange, and it struck me that this combo would make a refreshing frozen pop. Just watching T glide through this simple process inspired me to make her favorite drink into this easy, refreshing dessert.

1 Have ready six 4-ounce ice pop molds and make room in the freezer.

2 Working on a cutting board with a sharp knife, cut off the ends of the orange. Position the orange on one end and cut away all the zest and pith, following the fruit's contour. Thinly slice the orange. (You'll use 6 of the slices for this recipe so cover the remaining slices and save them for breakfast or a glass of iced green tea, Tierney-style.)

3 Tip the pop molds on one flat side and slide an orange slice into each mold so it is flush against the side. Arrange the molds, still on their side, in the freezer. Freeze until the orange slices are very hard, about 1 hour.

4 Put 1 cup of the green tea, the honey, lemon juice, and salt in a small saucepan. Cook, stirring, over medium heat until the honey is dissolved, about 1 minute. Slide the pan from the heat, add the remaining 1 cup green tea, and stir until blended. Set aside to cool completely.

to fill and freeze

1 Set the molds right side up (the oranges slices will stick to the sides of the molds), making sure they are level and secure.

2 Pour an equal amount of tea into the molds. Cover each mold with a lid that has a stem or with foil and push a wooden ice pop stick through the foil and into the middle of each pop. Freeze until firm, about 4 hours or up to 3 days.

3 To serve, remove the lids (or foil) and slip the ice pops from the molds.

1 small navel or Valencia orange

2 cups unsweetened green tea, divided

3 tablespoons honey

1½ teaspoons freshly squeezed lemon juice

Pinch of table salt

Makes six 4-ounce pops

twists
Instead of the orange slices, substitute the same amount of thinly sliced apple or ripe pear.

do ahead
• The tea can made and stored in the refrigerator for up to 1 day before continuing with the recipe.

• The pops can be prepared and frozen for up to 1 week, but they won't last that long.

KITCHEN WISDOM ☺☺
removing pop molds

While pop molds come in a variety of sizes, shapes, and materials, the goal is to remove the frozen treats easily and in one piece. Working with one pop at a time, dip the mold up to its rim into a tall bowl or glass of hot tap water for a couple of seconds. Remove and, holding the handle, gently wiggle until the pop feels loose, then slide it from the mold. Depending on your freezer and water temperature, you might need to repeat this process a few times.

Coconut Mango Ice Cream Sandwiches

The color of this ice cream is so vibrant that it will brighten even the dreariest of winter days. But make sure to serve these sandwiches year-round, as they make a very refreshing summertime treat.

1 Line a small cookie sheet or plate with plastic wrap and arrange in the freezer so it's level.

2 Cut both sides of the mangoes and discard the center pit. Cut the flesh of each mango half into 1-inch crosshatch without piecing the skin. Push up from the skin side (it will look like a porcupine) and cut away the mango from the skin. You'll have about 2 packed cups (about 12 ounces). Scrape the mango chunks onto the prepared sheet or plate and freeze until hard, about 3 hours. For longer freezing, pop the frozen mango pieces in a heavy-duty zip-top bag for up to 1 month.

3 Arrange a 4½x8¼-inch loaf pan (I like this shape because it makes scooping easy) in the freezer, making sure it's level. Pile the frozen mango chunks into a food processor and add the coconut milk, 3 tablespoons of the honey, and the salt (if your food processor is small, do this in batches; otherwise, you'll end up with coconut milk splatter over everything in your kitchen). Pulse until smooth, about 3 minutes. Taste and add more honey and salt, if needed. Scrape into the prepared pan and freeze until firm enough to scoop, 15 to 30 minutes.

4 Arrange 6 cookies, flat side up, on the counter. Using a large round ice cream scoop, portion the ice cream (about ⅓ cup per cookie) evenly onto the cookies. Top with the remaining cookies, flat side down. Press slightly to spread the ice cream to the edges. Arrange on the prepared cookie sheet and chill until firm. Serve immediately or wrap individually in plastic and stow in the freezer for up to 1 month.

FOR THE ICE CREAM
- 2 ripe mangos (12 ounces each)
- ⅔ cup coconut milk
- 3 to 4 tablespoons honey; more as needed
- Pinch of table salt

FOR ASSEMBLY
- 12 large (about 3-inch), store-bought soft ginger-molasses cookies

Makes 2 cups ice cream or 6 sandwiches

finishing touches
TOASTED COCONUT OR NUTS: After assembling the sandwiches, lightly roll the edges in 1¼ cups (3⅛ ounces) toasted, shredded sweetened coconut or toasted, chopped nuts (5 ounces).

twists
In place of the coconut milk, use ⅔ cup fresh orange juice or ⅔ cup half-and-half.

KITCHEN WISDOM ◎◎
coconut milk

Coconut milk is sold in cans and can often be found in the Asian or specialty food aisle in the grocery store. Not to be confused with cream of coconut, buy whole (not low-fat) coconut milk and be sure to give the can a good shake just before opening to blend the separated milk.

⅓ cup (1½ ounces) unbleached all-purpose flour

¼ teaspoon baking powder

Pinch of table salt

6 tablespoons (3 ounces) unsalted butter, cut into 4 pieces

⅓ cup (1 ounce) unsweetened natural cocoa powder, sifted if lumpy

¾ cup (5¼ ounces) granulated sugar

1 large egg, at room temperature

½ teaspoon pure vanilla extract

¼ cup (1 ounce) finely chopped toasted pecans

FOR THE ICE CREAM LAYER

1 container (28 ounces) coffee ice cream

⅔ cup chocolate-covered toffee bits

¾ cup colored sprinkles

Makes 64 bites

Coffee–Toffee Bonbon Bites

If your family, like mine, loves brownie ice cream sundaes, then stop right here and make this recipe. It's my version of a brownie sundae made into bite-sized squares—no spoon needed!

My family loves coffee ice cream so, for the filling, I've gussied up our favorite store-bought brand with lots of chocolate-covered toffee bits. They add a nice crunch and burst of flavor and partner nicely with the thin brownie base.

make the brownie-nut layer

1 Line a 9-inch-square baking pan (I like the straight-sided kind) with foil, leaving about a 1-inch overhang on two sides (see p. 5). Lightly grease the bottom and sides of the foil. Make room in the freezer for the pan so it's level and secure.

2 Whisk the flour, baking powder, and salt in a small bowl until well blended. Put the butter in a small saucepan and set over medium-low heat, stirring occasionally, until the butter is melted, about 2 minutes. Slide the pan from the heat and add the cocoa powder. Whisk until the mixture is smooth. Add the sugar and whisk until blended. Using your fingertip, check the temperature of the batter—it should be warm but not hot. If it's hot, set the pan aside for a minute or two before continuing with the recipe. Add the egg and vanilla and whisk until well blended. Add the flour mixture along with the nuts and stir with a rubber spatula until just blended.

3 Scrape the batter into the prepared pan and, using an offset spatula, spread evenly. Bake until a toothpick inserted in the center comes out with small bits of brownie sticking to it, 11 to 13 minutes. Move the pan to a wire rack and let cool completely.

4 Using the foil "handles," lift the brownie layer from the pan. Line the pan with a fresh piece of foil as directed in Step 1. Peel or tear away the foil from the brownie layer, then return the brownie layer to the pan with the fresh foil lining. Slide the pan into the freezer.

make the ice cream layer

1 Remove the ice cream from the freezer and let it soften at room temperature until it's just barely spreadable. Depending on your ice cream and kitchen's temperature, this can take 10 to 20 minutes. Using a large spade or large serving spoon, scoop the ice cream into a medium bowl and add the toffee bits. Using a chopping and stirring motion, work the ice cream until pliable but not melted, about 1 minute. (If at any time the ice cream starts to melt, pop it, bowl and all, into the freezer before proceeding.)

2 Set the brownie-lined pan on the counter. Working quickly, drop the ice cream in large scoopfuls over the brownie layer in the pan and, using an offset spatula, spread evenly to completely fill the pan. Evenly scatter the sprinkles over the ice cream, pressing lightly to make an even layer. Return the pan to the freezer and freeze until hard, about 3 hours or up to 3 days, before serving.

cut and serve

1 Line a small cookie sheet or plastic container with parchment or waxed paper and set it in the freezer.

2 Using the foil "handles," lift the ice cream from the pan onto a cutting board. Carefully peel or tear away the foil and toss it out. Using a ruler as a guide (or by eye) and a large knife, cut crosswise into 8 equal strips and then cut each strip into 8 pieces and arrange them on the small cookie sheet in the freezer. Keep the bites frozen until ready to serve, or stow in a covered container for up to 2 weeks.

twists

- Skip the nuts in the brownie layer.

- Instead of using toffee pieces in the ice cream, use the same amount of finely chopped bittersweet chocolate, mini chocolate chips, finely chopped toasted nuts, or sweetened shredded coconut, toasted.

- Instead of using sprinkles, use the same amount of toasted chopped hazelnuts, pistachios, pecans, or walnuts; or crushed peppermint candies; or chopped toffee pieces; or peanut butter chips.

- Instead of using coffee ice cream, use any flavor you like or use the Classic Chocolate Ice Cream (see p. 168) or the Tangy Vanilla Ice Cream (see p. 160).

FOR THE NUTELLA BITES

1½ cups plain yogurt (I like Greek style)

1 cup Nutella

FOR THE GLAZE

6 ounces bittersweet chocolate, chopped

4 teaspoons vegetable or canola oil

½ cup colored sprinkles

Makes 24 bites

twists

- **MAKE 'EM FINGER FOOD:** The bites can be made without the picks and eaten with your fingers.

- **INSTEAD OF MAKING INTO "BITES":** Before making the bite mixture, arrange a loaf pan in the freezer. Scrape the yogurt-Nutella mixture into the pan and freeze until firm enough to scoop, about 1 hour. Serve in Waffle Cones (p. 166) or between large soft chocolate or vanilla cookies.

- **INSTEAD OF DIPPING INTO THE BITTERSWEET GLAZE:** Use a half recipe of the white chocolate glaze from the Dulce de Leche Cake Bites (p. 98).

- **INSTEAD OF DIPPING INTO THE SPRINKLES:** Use the same amount of toasted chopped hazelnuts, pistachios, or walnuts.

Frozen Nutella Yogurt Bites

Long before my recipe for Nutella Brownie Bites from *Desserts 4 Today* went viral, I was a huge fan of this creamy chocolate-hazelnut spread. Its flavor is so bold that it needs very little additional ingredients to turn it into a knockout dessert. These little frozen bites are perfectly delicious even without the chocolate and sprinkles, but adding those really dresses them up.

make the bites

1 Lightly grease two plastic ice cube trays (12 cube spots per tray). Make room in the freezer for the trays so they are level and secure. Have ready short, heavy-duty wooden toothpicks.

2 Put the yogurt and Nutella in a medium bowl and whisk until well blended and smooth. Spoon into the prepared trays—they'll be about two-thirds full. Don't be tempted to fill them more or the frozen bite will be too big and cumbersome to eat. Tap the trays gently on the counter to settle the mixture, then slide the trays into the freezer. Freeze until the cubes are almost frozen, about 3 hours. Working in the freezer, carefully place a short wooden pick in the center of each cube, pushing it about three-quarters down into the mixture. If the pick wobbles, let the cubes freeze a bit longer and then try again.

3 Freeze until the bites are very hard, about 6 hours or up to 2 weeks. The bites can be served as is or dipped and sprinkled.

make the glaze and dip

1 Line a small cookie sheet with parchment or waxed paper and set it in the freezer. Melt the chocolate and oil in a small deep bowl in the microwave or over a pot of simmering water, stirring with a rubber spatula until smooth. Remove from the heat, set on a heatproof surface, and let cool slightly. Put the sprinkles in a small bowl.

2 Working with one Nutella bite at a time (keep the rest in the freezer), holding the bite by the pick, dip into the chocolate enough to come half to three-quarters of the way up the bite. Carefully drag the bottom of the bite across the bowl's edge so that the excess chocolate drips off and back into the bowl. Dip the bottom into the sprinkles and arrange the bite on the prepared cookie sheet in the freezer. Repeat with the remaining bites.

3 Freeze the chocolate-covered bites until the chocolate is set, about 1 hour. Serve immediately or arrange in a plastic container in layers separated with waxed paper or parchment. Stow in the freezer for up to 2 weeks.

Frozen Blueberry–Grape Bites

Every summer, I make an effort to freeze as many fresh berries as possible to have when the winter doldrums hit. This way, I can reach into the freezer and retrieve a hint of summer sunshine at a moment's notice. To make things easy, I wash, dry, and freeze berries in labeled 12-ounce containers so they're ready to go, but you can use store-bought frozen fruit as well.

These easy-to-prepare, healthy snacks are great to have at the ready for when my family needs a treat. Perfect on a hot summer day or when your kids are looking for an after-school treat, these mini-pop bites will bring a smile to every face. This recipe also makes delicious frozen pops.

1 Lightly grease two plastic ice cube trays (12 cube spots per tray). Make room in the freezer for the trays so they are level and secure. Have ready short, heavy-duty wooden toothpicks.

2 Put the frozen blueberries and sugar in a food processor and whiz until the berries are broken up, about 20 seconds. Add the grape juice and salt and whiz until blended and smooth (some tiny chunks of blueberries are good). Spoon into the prepared trays so each cup is about two-thirds full. Don't be tempted to fill them more, as the frozen bite will be too big and cumbersome to eat. Tap the trays gently on the counter to settle the mixture and slide them into the freezer. Freeze until the cubes are almost frozen, about 3 hours. Working in the freezer, carefully place a short wooden pick in the center of each cube about three-quarters of the way. If the pick wobbles, let the cubes freeze a bit longer and then try again.

3 Freeze until the cubes are very hard, about 6 hours or up to 2 weeks. Serve immediately or arrange in a plastic container with layers separated with waxed paper or parchment. Stow in the freezer for up to 2 weeks.

12 ounces frozen blueberries

⅓ cup (2⅜ ounces) granulated sugar

¾ cup white grape juice (preferably organic)

Pinch of table salt

Makes 24 bites

twists

INSTEAD OF BLUEBERRIES: Use the same amount of frozen pitted cherries or strawberries.

MAKE 'EM FINGER FOOD: The bites can be made without the picks and eaten with your fingers.

INSTEAD OF MAKING INTO "BITES": Before making the bite mixture, arrange a loaf pan in the freezer. Spoon the mixture into the pan and freeze until firm enough to scoop about 1 hour. Serve in Waffle Cones (see p. 166) or between large soft vanilla cookies.

·6·
Candies

....

GOOEY, CRISPY & CREAMY
CONFECTIONS

- **8** ounces bittersweet chocolate (70% cacao), chopped
- **1** cup coconut milk
- **2** tablespoons pure coconut oil
- **1½** cups unsweetened (desiccated, see p. 16) coconut, toasted

Makes 28 truffles

twists

- Instead of the 70% bittersweet chocolate, use the same amount of 62% bittersweet chocolate.
- Instead of the unsweetened coconut, substitute 1½ cups finely chopped toasted nuts.

KITCHEN WISDOM ☙☙
coconut oil

If you're unfamiliar with coconut oil, the first thing you should know is that unlike other oils, this is not liquid but a solid, scoopable ingredient. I buy it in a small tub at my grocery store in the health-food section, but any health-food store will carry it.

Bittersweet Chocolate–Coconut Truffles "Paleo"

These truffles were inspired by a conversation I had with my talented and lovely occupational therapist, Cory, who, while working my shoulder into submission, was telling me about the "paleo" diet she follows. Explaining that it's also called the "hunter-gatherer diet," she said that she only eats protein, nuts, and greens. My first reaction was "What! No dessert?" Cory explained that she indulges in this one very bittersweet chocolate-coconut confection that uses 70% bittersweet chocolate, contains no added sugar, and is made with only *four* ingredients. I've adapted Cory's recipe slightly, but they still are "paleo" friendly.

As an added bonus, these truffles are made with only coconut milk and oil—not a drop of dairy!

1 Put the chocolate, coconut milk, and coconut oil in a medium heatproof bowl and melt in the microwave or over simmering water. Remove from the heat and whisk until well blended and smooth. Set aside, stirring occasionally, until thick enough to scoop, about 2 hours. For faster cooling, set the bowl over a larger bowl filled with ice and a little water, stirring frequently and scraping the sides with a rubber spatula.

2 Line a cookie sheet with parchment or a nonstick liner or line a large flat plate with waxed paper or plastic wrap and make room in the refrigerator so the sheet will be level. (I arrange dairy containers that are the same height so that the sheet will sit on top.) Put the toasted coconut on a plate or in a shallow bowl. Using a 1-tablespoon mini scoop, shape the mixture into balls and roll in the toasted coconut, pressing gently to help it stick. Arrange close together on the prepared cookie sheet or plate and refrigerate until very cold and firm, about 4 hours, or arrange in a plastic container with layers separated with waxed paper or parchment. Stow in the refrigerator for up to 5 days. Serve slightly chilled.

Protein Bar Bark

I have yet to discover a store-bought protein bar that really hits the spot. To fill this void, I've adapted one of my bark recipes into a delicious snack that's also a great source of energy. I keep a batch of this bark in the refrigerator for whenever I need a quick charge up or for when I'm just looking for something sweet and salty to nibble on.

Either way, this is one of the fastest and easiest treats I make, and it's amazingly versatile. With dark chocolate as a base, the topping possibilities are endless. Chocolate and dried fruit are delicious companions and are also power boosters, especially when paired with a sprinkling of nuts, like pepitas or smoked almonds. Now, *that's* my kind of power bar.

1 Line a large cookie sheet with a nonstick liner and make room in the refrigerator.

2 Put the chocolate in a medium heatproof bowl and melt in the microwave or over simmering water. Remove from the heat and set aside to cool until it's no longer hot, about 5 minutes. Add the apricots and pretzels and stir until evenly coated. Scrape onto the center of the liner. Using an offset spatula, spread the chocolate mixture into a ½-inch-thick layer. Evenly scatter the pepitas over the bark, pressing gently into the chocolate.

3 Scrape the milk chocolate into one corner of a zip-top plastic bag, push out the air, and press the chocolate into the corner. Seal the bag and snip off a small piece of the corner. Pipe the chocolate in a zigzag pattern over the top of the bark. (There's no need for perfection here.) Sprinkle the fleur de sel evenly over the top.

4 Slide the cookie sheet into the refrigerator and chill until firm, about 20 minutes, or for up to 2 days. Cut or break into jagged pieces and serve cold.

8   ounces bittersweet chocolate, chopped

⅔ cup (6 ounces) chopped dried apricots, lightly packed

⅔ cup (1 ounce) coarsely chopped lightly salted pretzels

¼ cup (1¼ ounces) lightly salted pepitas

2   ounces milk chocolate, melted

Fleur de sel, for garnish

Serves 6

twists

- Instead of the apricots, pretzels, and pepitas, use up to 1⅔ cups of a combination of two or three of the following: dried dates, chopped; dried sweet cherries, chopped; shredded, sweetened coconut, toasted; chopped nuts, toasted (hazelnuts, pecans, pistachios, walnuts, or macadamias); smoked almonds; lightly salted peanuts; malted milk balls, coarsely chopped.

- Instead of the milk chocolate, use 2 ounces white chocolate.

8   ounces white chocolate
    (not chips), melted

2   ounces bittersweet chocolate,
    melted

¼   cup (2 ounces) peppermint candy
    chips (I like Kencraft® brand)

Pinch of fleur de sel

Serves 8 to 10

twists

- Instead of the 8 ounces white chocolate, use 8 ounces bittersweet chocolate.

- Instead of the 2 ounces bittersweet chocolate, use 2 ounces white chocolate.

- Instead of the peppermint candy chips, use one of the following or up to ⅔ cup of a combination: ½ up crushed toffee pieces or ½ cup chopped peanut butter chips.

White Chocolate Peppermint Bark

One of my closest childhood friends was Harriet "Hasty" Mays. Her house always seemed way cooler than mine. The Mays were (and still are) a very glamorous group, and their house exuded chic in every way—even when it came to food. For starters, they had a crisper, so no soggy crackers for that family! But the treat I remember most fondly was the stash of After Eight® mints they kept in an upper cabinet in the kitchen. Me being me, I freely dipped my hand into said stash and always reveled in the soft, melting texture and the subtle mint and chocolate flavor. The balance was just perfect. This chocolate confection is my ode to those lovely grown-up mints, though these taste even better than the originals.

1   Line a large cookie sheet with a nonstick liner and make room in the refrigerator.

2   Pour the melted white chocolate onto the center of the liner. Using an offset spatula, spread the chocolate evenly into a 12x10-inch rectangle (the chocolate will be about 3/16 inch thick).

3   Scrape the bittersweet chocolate into one corner of a zip-top plastic bag, push out the air, and press the chocolate into the corner. Seal the bag and snip off a small piece of the corner. Pipe the chocolate in a zigzag pattern over the top of the white chocolate (there's no need for perfection here). Sprinkle the peppermint candies over the top, pressing them gently into the chocolate.

4   Sprinkle the fleur de sel over the top. Slide the sheet into the refrigerator and chill until firm, about 20 minutes, or for up to 2 days. Cut or break into jagged pieces and serve cold.

> **KITCHEN WISDOM** ⌇ **making homemade candy chips**
>
> I like using prechopped candy "chips" because they're the perfect size for baking—and nibbling—but you can make your own chips, too. Put unwrapped peppermint hard candies in a heavy-duty zip-top bag, press out the air, and seal the bag. Using a mallet or a rolling pin, pound the candies until they are crushed. Set a strainer over a small bowl and pour in the crushed candies. Gently shake the strainer until the finely crushed candy is in the small bowl and only the pieces remain. Use the pieces for this bark and save the powdery remains in a airtight container to stir into hot chocolate or sprinkle over ice cream.

Fruit Leather

In southern New England, where I live, we wait all year for those precious few months of summer produce and then—bam!—one fruit is abundant and then quickly disappears just before the next fruit hits. Regardless of where you live, though, capturing and savoring fruit is top of mind during produce season. I recommend you add this fruit leather to your list.

Any fruit can be transformed into rolled-up goodness so experiment with whatever your CSA (community-supported agriculture) or local market has to offer. For even cooking/drying, it's important to spread the fruit purée as evenly as possible; don't obsess about this—you'll get a bit better with every batch. Speaking of batches, you can double, triple, or quadruple this recipe; just make sure you use a separate cookie sheet and liner for each batch. The sheets can all bake/dry at the same time; simply rotate the pans' position in the oven several times throughout baking.

1 Put the fruit in a food processor (a blender also works) and whiz until it's completely smooth, 1 to 2 minutes. Pour the fruit purée into a medium saucepan, stir in the lemon juice, and bring to a boil over medium-high heat, stirring occasionally. Reduce the heat to low and cook, stirring often, until it's very thick and reduced to $2/3$ cup, 20 to 26 minutes. Slide the pan from the heat, add the agave or honey to taste and the salt, and stir until well blended.

2 Position an oven rack in the center of the oven and heat the oven to 175°F. Line a cookie sheet with a nonstick liner. Scrape the purée onto the center of the sheet and, using a small offset spatula, spread evenly into an 8x12-inch rectangle (it will be about $1/8$ inch thick).

3 Bake until the purée looks dry and is tacky but not sticky when you touch it with your fingertips, 2 to $2\frac{1}{2}$ hours. Turn off the oven and let the fruit leather cool in the oven (it will continue to dry out). After 2 hours, test the leather. It should feel mostly dry and peel easily from the liner. If not, then leave it in the oven for a few more hours or even overnight.

4 Cut a piece of parchment into an 8x13-inch rectangle. Arrange on top of the dried leather, leaving about a 1-inch overhang on one long side, and press gently to smooth out any wrinkles in the leather. Invert the nonstick liner so the parchment is on the bottom and carefully peel away the liner. Fold the overhang on top of the leather and, beginning with one long side, roll the leather and parchment together into a tight roll, jelly roll style. Using a sharp knife, cut the leather into 1-inch pieces and stow in a zip-top plastic bag at room temperature for up to 3 weeks.

1 pound fresh strawberries, hulled and halved

1 teaspoon freshly squeezed lemon juice

2 to 3 tablespoons agave nectar or honey

Pinch of table salt

Makes twelve 1-inch-wide strips

twists
Instead of the strawberries, use 1 pound of peaches or apricots, pitted and quartered, or blueberries or raspberries.

Spread the purée into an even layer about $1/8$ inch thick.

4½ cups freshly popped popcorn (store-bought or homemade; see the recipe on the facing page)

½ teaspoon baking soda

¼ teaspoon table salt

¼ teaspoon ground cayenne

½ cup (3½ ounces) firmly packed light brown sugar

½ cup (3½ ounces) granulated sugar

6 tablespoons (3 ounces) unsalted butter, cut into 6 pieces, softened

¼ cup water

3 tablespoons light corn syrup

1½ teaspoons pure vanilla extract

Makes about 12 ounces

finishing touches

Sprinkle the freshly made caramel popcorn with ⅛ to ¼ teaspoon fleur de sel.

twists

- **MAKE IT NUTTY:** Add ⅔ cup lightly salted nuts to the popcorn and mix well before pouring the caramel over the top (peanuts are traditional, but slivered almonds or chopped macadamia nuts are also delicious).

- Instead of the cayenne, use ¼ teaspoon curry powder (on the sweet side), or ¼ teaspoon chipotle chile powder, or ¼ teaspoon ground cinnamon.

do ahead

The popcorn will keep in an airtight container for up to 3 days.

Spicy Buttery Caramel Popcorn

My friends Polly and Stuart Tilghman are amazing cooks. They have a passion for the craft of cooking, and they savor the nuance and balance of the meals they make for family and friends. They share my belief that outstanding food doesn't have to be complicated, which leads me to my love of their popcorn. You might be thinking that popcorn is just popcorn, but in this case, the Tilghmans' popcorn has reached an artisanal level of excellence. It's perfectly balanced and sublime to eat unadorned (which I do any chance I get), and it's even better when coated with this luscious, spicy caramel. Thanks to Polly and Stuart for sharing their recipe here.

1 Line a cookie sheet with a nonstick liner (parchment won't work for this recipe). Grease the bottom of a wide, offset metal spatula. Put the popcorn in a large bowl. Put the baking soda, salt, and cayenne in a small ramekin and stir until blended.

2 Put the brown sugar, granulated sugar, butter, water, and corn syrup in a medium heavy saucepan. Cook, stirring, over low heat until the sugar dissolves. Increase the heat to high and bring to a boil. Boil, without stirring, until the sugar is about 280°F, about 5 minutes. (Note: Unlike traditional caramel, this is already on the dark side so you'll need to use a candy thermometer.)

3 Slide the pan from the heat and add the vanilla and baking soda-cayenne-salt mixture. Using a heatproof spatula, stir until just blended and the caramel is foamy. Pour the caramel over the popcorn and stir until the caramel evenly covers the popcorn. Carefully pour the mixture onto the prepared baking sheet and, using the metal spatula, spread into an even layer.

4 Set aside at room temperature until completely cool, about 1 hour. Break or cut into small pieces and serve.

homemade popcorn

Many of the large health-food super stores like Whole Foods sell freshly popped, unsalted or buttered popcorn. It's always fresh and is perfect for this recipe. If you don't have access to one of these shops, use organic, unflavored microwave popcorn for this recipe. If you'd like to make your own, here's the Tilghmans' recipe.

Heat the oil and salt in a 6-quart heavy-duty pot over medium-high heat. Add 1 or 2 kernels and cover the pan tightly. When the kernels pop, add the remaining kernels and cover with the lid. Gently shake the pot, sliding over the burner, until the popping slows to a few seconds between pops. This should take about 6 to 9 minutes. Move the pan from the heat, dump the popcorn onto a large baking sheet and pick out any burnt or unpopped kernels.

2 tablespoons oil (I like olive oil but canola or vegetable is good, too)

¼ teaspoon table salt

⅓ cup (2½ ounces) organic corn kernels

Makes about 5 cups

4½ cups freshly popped popcorn

6 ounces white chocolate, chopped

1 cup (6 ounces) dried cherries

¼ teaspoon finely crushed fleur de sel

Makes about 8 cups of clusters

finishing touches

Put 2 ounces chopped bittersweet chocolate in a small heatproof bowl. Melt over simmering water or in a microwave. Scrape the melted chocolate into one corner of a heavy-duty zip-top bag, press out the air, and seal. Snip off a small piece of the corner and drizzle the chocolate casually over the popcorn. Set aside until both chocolates firm up.

twists

• **MAKE YOUR OWN POPCORN:** See Homemade Popcorn on p. 191.

• Instead of the white chocolate, use the same amount of bittersweet chocolate or milk chocolate.

• Instead of the cherries, use the same amount of one of the following or a combination: chopped dried apricots, dried cranberries, chopped dried apples, chopped pretzels, chopped crystallized ginger.

• **MAKE IT NUTTY:** Sprinkle ½ cup lightly salted cashews or peanuts over the popcorn along with the cherries.

White Chocolate– Cherry Popcorn

When I was testing the Tilghmans' recipe for popcorn (see p. 190), I ended up with a ton of extra popcorn and, as I never like anything to go to waste, I came up with this quick and easy popcorn "bark." Coating the freshly popped kernels and sweet-tart dried cherries with white chocolate and a sprinkle of salt creates clusters of sweet and salty deliciousness that your family and friends will love.

1 Line a cookie sheet with a nonstick liner or parchment. Put the popcorn in a large bowl.

2 Put the white chocolate in a medium heatproof bowl and melt in the microwave or over simmering water. Remove from the heat and whisk until well blended and smooth.

3 Pour the white chocolate over the popcorn. Using a heatproof spatula, stir until just blended and the white chocolate evenly but lightly covers the popcorn. Add the cherries and stir until they're lightly coated with the chocolate. Scrape the mixture onto the prepared cookie sheet and, using a plastic spatula, spread into an even layer. Sprinkle with the fleur de sel.

4 Slide the sheet into the refrigerator and chill until the chocolate is firm, about 1 hour. Break into small pieces (some popcorn kernels will break off) and stow in an airtight container for up to 3 days.

4 jars (3½ ounces each) colored sugars

1¼ cups water, divided

3 packages (¼ ounce each) unflavored powdered gelatin

1 large vanilla bean, seeds scraped, or 1½ teaspoons pure vanilla bean paste

   Pinch of table salt

2 cups (14 ounces) granulated sugar

½ cup light corn syrup

About 96 mini chocolate chips or mini M&M's®

Makes forty-eight 3-inch marshmallows

Gluten Free/Egg Free
Homemade Marshmallow Chicks

I've been making marshmallows for years. The taste and texture (to say nothing about the all-natural ingredients) are so much better than the store-bought variety that it would be a shame not to make them from scratch. I used to make them with gelatin and egg whites, but it was a cumbersome and awkward procedure so I began making the non-egg white version given here. It's much easier to work with, and the process flows smoothly.

A note to perfectionists: Not every homemade chick will be perfect, nor will they all look the same. Once they are coated with sugar and the little eyes are in place, they will look adorable.

1 Line two cookie sheets with nonstick liners and lightly grease. Put the colored sugars in separate shallow bowls.

2 Pour ¾ cup of the water into bowl of a heavy-duty mixer fitted with whisk attachment and sprinkle the gelatin over the water. Let sit until the gelatin is moist and plump, about 5 minutes. Add the vanilla bean seeds and salt. (They'll stay on top of the gelatin for now.)

3 Put the remaining ½ cup water, the sugar, and corn syrup in a medium heavy saucepan. Cook, stirring, over low heat until the sugar dissolves. Set a candy thermometer in the pan and increase the heat to high and bring to a boil. Boil, without stirring, until the hot syrup is 258°F.

4 With the mixer on medium-low speed, slowly pour the hot syrup into the gelatin mixture in a thin stream down the side of the bowl (avoid pouring syrup onto the whisk, as it will splash against the sides of the bowl). Gradually increase the speed to medium-high and beat until the mixture is very thick, about 10 minutes. The outside of the bowl will still feel quite warm. It's important to work with the marshmallow while it's still warm—it's difficult to pipe when it's cold and stiff.

5 Fit a large round tip ½- or ⅔-inch (I use an Ateco #5 or #7) into a pastry bag and fill the bag with some of the marshmallow (see the sidebar on p. 194). Pipe the marshmallow into 3-inch-long by 1-inch-wide logs, spacing them about 1 inch apart on the prepared cookie sheets. As you reach the end of a log, keep pressure on the bag and in one continuous motion, lift the pastry tip up and pipe more marshmallow on top of the log going back about 1 inch. Release any pressure on the pastry bag and pull the tip up and out to form a beak. Reload the pastry bag with marshmallow as needed.

recipe continues

Pipe marshmallow and lift from the log in one continuous motion.

Pat the sugar onto the marshmallow shape so that it sticks.

6 Sprinkle each shape with colored sugar, using your fingers to pat the sugar onto the marshmallow to cover almost completely, then set the cookie sheets aside until the shapes are completely cool but still tacky, about 1 hour. Using your fingers and working with one marshmallow at a time, lift the marshmallows from the sheets and roll in the bowl of colored sugars, pressing the shapes into the sugar lightly to cover completely. Return the shapes to the same sheets. Dab a bit of the remaining marshmallow from the bowl onto the flat side of the mini chocolate chips and press onto the shapes to form "eyes." Set the sheets aside until the marshmallows are completely cool and no longer tacky, about 2 hours. Stow in an airtight container for up to 1 week.

twists

- **MAKE THEM LEMON OR ORANGE FLAVORED:** Add 2 teaspoons finely grated lemon zest or 1 tablespoon finely grated orange zest along with the vanilla bean seeds and salt in Step 2.

- **MAKE TRADITIONAL MARSHMALLOWS:** Sift together 1/2 cup cornstarch and 2/3 cup confectioners' sugar. Lightly grease a 9x13-inch baking dish and dust the bottom with about one-third of the cornstarch-confectioners' sugar mixture.

Follow the recipe through Step 4. Scrape the cooked marshmallow mixture into the pan and, using a large offset spatula, spread evenly. Set aside, uncovered, and at room temperature until the marshmallow is completely cool and firm to the touch, about 4 hours.

Run a sharp knife between the marshmallow and the sides of the pan. Dust the top of the marshmallow with some of the cornstarch-confectioners' sugar mixture. Put a large cutting board on top of the pan and invert the pan onto the cutting board. Lift off the pan.

Using a lightly greased, sharp knife, trim the edges of the marshmallow, then cut into even strips about 1 to 1 1/2 inches wide and then into squares. Toss the marshmallows, in batches, in the remaining cornstarch-confectioners' sugar mixture until coated. The marshmallows will keep in an airtight container at cool room temperature for 1 week.

- ⅔ cup (2⅝ ounces) confectioners' sugar
- ½ cup (2 ounces) cornstarch
- ¾ cup water
- 3 packages (¼ ounce each) unflavored powdered gelatin
- Pinch of table salt
- 2 cups pure maple syrup (grade B)
- ⅔ cup (2⅝ ounces) finely chopped walnuts, toasted
- 1 teaspoon pure vanilla extract

Makes 60 marshmallows

twists
Skip the nuts or, instead of the nuts, add in ⅓ cup finely crushed cocoa nibs.

Gluten Free/Egg Free

Toasted Walnut Maple Marshmallows

I am fond of concentrating flavors to maximize their boldness, and the maple flavor in these marshmallows is testament. Boiling the maple syrup not only intensifies the flavor, but by bringing it up to 248°F, we can make marshmallows with it. How much fun is that?

Serve these marshmallows on their own or drop a few into your next mug of hot bittersweet or white chocolate and you'll be a believer.

1 Put the confectioners' sugar and cornstarch in a small bowl and whisk until blended. Lightly grease a 9x13-inch baking pan (I use a straight-sided type for nice, straight-sided marshmallows) and sift about one-third of the sugar-cornstarch mixture evenly over the bottom of the pan.

2 Pour the water into bowl of heavy-duty mixer fitted with whisk attachment and sprinkle the gelatin over the top. Let it sit until the gelatin is moist and plump, about 5 minutes. Add the salt. (The granules will stay on top of the gelatin for now.)

3 Put the maple syrup in a large heavy saucepan. Set a candy thermometer (see p. 207) in the pan and cook, without stirring, over medium heat until boiling. Boil, without stirring, until the syrup reaches 248°F. Keep an eye on the pot as the syrup bubbles up high and reduce the heat slightly if the syrup gets too close to bubbling over.

4 With the mixer on medium-low speed, slowly and carefully pour the hot syrup into the gelatin mixture in a thin stream down side of bowl (avoid pouring the syrup onto the whisk, as it will splash against the sides of the bowl). In the beginning, the syrup will be thick and drop in clumps but it will smooth out toward the middle of pouring. Gradually increase the speed to medium high and beat until the mixture is very thick and light in color, about 10 minutes. The outside of the bowl will still feel quite warm. Add the walnuts and vanilla and beat until blended, about 1 minute. It's important to work with the marshmallow while it's still warm—the colder it gets, the stiffer and more difficult it is to spread.

5 Scrape the cooked marshmallow mixture into the pan and, using an large offset spatula, spread evenly. Set aside, uncovered and at room temperature, until completely cool, firm to the touch, and no longer tacky, about 4 hours.

6 Using your fingers, peel the marshmallow away from the edges of the pan. The marshmallow will fall back to the edge but it will no longer be stuck. Sift about half of the remaining sugar-cornstarch mixture over the top of the marshmallow and sift the remaining mixture into a medium bowl. Put a large cutting board on top of the pan and invert the pan onto the cutting board. Lift off the pan, using your fingers to help peel the marshmallow away from the pan, if necessary.

7 Using a lightly greased, sharp knife, trim the edges of the marshmallow, if necessary; cut the marshmallow lengthwise into 6 equal strips and then cut each strip into 10 pieces. Toss the marshmallows, in batches, in the remaining cornstarch-sugar mixture until lightly but thoroughly coated. The marshmallows will keep in an airtight container at room temperature for up to 1 month.

8   tablespoons (4 ounces) unsalted
    butter, cut into 6 pieces
    + 2 tablespoons, softened, for
    greasing the foil

1½ cups (10½ ounces) granulated
    sugar

⅓   cup Lyle's Golden Syrup

¼   cup water

1½ cups heavy cream, at room
    temperature, divided

¼   cup bourbon

½   teaspoon table salt

Makes about 81 pieces

finishing touches
Just before wrapping the caramels,
sprinkle evenly with crushed fleur
de sel.

twists
• Use 1½ teaspoons pure vanilla
  extract instead of the bourbon.
• **MAKE IT NUTTY:** Scatter 1 cup
  (4 ounces) toasted slivered
  almonds evenly in the prepared
  baking pan and pour the caramel
  on top, being careful not to jostle
  the nuts.

do ahead
Stow in an airtight container
at room temperature for up to
1 month.

Buttery Bourbon Caramels

The flavor of these caramels is quite sophisticated. While they contain a good splash of booze, the bourbon really doesn't stand out. In fact, the butter softens the bourbon's heat and, with the addition of cream, the flavors mellow into a silky-textured caramel. This is one of my favorites, for sure.

It's important to keep a close eye on the temperature for these caramels—a couple of degrees higher than what's called for and the caramel overcooks and goes from soft and tender to hard. Be sure to avoid pouring any darker-colored caramel into the baking dish as well.

1 Line the bottom and sides of an 8-inch-square baking pan (I like the straight-sided kind) with foil, leaving about a 1-inch overhang on two sides (see p. 5). Generously grease the bottom and sides of the foil with the 2 tablespoons softened butter (cooking spray works as well, but the butter tastes so good).

2 Put the sugar, Lyle's Golden Syrup, water, and ½ cup of the cream in a large heavy saucepan. Cook, stirring, over low heat until the sugar dissolves. Cover the pan and increase the heat to medium. Cook, covered, for 2 minutes (this helps dissolve any pesky sugar crystals stuck on the sides). Uncover the pot, attach a candy thermometer, and boil without stirring until the mixture reaches 236°F, 3 to 5 minutes. Swirl the pan over the heat until the caramel is an even deep amber, about another 3 minutes. Carefully slide the pan from the heat and slowly add the remaining heavy cream, the remaining butter, the bourbon, and the salt. (Careful—the steam is hot.) Using a clean heatproof spatula, stir (avoiding the sides) until well blended.

3 Return the saucepan to medium-high heat, attach a candy thermometer, and bring the mixture to a boil. Boil, without stirring, until the caramel is 248°F, about 5 minutes. Pour the caramel into the prepared baking pan without scraping the bottom or sides of the saucepan and leaving behind any darker caramel. It's going to be very tempting to not leave any deliciousness behind in the saucepan, but resist because the mixture on the sides can cause your finished caramel to be grainy and hard. Set aside to cool completely. Depending on your kitchen temperature, this will take 3 to 4 hours or overnight.

4 To cut and serve, use the foil "handles" to lift the caramel from the pan. Carefully peel or tear away the foil and toss it out; put the caramel on a cutting board. If the caramel is sticking to the cutting board, spray the board with a little baking spray. Using a ruler as a guide (or by eye) and a long, sharp knife, cut crosswise into 9 equal strips and then cut each strip into 9 pieces. Serve immediately or wrap in small pieces of waxed paper or cellophane (2¾-inch squares are the perfect size).

Soft Honey–Orange Cream Caramels

This caramel has its own unique character. The honey makes the texture tender-soft and, when paired with some orange zest, the flavor is really bright and sunny. This is a special confection that is super easy to make.

1 Line the bottom and sides of an 8-inch-square baking pan (I like the straight-sided kind) with foil, leaving about a 1-inch overhang on two sides (see p. 5). Generously grease the bottom and sides of the foil with the 2 tablespoons softened butter (cooking spray works as well, but the butter tastes so good).

2 Put the sugar, honey, heavy cream, butter, orange zest, salt, and vanilla in a large heavy saucepan. Cook, stirring, over low heat until the sugar dissolves. Cover the pan and increase the heat to medium. Cook, covered, for 2 minutes (this helps dissolve any pesky sugar crystals stuck on the sides). Uncover the pot, attach a candy thermometer (see p. 207), and boil without stirring until the mixture reaches 242°F, 4 to 7 minutes. Continue cooking the caramel until it reaches 248°F, carefully swirling the caramel in the pot over the heat to even out the color.

3 Pour the caramel into the prepared baking pan without scraping the bottom or sides of the saucepan. It's going to be tempting to not leave any deliciousness behind in the pan, but the mixture on the sides can cause your finished caramel to be grainy and hard. Put the baking dish on a wire rack and set aside, without stirring or jostling the pan, until completely cool. Depending on your kitchen temperature, this will take 3 to 4 hours or overnight.

4 To cut and serve, use the foil "handles" to lift the caramel from the pan. Carefully peel or tear away the foil and toss it out; put the caramel on a cutting board. If the caramel is sticking to the cutting board, spray the board with a little oil. Using a ruler as a guide (or by eye) and a long, sharp knife, cut crosswise into 9 equal strips and then cut each strip into 9 pieces. Serve immediately or wrap in small pieces of waxed paper or cellophane (2¾-inch squares are the perfect size).

8 tablespoons (4 ounces) unsalted butter, cut into 6 pieces, softened + 2 tablespoons, softened, for greasing the foil

1½ cups (10½ ounces) granulated sugar

½ cup honey

1½ cups heavy cream, at room temperature

1 tablespoon finely grated orange zest

½ teaspoon table salt

1 teaspoon pure vanilla extract

Makes about 81 pieces

finishing touches
Just before wrapping the caramels, sprinkle evenly with crushed fleur de sel.

twists
- Leave out the orange zest.
- Instead of the orange zest, use the same amount of finely grated fresh ginger.
- **MAKE IT NUTTY:** Scatter ⅔ cup (3⅜ ounces), toasted, chopped, lightly salted macadamias evenly in the prepared pan and carefully pour the caramel on top, being careful not to jostle the nuts.

do ahead
Stow in an airtight container at room temperature for up to 1 month.

12 tablespoons (6 ounces) unsalted butter, cut into 6 pieces + 2 tablespoons, softened, for greasing the foil

1⅓ cups (9¼ ounces) firmly packed dark brown sugar

¾ cup heavy cream

½ cup Lyle's Golden Syrup

1½ cups puffed rice cereal

1½ teaspoons pure vanilla extract

¼ teaspoon table salt

FOR THE CHOCOLATE GANACHE

8 ounces bittersweet chocolate, chopped

1 tablespoon vegetable oil

Makes 48 pieces

twists

- **MAKE STRAIGHT-UP BUTTERSCOTCH CARAMELS:** Omit the puffed rice cereal and the chocolate ganache and sprinkle the top of the still-warm caramel with finely crushed fleur de sel, if you like.

- **MAKE ORANGE-FLAVORED BUTTERSCOTCH CARAMELS:** Reduce the vanilla to ¾ teaspoon and add 1 teaspoon pure orange extract.

do ahead

Stow in an airtight container at room temperature for up to 1 month.

Cut strips of caramels with a greased sharp knife.

Chocolate-Covered Crispy Butterscotch Caramels

This is the easiest, most melt-in-your-mouth butterscotch caramel that you will ever make. It has a rich buttery flavor, supple texture, and a touch of crunch and is as easy as piling the ingredients into a large saucepan and cooking until a candy thermometer registers 250°F. All that's needed is a little puffed rice cereal and a decadent chocolate topping.

make the caramel-puffed rice layer

1 Line an 8-inch-square baking pan (I like the straight-sided kind) with foil, leaving about a 1-inch overhang on two sides (see p. 5). Generously grease the bottom and sides of the foil with the 2 tablespoons of softened butter (cooking spray works, too).

2 Put the remaining butter, brown sugar, heavy cream, and golden syrup in a large heavy saucepan. Cook, without stirring, over low heat until the butter is melted, about 5 minutes. Increase the heat to medium high and bring to a boil. Boil, without stirring, until a candy thermometer registers 250°F, about 5 minutes.

3 Slide the pan from the heat and add the puffed rice, vanilla, and salt. Be careful— the mixture will bubble up, and the steam is super hot. Using a heatproof spatula, stir, without scraping the bottom and sides (see Kitchen Wisdom on p. 208), until blended. Pour the crispy caramel, without scraping the bottom or sides of the saucepan, into the prepared baking pan. Set aside to cool until warm to the touch, about 45 minutes.

make the ganache

Melt the chocolate and oil in a small heatproof bowl (I use the microwave, but an improvised double boiler works just fine). Whisk until well blended and smooth. Pour over the still-warm caramel. Using an offset spatula, spread the ganache evenly. Set aside to cool completely, about 4 hours.

finish the caramel

1 Use the foil "handles" to lift the entire caramel from the pan. Carefully peel or tear away the foil and discard; set the caramel, chocolate side up, on a cutting board.

2 Grease the blade of a long, sharp knife with butter or cooking spray and, using a ruler as a guide (or by eye), cut crosswise into 8 equal strips and then cut each strip into 6 pieces. Serve immediately or wrap in small pieces of waxed paper or cellophane (2¾-inch squares are the perfect size). Serve in mini cupcake wrappers, if you like.

2 tablespoons (1 ounce) unsalted
   butter, softened, cut into
   2 pieces + 2 tablespoons,
   softened, for greasing the foil

1¼ cups (8¾ ounces) granulated
   sugar

1¼ cups heavy cream

⅓ cup Lyle's Golden Syrup

4 ounces unsweetened chocolate,
   chopped

1 teaspoon pure vanilla extract

½ teaspoon table salt

Makes about 81 pieces

finishing touches
Just before wrapping the caramels,
sprinkle evenly with crushed fleur
de sel.

twists
• Use 2 tablespoons bourbon
  instead of the vanilla extract.
• **MAKE IT NUTTY:** Scatter 1 cup
  toasted slivered almonds evenly
  in the prepared pan and pour the
  caramel on top, being careful not
  to jostle the nuts.

do ahead
Stow in an airtight container
at room temperature for up to
1 month.

Bittersweet Chocolate Cream Caramels

When I was a kid, my mom volunteered at our local Women's Exchange shop, and I'd always happily tag along. If you knew the shop, you'd know that a young girl must have had an ulterior motive to go along voluntarily—I did indeed. My visits were all about scoring some of the chocolate-marshmallow caramels stowed in a wicker basket by the register. Back in the day, they cost a dime a piece and before leaving home for the shop, I'd scour around for stray change. After dropping my money in the basket, I would select what I thought were the biggest pieces (they were all the same size of course) and reverently place the waxed paper–wrapped caramels in my hand. Mom would always ask me to "please save them for after dinner, Abby," but there was no way to resist these gems—I devoured them immediately.

These soft, chewy candies remind me of the Exchange caramels—luscious, chocolaty, and creamy, with just the right amount of salt. Pure heaven.

1 Line the bottom and sides of a 8-inch-square baking pan (I like the straight-sided kind) with foil, leaving about a 1-inch overhang on two sides (see p. 5). Grease the bottom and sides of the foil with the 2 tablespoons softened butter (cooking spray works).

2 Put the sugar, heavy cream, Lyle's cane syrup, chocolate, the remaining butter, the vanilla, and salt in a large, narrow, heavy saucepan. Cook, stirring, over low heat until the sugar dissolves and the chocolate is melted. Cover the pan and increase the heat to medium. Cook, covered, for 2 minutes (this helps dissolve any pesky sugar crystals stuck on the sides). Uncover the pot, attach a candy thermometer (see p. 207), and boil the mixture without stirring until the mixture reaches 238°F, 3 to 5 minutes. Continue cooking the caramel until 242°F while carefully swirling the pot over the heat to even out the caramel.

3 Pour the caramel into the prepared baking pan without scraping the bottom or sides of the saucepan and leaving behind any darker caramel. It's going to be very tempting to not leave any deliciousness behind in the saucepan, but resist because the mixture on the sides can cause your finished caramel to be grainy and hard. Set aside to cool completely. Depending on your kitchen temperature, this will take 3 to 4 hours or overnight.

4 To cut and serve, use the foil "handles" to lift the caramel from the pan. Carefully peel or tear away the foil and toss it out; put the caramel on a cutting board. If the caramel is sticking to the cutting board, spray the board with a little oil. Using a ruler as a guide (or by eye) and a long, sharp knife, cut crosswise into 9 equal strips and then cut each strip into 9 pieces. Serve immediately or wrap in small pieces of waxed paper or cellophane (2¾-inch squares are the perfect size).

Bourbon Chocolate Truffles

When I was running the bakery at Hay Day Country Market (now owned by Balducci's), I developed a line of chocolate truffles. They became so popular that I designated two staffers as "truffle folk" and, two days a week, their job was to—you guessed it—make sure the three stores in the chain always had a full complement of truffles. That's a ton of truffles.

Luckily, this recipe won't require you to hire a staff to prepare. The bittersweet filling can be flavored in any number of ways, and I also give several options for coating the finished candies (see Twists at right). You might notice that I haven't included one normally popular covering on my options list: unsweetened cocoa powder. For me, truffles rolled in this bitter powder are, well, too bitter for my taste.

1 Put the chocolate, milk, and butter in a medium heatproof bowl and melt in the microwave or over simmering water. Remove from the heat. Add the bourbon and salt and whisk until well blended and smooth. Set aside, stirring occasionally, until thick enough to scoop, about 2 hours. For faster cooling, set the bowl over a larger bowl filled with ice and a little water, stirring frequently and scraping the sides with a rubber spatula.

2 Line a cookie sheet with parchment or a nonstick liner and make room in the refrigerator so the sheet will be level. (I arrange dairy containers that are the same height so that the sheet will sit on top.) Put the nuts on a plate or in a shallow bowl. Using a 1-tablespoon mini scoop, shape the mixture into balls and roll in the chopped nuts, pressing gently to help them stick. Arrange close together on the prepared cookie sheet and refrigerate until very cold and firm, about 4 hours, or arrange in a plastic container with layers separated with waxed paper or parchment. The prepared truffles can be stowed in the refrigerator for up to 5 days. Serve slightly chilled.

12 ounces bittersweet chocolate, chopped

1 cup whole milk

4 tablespoons (2 ounces) unsalted butter, cut into 4 pieces

4 teaspoons bourbon

¼ teaspoon table salt

1½ cups (6 ounces) finely chopped toasted nuts (hazelnuts are my favorite)

Makes 34 pieces

twists

• Instead of the bourbon, chose one of the following: 1 teaspoon pure vanilla extract or 4 teaspoons any type of liqueur or 1 tablespoon finely grated orange zest or ¼ teaspoon pure peppermint oil.

• Instead of using a 1-tablespoon scoop, use a 1- or 2-teaspoon scoop (a small or large melon baller works well).

• Instead of the finely chopped nuts, choose one of the following: 1½ cups colored sprinkles or 1½ cups confectioners' sugar (plus more for re-rolling before serving) or 1½ cups toasted unsweetened (desiccated; see p. 16) coconut or 1½ cups crushed peppermint candies.

Salty Mixed Nut Brittle

Making caramel is one of my favorite "kitchen magic" moments. It seems impossible to believe that granulated sugar will melt and transform into bittersweet, rich caramel but it does. Resist the urge to stop cooking the sugar too soon. If you do, your brittle will be sticky and too sweet. The finished brittle should be a deep amber color.

A quick mention about the baking soda that I add at the end of cooking: This makes the finished brittle a bit airier and less sticky than traditional brittle, and, therefore, it's a bit easier on your teeth.

1 Line a cookie sheet with a nonstick liner (parchment won't work for this recipe). Grease the bottom of a wide, offset metal spatula.

2 Put the sugar, butter, water, and Lyle's Golden Syrup in a large heavy saucepan. Cook, stirring, over medium-low heat until the sugar dissolves. Increase the heat to high and bring to a boil. Boil, without stirring, until the sugar begins to color around the edges of the pan, about 5 minutes. (Note: Unlike traditional caramel, this will look foamy and opaque.) Swirl the pan over the heat until the caramel is an even deep amber, about another 3 minutes.

3 Slide the pan from the heat and add the nuts and baking soda. Using a heatproof spatula, stir until just blended and the caramel is foamy and evenly covers the nuts. Carefully pour the mixture onto the prepared cookie sheet and, using an offset spatula, spread into a thick (about ½ inch) layer. Sprinkle with the salt.

4 Set aside at room temperature until completely cool, about 2 hours. Break or cut into small pieces and stow in an airtight container for up to 3 days.

KITCHEN WISDOM ✆ making brittle

Like all caramels, brittles don't behave well in humid conditions so, for best results, avoid making them during the summer months.

- **1** cup (7 ounces) granulated sugar
- **4** tablespoons (2 ounces) unsalted butter, softened and cut into 2 pieces
- **⅓** cup water
- **¼** cup Lyle's Golden Syrup
- **2** cups (10 ounces) lightly salted mixed nuts
- **½** teaspoon baking soda
- **⅛** to ¼ teaspoon fleur de sel

Makes 1¼ pounds

twists

- Instead of the mixed nuts, use one of the following or a combination of two or three to add up to 2 cups (10 ounces): toasted chopped macadamia nuts, lightly salted peanuts, chopped toasted walnuts. (If the nuts you choose are unsalted, double the amount of fleur de sel.)

- For a less chewy brittle, add another ½ teaspoon baking soda and proceed as directed. This will make the brittle even more airy.

Cook the caramel until it's dark amber.

- 3¼ cups (22¾ ounces) granulated sugar
- 2 tablespoons unsweetened natural cocoa powder, sifted if lumpy
- 1 tablespoon instant espresso granules
- ½ teaspoon table salt
- 1¼ cups half-and-half
- ¼ cup Lyle's Golden Syrup
- 4 ounces unsweetened chocolate, finely chopped
- 4 tablespoons (2 ounces) unsalted butter, cut into small cubes and chilled

Makes 36 pieces

do ahead
The fudge can be stowed in the refrigerator for up to 5 days. Arrange in a plastic container with layers separated with waxed paper or parchment.

Double Chocolate Espresso Fudge

Serving fudge at Thanksgiving has become a running joke between me and my brothers. Every year, my oldest brother, Darv, arrives all but empty-handed save the perennial box of fudge from a shop in Williamstown, Massachusetts. Mind you, Darv has never been tasked with this assignment, but bring it he does. This year, I decided to turn the tables on him and serve up a batch of fudge similar to the type my mom and I used to make. Rich, chocolaty, and sweet, this fudge has a velvety texture along with a hint of coffee flavor. I think we all agreed that my homemade version was far better than the store-bought. Looks like we have a new Thanksgiving fudge tradition!

1 Line the bottom and sides of a 8-inch-square baking pan (I like the straight-sided kind) with foil, leaving about a 1-inch overhang on two sides (see p. 5), and lightly grease the bottom and sides of the foil.

2 Put the sugar, cocoa powder, espresso granules, and salt in a large saucepan and whisk until blended. Add the half-and-half, golden syrup, and chocolate and whisk until well blended. Cook over low heat, stirring frequently with a heatproof rubber spatula until the sugar is dissolved (when you press the tip of the spatula across the bottom, the mixture won't feel granular) and the chocolate is melted.

3 Cover the pan and increase the heat to medium. Cook, covered, for 2 minutes (this helps dissolve any pesky sugar crystals stuck on the sides). Uncover the pot, attach a candy thermometer, and boil without stirring until the mixture reaches 236°F, 3 to 5 minutes. Carefully slide the pan from the heat and drop the cold butter into the fudge but do not stir. Set aside, without stirring or jostling the pan, until the fudge has cooled to about 110°F. Depending on your kitchen temperature, this will take 1 hour to 1 hour 45 minutes.

4 Holding the pot with two hands (use potholders), tip the saucepan over a large bowl and gently nudge the fudge into the bowl with a rubber spatula. It's okay to scrape the bottom of the saucepan but don't touch the sides. It's going to be tempting to not leave any deliciousness behind in the pan, but the mixture on the sides can cause your finished fudge to be grainy. Beat with an electric mixer fitted with the paddle attachment on medium speed until the fudge is the color of milk chocolate, less shiny, and hold its shape when scooped with a tablespoon, 8 to 12 minutes. The outside of the bowl will feel warm but no longer hot.

5 Scrape the fudge into the prepared pan (it's okay to scrape the bottom and the sides of the bowl) and, working quickly, spread into an even layer. Put the baking dish on a wire rack and set aside until completely cool. Cover and refrigerate until chilled, about 6 hours or up to 1 week.

6 To cut and serve, use the foil "handles" to carefully lift the fudge from the pan. Carefully peel or tear away the foil and toss it out. Using a ruler as a guide (or by eye) and a long, sharp knife, cut crosswise into 6 equal strips and then cut each strip into 6 pieces.

KITCHEN WISDOM ◎◎ candy thermometers

Using a candy thermometer is important in candy recipes to ensure that the sugar mixture is cooked to a specific stage; otherwise, your fudge or caramel will be too soft (undercooked) or too hard (overcooked). Whether you are using a digital or mercury-filled thermometer, be sure to use one that clips securely to the side of the pot and that can be adjusted so the base doesn't touch the bottom of the pan but is fully covered by the liquid. Before using, test the thermometer's accuracy in boiling water. It should read 212°F (at sea level).

twists

- **MAKE IT STRAIGHT-UP CHOCOLATE:** Omit the espresso granules.

- **MAKE IT MINT:** Instead of espresso granules, add 1/2 teaspoon pure peppermint oil to the fudge along with the butter. After pouring the fudge into the pan, sprinkle the top evenly with 1/2 cup (3 ounces) chopped peppermint candy chips, pressing gently on them so they stick.

- **MAKE IT ORANGE:** Instead of the espresso granules, add 2 tablespoons finely grated orange zest and 1 tablespoon orange liqueur to the fudge along with the butter. Just before pouring the fudge into the pan, stir in 1 1/2 cups mini marshmallows (store-bought or homemade, see p. 193) or toasted sweetened shredded coconut, if you like.

- **MAKE IT BOOZY:** Add 1 tablespoon coffee liqueur, bourbon, or hazelnut liqueur to the fudge along with the butter.

- Instead of the half-and-half, use 1 1/4 cups whole milk or 1 1/4 cups heavy cream.

- Just before pouring into the pan, stir in one of the following or up to 1 1/2 cups total of two or three: 1 1/2 cups toasted chopped nuts, 1 1/2 cups mini marshmallows, 1 1/2 cups lightly salted peanuts, 1 1/2 cups sweetened shredded coconut, toasted.

- 12 ounces bittersweet chocolate, chopped
- 4 tablespoons (2 ounces) unsalted butter, cut into 6 pieces
- 2 tablespoons unsweetened natural cocoa powder, sifted if lumpy

Pinch of table salt

- 1 can (14 ounces) sweetened condensed milk
- 1 teaspoon pure vanilla extract
- 1 cup mini marshmallows
- 4 ounces milk chocolate, chopped
- ½ cup (2½ ounces) coarsely chopped, lightly salted peanuts

Makes 32 pieces

twists

- Instead of the vanilla extract, use 1½ tablespoons dark rum, brandy, or hazelnut liqueur.
- Instead of the mini marshmallows, use the same amount of chopped homemade marshmallows (see p. 193).
- Instead of the milk chocolate and peanuts, you can use up to 1¼ cups of any combination of good stuff to make this fudge. Consider using: white chocolate or dark chocolate, coarsely chopped; peanut butter or butterscotch chips; coarsely chopped malted milk balls; coarsely chopped pretzels; coarsely chopped thin mint cookies; coarsely chopped homemade caramels (see the caramel recipes in this chapter).

do ahead

The fudge can be prepared, covered, and stowed in the fridge for up to 5 days.

Rocky Road Fudge

This fun little recipe is meant to inspire your whimsical, creative side. As with all of my recipes, I encourage you to add your own twists and to experiment with your own favorite flavors. The add-in possibilities for this easy-to-make fudge are practically endless, so switch in whatever you have in the pantry—even gummy worms would work! The only thing I wouldn't take out would be the marshmallows—they're too iconic to eliminate, but that's just this baker's opinion.

1 Line an 8-inch-square baking pan (I like the straight sided kind) with foil, leaving about a 1-inch overhang on two sides (see p. 5). Lightly grease the bottom and sides of the foil.

2 Put the chocolate and butter in a large heatproof bowl and melt in the microwave or on top of simmering water. Remove the bowl from the heat and sprinkle the cocoa powder and salt over the top. Add the condensed milk and vanilla and stir with a heatproof spatula just until well blended and smooth. If the fudge feels hot to the touch, set aside, stirring frequently, 1 to 2 minutes. Adding the rocky road ingredients to a too-warm fudge would melt them.

3 Add the marshmallows, chocolate chips, and peanuts and mix briefly until blended. Scrape into the prepared pan and spread evenly. Refrigerate until chilled and firm, about 6 hours or up to 2 days.

4 Use the foil "handles" to lift the fudge from the pan. Carefully peel or tear away the foil and toss it out; set the fudge on a cutting board. Using a ruler (or by eye) and a large knife, cut the fudge crosswise into 4 equal strips and then cut each strip into 8 pieces. Cover and stow in the refrigerator for up to 5 days. Serve slightly chilled.

KITCHEN WISDOM ◎◎ **making fudge and caramels**

Contrary to most baking recipes where I remind you to scrape down the sides of the bowl, it's very important to *not* scrape the sides and bottom of the pan during the final steps of making fudges and caramels. The sugar mixture on the bottom and sides continues to cook and, therefore, results in a different, firmer texture than the caramel in the center of the pot. Mixing the two together makes for an oddly textured candy.

Essential Equipment

While fancy, expensive machines aren't necessary for my recipes, a few well-chosen items will make your dessert making easier and more consistent. As with your ingredients, be choosy and purchase the best equipment your budget can support.

BAKING AND COOKIE SHEETS

These are not the same thing! A baking sheet (a.k.a. jelly roll pan) has four 1-inch-high sides. I have a large one (12½x17½), also known as a half-sheet pan, and a small one (9x12½), known as a quarter-sheet pan. They are great for baking as well as for toasting nuts. For cookie baking, purchase cookie sheets with one raised edge. The edge allows for easy handling, and the remaining rimless edges allow for even cooking. Choose both types made from heavy-duty, shiny (not dark) aluminum.

BAKING PANS

As with other equipment, select heavy-duty, affordable ones and only in the quantity that your space permits. Here are a few to have on hand: regular-sized muffin pans with 2¾-inch diameter cups; mini muffin pans with 1⅞-inch diameter (or 3-tablespoon volume) cups; a Pyrex® 8½x4½-inch loaf pan; a 9-inch pie plate; 8- and 9-inch-square pans; and 9-inch-round cake pans.

BLENDER OR FOOD PROCESSOR

It's close to impossible for me to choose between these two power tools. They both have a place in my kitchen. That said, a food processor is more versatile. For the most flexibility, choose one that has a variety of workbowl sizes. I have a 14-cup Cuisinart® with two smaller bowls. I most often use it for cutting butter into flour for scones and pastry dough and whizzing granulated sugar into superfine, but it's also useful for puréeing fruits and chopping nuts.

CUTTING BOARDS

I keep a small and large plastic one on hand for all my chopping and cutting duties. They are lightweight and dishwasher-safe. Always remember to place a damp piece of paper towel under the cutting board on your counter to keep it secure and prevent wobbling.

ELECTRIC MIXER (HAND-HELD OR STAND)

Everyone needs one, but you don't have to break the bank to get a good-quality model. If you have the counter space, I urge you to buy a freestanding mixer. My KitchenAid® has been working hard for over 30 years, and Sunbeam® makes a great mixer, too. If a hand-held mixer fits your space and budget restrictions, look for one with a comfortable handle, sturdy beater blades, and multiple speeds.

KNIVES

Yup, even bakers need a few good knives. I suggest stowing a chef's knife, a paring knife, and a serrated (bread) knife, as well as a good pair of scissors, in your drawer or block and keep them sharp. A dull knife causes more injuries than a sharp one, and it will only slow your work. I take mine to my local butcher when they need a new edge or a quick professional sharpening.

MEASURING TOOLS

You'll achieve the most accurate and consistent results if you weigh your ingredients. My Salter® scale has a big digital read-out (no reading glasses necessary), and it measures in grams as well as ounces. You also need both glass and metal measures. Glass (Pyrex) measuring cups are for all liquids, and metal measures are for dry ingredients and thicker creamy items like yogurt, crème fraîche, and mascarpone. You'll also need at least one set (I suggest two) of standard measuring spoons. Stay away from the decorative ones—they may be cute, but they're not always accurate.

MIXING BOWLS

You'll need at least one of each size: small, medium, large. I prefer Pyrex heatproof bowls for mixing. They can go in the microwave, on top of simmering water, in the dishwasher, and, heck, they can even go in the oven. Metal bowls are good, too. They are lighter weight than Pyrex, but they aren't microwave-safe. Stay away from plastic bowls, as they aren't as sturdy, stain easily, and can hold onto strong odors.

NONSTICK LINERS

Used to line cookie sheets, baking sheets, and pans, there are two nonstick varieties that I recommend—silicone-coated fiberglass baking mats and kitchen parchment; each is available in many brands. All share common goals: They keep the baked goods from sticking and make cleanup easy-breezy and, unless otherwise noted, they are interchangeable. Silicone baking mats come in many sizes and are sturdy, washable, and reusable. Parchment (or baking paper) is silicone-coated paper that can withstand oven temps up to 450°F. Available in many forms, I find the flat sheets the easiest to work with, and they can be cut to fit any pan. They can be ordered online or purchased at a restaurant-supply store. P.S.: Waxed paper is *not* a substitute!

STRAINERS

Most likely, you already have a large colander in your cupboard. It's what you use to drain your cooked pasta and rinse and drain your fruit. I also recommend keeping a medium-sized fine-mesh sieve for straining liquids, custards, and purées.

WIRE RACKS

If I'm baking just one sheet of cookies or one small baking dish, I'll occasionally let the grates on my cold cooktop stand in as a cooling rack. But you can't always count on a cold cooktop or only needing room for one hot-from-the-oven item, so have one or two large racks at the ready. They are inexpensive and will last a lifetime.

Small Gadgets

HEATPROOF SILICONE SPATULAS

These "rubber" spatulas are the most durable on the market. They can withstand temperatures up to 350°F (or higher, in some cases), making them perfect for stirring hot custards or sugar syrups.

MICROPLANE ZESTER

While zesters come in a variety of shapes and sizes, I like a wide, stainless-steel blade with very small and extremely sharp holes or rasps for finely grating zest or ginger. A rubber-coated handle keeps this very sharp tool in control.

OFFSET SPATULA

The metal blade of this handy tool jogs out from its handle at about a 45-degree angle and then continues out to flat, dull blade. I have long and short ones in my drawer. Nothing is better for spreading soft dough, creamy fillings, batters, frosting, or glazes.

PASTRY BRUSH

Choose natural-bristled brushes with sturdy handles. I suggest having a small one for brushing water or egg wash on pastry borders and a medium one for brushing egg wash on larger surfaces.

PEELER

The Y- or U-shaped types with a ceramic blade are my peeler of choice because they afford the most control and have a stay-sharp blade.

ROLLING PIN

I use a straight wooden cylinder without handles or tapered ends. With my hands placed on the pin directly over the dough, I get a better feel for the evenness of the dough, and I'm also better able to apply even pressure as I roll. Stay away from the pins with deeply tapered ends. They offer a small rolling surface and therefore can cause your dough to be uneven. In a pinch, a straight-sided wine bottle, carefully handled, will also get the job done.

RULER

I want your results to be the same as mine, so please have a 20-inch wooden or plastic ruler at the ready. It's the only way you'll know that your pan or pastry dough is the same size that's called for in the recipes.

TIMER

Although your oven or microwave has one, a separate, freestanding timer is great to carry with you if you have to leave the kitchen—it's even better if it clips to your shirt or sweater.

WHISKS

Wire whisks are great for blending ingredients. I have a very small one that I use to combine dry ingredients, as well as small and medium sizes.

metric equivalents

liquid/dry measures

U.S.	METRIC
$1/4$ teaspoon	1.25 milliliters
$1/2$ teaspoon	2.5 milliliters
1 teaspoon	5 milliliters
1 tablespoon (3 teaspoons)	15 milliliters
1 fluid ounce (2 tablespoons)	30 milliliters
$1/4$ cup	60 milliliters
$1/3$ cup	80 milliliters
$1/2$ cup	120 milliliters
1 cup	240 milliliters
1 pint (2 cups)	480 milliliters
1 quart (4 cups; 32 ounces)	960 milliliters
1 gallon (4 quarts)	3.84 liters
1 ounce (by weight)	28 grams
1 pound	454 grams
2.2 pounds	1 kilogram

oven temperatures

°F	GAS MARK	°C
250	$1/2$	120
275	1	140
300	2	150
325	3	165
350	4	180
375	5	190
400	6	200
425	7	220
450	8	230
475	9	240
500	10	260
550	Broil	290

index

If you like this cookbook then you'll love everything about *Fine Cooking* magazine

Fine Cooking magazine is the choice for people who love to cook. And there's even more beyond our award-winning pages: With our apps, e-newsletters, interactive web tools, and online recipe search, we're ready to help you cook great food every day.

Discover all that *Fine Cooking* has to offer.

Subscribe today at **FineCooking.com/more**